All the sounds of the world yearn t⟨
still and marginal. The immensity of
I do not know how to begin it. But I l
my absence and enveloping it with dis
mately evocative. As the summer sunse   ⸺gination
with bright memories of my mother a⟨   ⸺, their souls on their faces, so
quiet and peaceful, yet so fertile for the growth of poetry, I embrace the seeds
of my fate in their light and wander the earth so their silence may become my
language. With this and what perhaps awaits, I begin.

POETRY AND POLITICS IN THE MODERN ARAB WORLD

ATEF ALSHAER

Poetry and Politics in the Modern Arab World

HURST & COMPANY, LONDON

First published in the United Kingdom in 2016 by
C. Hurst & Co. (Publishers) Ltd.,
41 Great Russell Street, London, WC1B 3PL
© Atef Alshaer, 2016
All rights reserved.
Printed in India

Distributed in the United States, Canada and Latin America by
Oxford University Press, 198 Madison Avenue, New York, NY 10016,
United States of America.

A Cataloguing-in-Publication data record for this book is
available from the British Library.

ISBN: 978-1-84904-319-9 *hardback*

This book is printed using paper from registered sustainable
and managed sources.

www.hurstpublishers.com

To the bright soul of my friend in the infinite space of peace,

Nick Pretzlik (30 July 1945—11 July 2004)

CONTENTS

ACKNOWLEDGMENTS

I am deeply grateful to my dear friend Robert Anderson. Thanks will never do justice to this truly gifted and dedicated man who experienced many worlds, cultures, languages, and put them generously into the service of others. Ursula Pretzlik too has always supported me in my studies. I appreciate and value her help and acknowledge my gratitude to her, to her late husband Nick Pretzlik (to whose soul I dedicate this book), and to her son Luke, a dear friend. I am further grateful to Alison Phillips, the gentlest soul I have ever met. I could not have done it without your help.

Many friends made this task easier and more enriching, and I would like to express my affection towards them: Fernando Mariño, Ahmad Joumma, Tim Kay, Julio Pinna, Sahar Rad, Jennifer Griggs, Sara Vaghefian, Yuko Fujita, Tahani Mustafa, Mohammed Moussa, Hannes Bouman, Kareem Dennis, Toufic Haddad, Aicha Belkadi, Souad Lamrani, Zahera Ali, Hamza Almalik, Nisreen Alrifaei, Ali Zaherinezhad, Husam Almallak and Sarah Elibiary.

I am thankful to my friend Dominique Shane Oliver for proofreading several chapters of this book. His interest and warmth are deeply appreciated. I am grateful to Hilary Wise for proofreading some chapters and for making them read more fluently. Thanks are also due to Corinna Mullin for proofreading earlier versions of chapters four and seven.

To Ilana Webster-Kogen and Simon Webster-Kogen: thank you for your encouragement and for reading parts of this book.

I am very thankful to my friend Dina Matar of SOAS, whose support I acknowledge with deep gratitude. Thanks are also due to many colleagues for their support: Arshin Adib-Moghaddam, Mohammad Said, Karima Laachir, Martin Erwin, Stefan Sperl, Mark Weeden, Ayman El-Desouky, Gilbert Achcar, Peter Hartung, Ahmad Alkhashem, Chris Lucas and Nora Parr.

ACKNOWLEDGMENTS

I thank Caroline Rooney at Kent University for her encouragement and comments.

I thank Michael Dwyer and his team at Hurst for their patience and cooperation. I am grateful to Brenda Stones who thoroughly edited the entire manuscript, improving it in quality and style. And I also thank emphatically the anonymous reviewers for their encouraging and constructive remarks. Any failings in this book remain mine.

Last but not least, my family. My family in Gaza (Rafah), whom I have not seen for more than ten years, have been my constant source of inspiration. I have revisited their faces and their words many times in order to remember what they look like, how they speak and how they interact with their (our) neighbours. This has enabled me to practise 'science as practice'. My family deserve my deepest gratitude and admiration. No matter what problems I have encountered while away from them, I have always tried to remember that these are insignificant compared to the challenges they face. Their undefeated, unmistakable sense of optimism and steadfastness in the face of inhumanity is a fountain of inspiration and hope. To them, to the dear souls of my father, my mother and my brother, to the Palestinians of Gaza and to Palestinians everywhere, every well-placed word, sentence and every good idea in this book is dedicated. With humility and humanity, we shall overcome.

NOTES

All translations are the author's, unless otherwise indicated. The book draws on a number of sources in Arabic and English, as indicated in the references.

Regarding transliteration, I use a simplified version of the IJMES.[1] I leave familiar names such as Adonis and Mahmoud Darwish without transliteration.

Shorter versions of the following chapters in the book appeared in earlier publications, as acknowledged below:

Chapter Four: Humanism, Nationalism and Violence in Mahmoud Darwish's Poetry, in Hugh Kennedy (ed.), *Warfare and Poetry in the Middle East*, London: I. B. Tauris, 2013, pp. 257–283.

Chapter Five: The Poetry of Hamas, in *Middle East Journal of Culture and Communication*, Leiden: Brill, 2 (2), 2009, pp. 214–30.

Chapter Six: The Poetry of Hizbullah, in Lina Khatib and Dina Matar and Atef Alshaer, *The Hizbullah Phenomenon: Politics and Communication*, London: Hurst & Co., 2014, pp. 119–153.

Chapter Seven: Poetry and the Arab Spring: A Historical Perspective, in Larbi Sadiki (ed.), *Routledge Handbook of the Arab Spring: Rethinking Democratization*, 2015, pp. 392–408.

INTRODUCTION

Poetry has been a force of timeless and universal value. No other of language's many faces has so often expressed the innermost dimensions of human life. Through and with it, religions are founded and constituted; truths discovered; entire edifices of visual and psychological perceptions formed, with consequences ranging from peace to war to truce to love to inner euphoria to infinite serenity. One fundamental value of poetry is that it renders visibly alive both the silent and the unconscious alongside the spoken and the conscious. It brings to life an entire picture or perception of human reality, even if an ephemeral one. In this sense, poetry liberates the embodied human of the burden of embodiment. Summarising Heidegger's liberationist view of poetry, Vincent Leitch wrote:

> Poetry is the source and foundation of language and art and history and being and time and truth. It is primordial founding, establishing, situating, naming. It brings forth existence. It produces thinking. There is nothing outside poetry. Strictly conceived, there is no 'outside poetry'; not even 'nothing' is outside poetry.[1]

Indeed, so much of Arab life has been established, situated and named through poetry that even personal names tend to carry poetic virtues, attesting to poetry's lasting power in Arab culture.[2] Arabic poetry is a genuine example of a literary tradition in which words, woven into poetic constructions, are impregnated with meanings steeped in both psychological and socio-political implications.[3] Poetry is often unquantifiable in terms of its material weight, but the fact that it has lasted for as long as humankind has been using language suggests that its value lies in its presence as a fact of language within which people search for meanings, for echoes to the sounds of their souls and the music of their minds.

1

Beginning in the fifth century, pre-Islamic poetry was an early poetic rendering of Arab life and thinking that set the scene for an enduring and expansive tradition, originally oral, whose living power never ceased to be reproduced in congruence with socio-political, economic, and aesthetic influences and adaptations. The orality of poetry was facilitated through formulaic constructions based on metrical and rhythmic orders that engender different moods and effects. Poetry was crafted to be memorised and recited.[4] Thus, listening and reproducing poetry was from the outset an embodied social act. That poetry was composed to be heard and to have immediate effect is a recurrent Arab pattern; hence the embodiment of sound and aesthetics in the socio-political milieu of Arab culture, defined as that reproduced compendium of past echoes and habits as congruent with present orientations and aspirations.[5] To this end, intuitions were honed and tuned towards individual and collective understanding. They were endowed with form, voice and affective resonance and could therefore institute wider social and political cohesion and solidarity. In this sense, Arabic poetry, both early and modern, is embedded within a culture of communication that allowed early poetic composition, as enshrined in the *Qaṣīdah* with its metrical and rhythmical pattern, a prime position. The poetic ingredients of this culture are eloquently captured in a passage by the great fourteenth-century thinker and writer Ibn Khaldun (AD1332–1406). This passage is truly remarkable for its timeless perceptiveness regarding Arabic poetry, be it classical or modern, and particularly concerning its technical aspect, which is intertwined with conceptual content and the auditory basis of Arabic poetry's orality. Ibn Khaldun writes:

> Let us mention the significance of the word 'method' as used by poets, and what they mean by it.

> It should be known that they use it to express the loom on which word combinations are woven, or the mould into which they are packed. It is not used to express the basis upon which the meaning [of a word rests]. That is the task of the vowel endings. It also is not used for perfect expression of the idea resulting from the particular word combination used. That is the task of eloquence and style. It also is not used in the sense of meter, as employed by the Arabs in [connection with poetry]. That is the task of prosody. These three sciences fall outside the craft of poetry.

> [Poetical method] is used to refer to a mental form for metrical word combinations which is universal in the sense of conforming with any particular word combination. This form is abstracted by the mind from the most prominent individual word combinations and given a place in the imagination comparable to a mould or loom. Word combinations that the Arabs consider sound, in the sense of having the [cor-

rect] vowel endings and the [proper] style, are then selected and packed by [the mind] into [that loom], just as the builder does with the mould or the weaver with the loom. Eventually, the mould is sufficiently widened to admit the word combinations that fully express what one wants to express. It takes on the form that is the sound in the sense [that it corresponds to] the Arabic linguistic habit...the [poetical] methods that we try to establish here have nothing to do with analogical reasoning. They are a form that is firmly rooted in the soul. It is the result of the continuity of word combinations in Arabic poetry when the tongue uses them. Eventually the form of [those word combinations] becomes firmly established. It teaches [the poet] the use of similar [word combinations]. [It teaches him to] to imitate them for each word combination that he may use in his poetry.[6]

If Ibn Khaldun emphasises the conceptual and habitual methods through which poetry gained a uniquely everlasting foothold in Arab culture, other thinkers reflect directly on the socio-political functions of poetry in Arab culture. When recalling these functions, as recorded by the ninth century Muslim scholar Ibn Rashīq (AD1000–1063) in his commentary on pre-Islamic poetry (which is the foundational wellspring of Arabic poetry), parallels can be drawn with modern ages. In this respect, continued access to the Arabic language and the literary heritage associated with it allowed for an organic process of poetic creativity and development that resumed in the nineteenth century and carried the distant past into present Arab life in many ways. This transference occurred despite political interruptions and upheavals that obstructed and diffused the flow of the original Arabic *Qaṣīdah* around the thirteenth-century (though the *Qaṣīdah* did continue to be known in Andalucía, where Muslims remained until the fall of Granada in 1492). Ibn Rashīq's observations on pre-Islamic poetry continue to bear relevance to modern Arabic poetry and life, although their relevance has shifted given the different socio-political formations of the Arab past and present:

> The Arabs needed to sing about the nobility of their character, the purity of their blood, and to recall their good battle days and faraway abodes, their brave horsemen and compliant steeds, in order to incite themselves to nobility and direct their sons toward good character [...] to perpetuate memorable deeds, strengthen their honour, guard the tribe and inspire the awe of it in other tribes, since others would not advance against them for fear of their poet.[7]

The old ethos of singing for the tribe has been transformed in the modern period into singing for the nation-state, with poets highlighting its virtues and woes, and engaging with colonialism, modernity, religion and ideology. In addition, projection of the self and the other continued unabated, revealing Arab culture to be a historic one in which the past is integrated into the present by virtue of continuity of language. The same cannot be said of Western cultures. The metamorphoses of Latin into several languages caused fragmentation in Europe's cultural consciousness, alongside the development of capitalist modes of existence that made Europe less prone to oral and performative poetry. In the Arab world the nation-state continued in a state of flux, and ideologically the spiritual and the material have yet to occupy separate spheres of reasoning, as they largely do in Europe. Thus, while poetry is foundational for human perception, sense, and indeed civilisation, in a universal sense,[8] in the Arab world it has also carried socio-political importance as an oral and later a written tradition, performed, shared, sung and imagined within a symbiotic relationship binding the individual to the language of his community. This can be traced back to Islam.

Following the spread of Islam from the seventh century onwards, the tradition of poetry continued and expanded, directly involving kings and rulers who derived and sustained their legitimacy through the praise of poets. The latter thrived on being sponsored by the former within a system of patronage permeated with divine, political and mythic attributes that consolidated authority and perpetuated one particular political and understanding order over another.[9] This tradition of court poetry, exemplified by illustrious poets such as al-Buḥturī (AD820–897) and Abū al-Tayyeb al-Mutanabbī (AD915–965), added to the political-poetic confluence that their times are famous for. When remembering a ruler from these times, one tends to recall them in relation to their poets—most famously, the ruler Abū Firās al-Ḥamadānī is associated with the poet Abū al-Tayyeb al-Muttanabī.[10] The seismic shift that occurred in the seventh century was therefore radically holistic, in a manner championed by the linguistic ingenuity expressed and indeed immortalised in the Qur'an. The particular Qasīdah form, which began in the pre-Islamic age with its metrical characteristics and its chivalric, ritualistic and rebellious themes, acquired new dimensions and became associated with literary genres and commentaries.

It is notable that from the earliest days of Arab culture, poetry supported aesthetic and political powers, suggesting that no existing or aspiring political order could flourish without it. In this, poetry functioned as an ingredient of legitimacy and intersubjective truth; hence its widespread orality and its role in inaugurating the belief that without a hold on language, there is no hold on politics.[11] The shift from the pre-Islamic period to the Islamic one, most notably through the medium of the Qur'an—a challenging linguistic phenomenon in the first place—starkly materialised the significance of seizing language for political and social power.

The Qur'an, the principal sacred book of Islam, shows perhaps the most important conceptual shift in the history of the Arab and Islamic worlds. It introduced a linguistic medley, infusing poetry and prose in ways that broke away from the poetry-laden, pre-Islamic past. Such an inimitable mixture encapsulated teachings and exhortations about the virtues of monotheism, piety, and political and social justice, all in accordance with divine order. Meanwhile, the manner of Qur'anic expression has led to interpretations and qualifications throughout the ages that now run into almost endless numbers of volumes. There has therefore always been a weighty sensitivity to language in the Arab world: so much so that it resonates even today with both past and present values and judgments.[12] The Qur'an represents at heart a case of the affective power of the use of language, and of its the conceptual and creative possibilities. Against this background, modern Arabic poetry since the nineteenth century, with which this book is concerned, combines facets of power relations with changes in political and aesthetic perceptions of the Arab world. This period produced Arab voices that yearn for independence and sing for its realisation; their hope is to regain the Arab glory of past centuries, when the Arabs excelled in several fields of knowledge, and science and poetry were its crowning glories.

From the tremendous advancement of culture and science during the Umayyad (AD661–750) and the Abbasid periods (AD750–1258), the Arabs inherited a sense of mature genius sharpened by the poetic achievements of these times; a spirit of nostalgia and the possibility of greatness has overshadowed their lives ever since.[13] With the decline of the Ottoman Empire (AD1453–1923) and the rise of Arab nationalism in the nineteenth century, the Arab world felt emboldened to return to its past; the educated believed that the present and the future for the Arabs could be revitalised. As a result, the intellectual, political and literary efforts of this period constituted an Arab renaissance; remoulding past ways of living and thinking; influenced by new inflections of nationalism, literary developments and the interaction with European culture. Arabic poetry was inherited from the pre-Islamic, the Umayyad, and the Abbasid epochs, from the essence of their expressive entities. The Palestinian poet and novelist Ibrahim Nasrallah calls poetry 'the spiritual record of the Arab peoples';[14] as Marlé Hammond put it, '[poetry] was a form of art which assumed great importance in public discourse, for it served not only as a crucial method of communication but also as the storehouse for collective memory',[15] It inspired the Arab poets of the nineteenth and twentieth centuries to substantiate cultural and political developments with revived and expanded poetic meanings. To this end, several famous modern Arab poets were patronised by rulers in order to give their regimes legitimacy. Yet, with time, Arab poets developed independent sensibilities that responded to their own perception of aesthetics and politics, rendering the landscape of modern Arab poetry both diverse and deeply instructive with regard to the multifaceted life of the Arab world. It is not possible to name every Arab poet who contributed to this period of revival. Many people tapped into the power of language in order to discover and express their beliefs and views, holding a mirror to themselves and their situations. A culture as language-minded as that of the Arab world gave rise to countless voices with varying degrees of quality, breadth and influence. This book is intended to shed a concentrated light on notable aspects of modern Arabic poetry, as related to political changes and influential figures at certain events, and on poets whose roles have resounded at aesthetic, political or strictly ideological levels within the realm of current Arab life. The book is inevitably selective and discursive, and necessarily has to limit its scope, with apologies to those poets and writers whose names have not been included. Its compass is the poetics of the political milestones, ideas and discourses that have shaped and preoccupied the Arab world since the nineteenth century.

Politics is often understood as a realm of power and power relations, interlocked within varying degrees of domination and resistance. The French philosopher Michel Foucault emphasised in the 1970s and 1980s the extensive and dense meanings of power, and a parallel can be drawn between his argument and the multiple and diverse ways in which modern Arabic poetry began and developed. Modern Arabic poetry can be viewed as a vessel of power and resistance situated within the field of language, which is an infinite site of structural and semantic power, conjuring up events and insights, and widening the possibilities for existential understanding within political contexts, which have often been narrow and perplexing. Foucault writes:

> [P]ower is co-extensive with the social body; there are no spaces of primal liberty between the meshes of its network [yet] one should not assume a massive and primal condition of domination, a binary structure with 'dominators' on one side and 'dominated' on the other, but rather a multiform production of relations of domination which are partially susceptible of integration into overall strategies [...] there are no relations of power without resistances; the latter are all the more real and effective because they are formed right at the point where relations of power are exercised; resistance to power does not have to come from elsewhere to be real, nor is it inexorably frustrated through being the compatriot of power. It exists all the more by being in the same place as power; hence, like power, resistance is multiple and can be integrated in global strategies.[16]

Modern Arabic poetry is located at the intersections of colonialism, post-colonialism, nation-state constructivism, traditionalism, modernity and post-modernity. It comes with these legacies from within an Arab world at the mercy of forces both internal and external that have affected its identity, its very expressions of itself. Thus situated, modern Arabic poetry offers illustrative examples of various configurations of power and resistance.[17] Yet particular types of poetry, such as the avant-garde, should be seen through more lenses than simply those of power and resistance. The grand scale of such poetry offers expressions of liberation and transcendence beyond what can be captured solely by the dialectic of power and resistance. In particular, analysis of the Arabic avant-garde calls for an expanded sense of political understanding; for an awareness of an element of existential empowerment in the poetic product of language, an empowerment that has saved many an Arab individual amidst their crushing socio-political conditions. Indeed, the performative, lyrical and philosophical dimensions of avant-guard Arabic poetry cannot be emphasised enough. The great modernist Arab poet Adonis expressed the unmatched significance of this poetry for Arab culture, while registering dismay at the intrusion of politics on its aesthetics. Adonis looks for further exploration of the innovative and unknown as something that resides within the metaphysics of language, decrying the narrowness of politics:

> My admiration and enthusiasm for Arabic poetry increases as I gain more consciousness and conviction that among the creative means of Arab expression, poetry is the most authentic and comprehensive, the most present and illustrious. I imagine that at the end of this century (the 20th century), poetry is the only medium that gives this Arab energy its humanist and universal dimensions at the same time [...] seen from this perspective and at this level, Arabic poetry is the cleanest air, which the lung of Arab creativity inhales. However, this air is tied down, besieged; and it is almost imprisoned in the chains of politics, which does not see beyond its chair of domination. This is in addition to the blind ideology and the distortive taste, and the [political] criteria that do not see in the creative artistic aesthetic except what benefits its direct effectiveness and functionality. This makes the lung shrink and agitates to the point of suffocation [...] Suffice for me to say that the death of poetry among the Arabs is the death of the Arabic language, or it is at least an end to the great aesthetic trigger with which we lived as Arabs for twenty centuries.[18]

Yet although Adonis does not perceive a place for politics in poetry, considering the serious abuse narrow ideologies cause to art, many important Arab poets have come to show how poetry can include all experiences and perceptions. If the Arabs have developed acute sensibilities towards their language and its importance, they have also been immersed in political conditions that overwhelmed them and affected their very subjecthood as people, in a way that could not escape their most important and historic medium of expression—poetry. Thus, while Adonis's voice and indeed practice of poetry is indispensable to the development of modern Arabic poetry, other poets, such as the Palestinian poet Mahmoud Darwish, have shown an extraordinary poetic range, reflecting political and existential Arab concerns in an innovative fashion as well as the sublime aesthetic of language as conversant with people's lives, collective imaginations, and individual dispositions and hopes.[19]

Against this background, the first chapter of the book opens within the context of the Arab world under Ottoman rule. Arabic poetry started to assert its presence at the confluence of a political transition, when Arab nationalism was on the rise while the Ottoman Empire was giving way to the European empires in Arab lands. The Arabic poetry of the time was integrated into the expression of Arab identity in general. During this period, Arab poets resorted to invoking the medieval Arabic classical tradition, and to using its binary formulaic prosodic system. The themes that preoccupied Arab poets included granting legitimacy to one political order rather than another, and asserting characteristic Arab traits such as generosity and loyalty as well as Islamic values of piety, unity and honesty. Gradually, the neo-classical tradition in Arabic poetry admitted into the cultural landscape an independent Arabic poetry with Arabic themes that celebrated the achievements of the classical age while adding new elements from the modern period, which was beginning to interact with European culture. During this period, which extended from the middle of the nineteenth century through to the 1930s, Arabic poetry preoccupied itself with various nationalist, social and religious themes that corresponded to the political and intellectual currents of the time.

While proponents of Arab nationalism tended to promote a range of nationalist agendas covering pan-Arab, nation-statist nationalism and regional Arabism based on geographical or ideological proximity, Arab poets tended to be pan-Arabist by nature. But each Arab poet from the neo-classical generation focused on the travails of their own nations and the particular events that shaped them. The central source of pan-Arabism amongst poets was, however, historical Arab culture itself, and its embodiment within the Arabic language; this made poets combine or single-handedly reflect shared Arab facets and concerns, such as the state of the Arabic language, the social customs and the necessity of Arab-inspired renewal. Another significant focus in neo-classical poetry was resistance against colonialism and its violations of the Arab land. In this respect, Arabic poetry carried the torch of Arab nationalism and resistance, particularly in countries such as Iraq, Egypt, Algeria and Palestine. The Palestinian scholar Yasir Suleiman reflects on the role of literature in creating and reinforcing common bonds for the nation:

> Literature is an important channel of communication in nation building...It helps foster a national consciousness, a national sentiment, a shared cultural inheritance and a shared destiny, and it does so through a shared idiom that resonates with members of the nation. To achieve this, nationalist literature aims at mobilisation and political activism by bonding the present to the past for reinforcement, legitimatisation and inspiration purposes.[20]

These remarks apply both to the neo-classical period, in reflecting shared and constant Arab attempts at mobilisation against an outside enemy in favour of a united Arab culture and life; and also to the modern period, particularly after the 1950s, when the nation-state in the Arab world was becoming independent and consolidated. Furthermore, Suleiman explains the aforementioned nationalist functions as follows:

> Reinforcement aims at using the past to cull symbols and capture moments of glory, which the poet deploys to give the nation reasons to be proud of who it is...poetic compositions of this kind play a motivational role in society by turning the past, which is both to be emulated and surpassed, into a springboard for action. Legitimisation is intended to lend validity to the claims of the nation and its pedigree, so that it can move forward in an assured way. Inspiration is likened to task-orientation: it works through affect, resonance and impact.'[21]

Indeed, these functions have been significant within the context of the Arab nation-state and nationalism in general. Yet at the same time, modern Arabic poetry after the forties nurtured some important avant-garde poets who acquired and deployed individual impulses and visions, while the nation was foregrounded within holistic tendencies. These tendencies are concerned with poetic aspirations relating to existential and aesthetic openness that is neither nation-bound nor task-orientated as such.

Thus, later poetic genres included the romantic, the symbolist, the social realist, the nationalist, the humanist nationalist and the existentialist, as well as the ideological. All these domains of poetry found proponents and opponents. Each introduced new dimensions and twists to Arabic poetry, enriching it through the incorporation of myths and philosophical ideals and adventures, experimentally and expansively. One notable difference that separates early poetry from later relates to form. Modernist Arabic poetry after the 1940s exhibited an impressive range of poetic techniques that stretched the scope of the prosodic system of Arabic poetry, thus adding to the richness of

Arabic poetry and the Arabic language itself.[22] Most significantly, the break from the mono-rhymed *Qaṣīdah* form was no less than revolutionary in stretching the poetic possibilities beyond the early metrical limits, thus ending the dominance of the fifteen-hundred-year-old *Qaṣīdah*, productive and immensely significant though it had been. In addition, many modernist poets have come to enliven and at times transcend the past by writing poetry brimming with an openness that could not be imprisoned by past or present references alone, opening up their poetry to aesthetics of existential empowerment and marvel. It is therefore limited, if not wrong, to consider Arab poets as inevitable prisoners of the past or present world. They took inspiration from both the past and the present but charged their poetry with energy that does not subscribe to periodic confinement—it is in this sense their poetry is one of aesthetic emancipation. Exemplars include modernist poets such as Badr Shākir al-Sayyāb of Iraq, Ṣalāḥ ʿAbd al-Ṣabūr of Egypt, Khalīl Ḥāwi of Lebanon, Nizār Qabbānī and Adonis of Syria and Mahmoud Darwīsh and Samīḥ al-Qāsim of Palestine. Moreover, it is notable that the modern Arabic novel also benefited from the developments in form in Arabic poetry. Such developments encouraged experiment in the narrative style of modern Arabic fiction, which at times incorporated poetic tendencies reminiscent of free verse modernist styles in poetry.[23]

To this end, the variety of themes, techniques and backgrounds that make up the story of modern Arabic poetry motivates one to consider this diversity on its own terms. This guards against the pitfall of limiting such significant poetic diversity, which has come to define the modern landscape of Arabic poetry, to a mere reflection of its past and present. In fact, if the promising future and openness of the Arab world has been seen anywhere, it is in the avant-garde creations of modernist Arab poets.

Against this background, the three chapters in Part One are devoted to exploring general trends in modern Arabic poetry, and the three chapters in Part Two offer case studies: chapter four focuses on one poet, the phenomenal Palestinian Mahmoud Darwish; and chapters five and six focus on two mainstream Islamist political movements, namely the Palestinian Islamist movement Hamas and the Lebanese Islamist movement Hizbullah. The last chapter offers a summary of the poetic trends that characterised the twentieth century, particularly in relation to the Arab Spring. This book will argue that revolution and change have been dominant themes throughout modern Arabic poetry. Many Arab poets aspired at least once in their lives to in time affect general sensibilities through their poetry, resulting in political changes of a profound nature. Their belief in the creative power of language and its capacity for revolutionary change echoes the ideas of the great American–British poet and critic T. S. Eliot, who wrote:

> [Poetry] may effect revolutions in sensibility such as are periodically needed; it may help to break up the conventional modes of perception and valuation which are perpetually forming, and make people see the world afresh, or some new part of it. It may make us from time to time a little more aware of the deeper, unnamed feelings which form the substratum of our being, to which we rarely penetrate; for our lives are mostly a constant evasion of ourselves, and an evasion of the visible and sensible world.[24]

PART ONE

1

POETRY IN THE SHADOW OF THE
OTTOMAN EMPIRE

Introduction

Soldiers! Behind you stretch the empty deserts,
Before you stands the craven foe.
Beyond the enemy is rich Egypt, avid to welcome you.
If you falter, death only shall be your lot.
Forward, for before you lies paradise![1]

These lines were uttered by an eminent Turkish figure in 1915, a mere eight years before the already weak Ottoman Empire collapsed. Their significance lies in their allusions to a history of empires jockeying for power in the Arab world, and to a narrative of resistance accentuated by poetry. The author, Ahmad Jemal Pasha, Maritime Minister in the Ottoman cabinet, was one of the many who wished to salvage the Empire from the hands of European powers, namely France and Britain. Keen as he was to preserve Egypt for the Empire because of its enduring political and cultural hold on the Arab world, Pasha took Egypt's loyalty for granted. He assumed that the price of letting Egypt go would be irredeemably high. His choices were extremely limited, and so his style is extravagantly declarative and assertive. He commands his soldiers, 'Forward, for before you lies paradise.'

The invocation of 'paradise' in this context is illuminating; it bears many associations. If poetry in the Arab world is 'the register of the Arabs' and an

15

exalted source of '*ilm*' or 'knowledge', it could be described as 'the paradise of the Arabs'. Pasha's use of the word affords multiple interpretations, beyond the fact that in Islamic culture 'paradise' is always a reference to the concept of martyrdom for a greater cause that concerns the collective. One of these possible interpretations relates to the fact that throughout Arab history, poetry often stood for higher states of existence; for high-flown description, reflection, introspection, engagement and verbal penetration; all of which attempt to establish a sense of spiritual ascendance and release, to compensate for earthly human existence through language that aspires to divine paradise. Such a paradise is not monolithic but is supported by a passionate involvement with the subject matter, which in return establishes psychological fulfilment or comfort through serene, temporal infinity. Such a seizure of infinity is taken to be heavenly, because it encompasses the earthly and the celestial. In origin, however, it is all earth-bound, enmeshed in the human pursuit of meaning and power.

In these lines 'paradise' literally means Egypt, but it is also poetry, the object of desire within language itself. The word and the dream of 'paradise' are vividly evoked in the Qur'an and the Muslim canon in general; and here 'paradise' is threatened. '[P]aradise' saturates the imagination with otherworldly abundance and infinite promise: it is a bright world of concrete imagery. Thus, it falls to the Arabs and Ottomans to liberate the Arab world from the Western powers that have divided and ruled it.

Still, the word deserves to be further deconstructed so that the bare essence of the unconscious, its power within the conscious, might be clarified. In the Arabic political poetry of the nineteenth century, and indeed later, claims for one power or another are often evident. The words of poetry are packaged within the accessible language of the ideologies and political discourses of the day. Yet, the ordinary language of poetry often shows an initial obsession with political power, which the poets embed within cultural narratives abounding with values and visions. It is not the intention of this chapter to delve into the psychological content of such poetry. Worthwhile though this might be, it would open up the enormous subject of motivation behind action, including poetry. The force of power in politics, and indeed in almost all domains of life, as the French philosopher Michel Foucault originally contended, operates and appears at its zenith in poetry and art in general. To this end, the desire for power in politics and its manifestation in poetry deserve further scrutiny. This is particularly so given the significance of the time in question, when the Arab world found itself between empires intent on devouring its land and resources, and struggling to reinvigorate its culture and political life with independence and renewed pride.

Thus, turning an actual, impending defeat or naked loss of power into an extraordinary ordeal, as happens in this particular poem, is what man does in the face of his demise. He cannot accept the defeat; he does not like to lose, particularly if the object of this loss is deeply imprinted in his psyche, historically interwoven within it. So for actual loss he substitutes extraordinary images of unfulfilled passions: the Ottoman Empire, which up until this point in history had been the centre of the Islamic Caliphate, becomes the guardian of paradise, which is Egypt itself. In the modern history of the Arab world, naked defeat and frustrations on social and political fronts have turned into poetic spectacles of triumphal sounds countless times, spectacles that managed to conceal the crushing burden of loss. Yet it is also fair to point out that several Arab poets saw themselves as the voice of the Arab conscience, strained as it was by untrammelled powers beyond the Arabs' ability to contest. To this end, much of the committed Arabic poetry of the nineteenth century is steeped in claims of legitimacy: the legitimacy of one order or another, be it a ruler, an empire or a set of values or ideas. This poetry therefore represents power relations at the political as well as cultural level.

Relatively speaking, Jamal Pasha is a secondary figure in the history of the Ottoman Empire. He was one of the last officials of the Ottoman Empire, which had ruled the Arab world for four centuries, from 1517 to 1923. The Ottoman Empire was the first great empire to rule the entire Arab world (excepting Morocco and Central Arabia, *Nejd*) under the name of Islam through non-Arab rulers from a non-Arab centre, Constantinople (now Istanbul). While some Arabs integrated themselves socio-politically and economically with this non-Arab but Muslim regime, others maintained positions of ambivalence or outright rejection. The numbers of the latter group increased as the Ottoman Empire began to tremble under the combined pressure of European colonial powers and rising Arab nationalism. Thus, although Pasha's evocation of 'paradise' can be considered effective in the intended religious sense, given the shared Islamic background of the Arab world and the Ottomans, rising nationalism was at that time altering narratives and replacing or nuancing them with specific connotations. At the heart of such change, in this example, was the Arabic language, where Islam was most integrated and represented.

There is a latent despair in Pasha's language: a lack of alternatives as well as humiliation and exaggeration accented with defiance. All of these are symptomatic of the Arabic poetry of that period, commonly described as the age of the renaissance or, simultaneously, awakening, *'asr al-Nahda*. The Ottoman

Empire was losing popularity by the time Pasha issued his commands. Throughout the nineteenth century, and indeed beyond, Egypt represented a centre of cultural and political weight, acting as the pivotal magnet of Arab identity and destiny. To this end, Egypt's historic power invited attention from all the powers of the day; once it started charting its own political path, Egypt stumbled upon enemies with various inclinations but ultimately led the Arab world towards a new era of nationalism, nation-statism, and significant shifts towards cultural modernity.

In this period it was Mohammad Ali (1769–1849) who opened up Egypt to Western civilisations, turning it into a cultural haven and shaking the declining Ottoman Empire to its roots. In fact, his period is one whose tensions are not so distant from those of the Arab world of today. He fought off the seeds of ambitious Islamism in Saudi Arabia and meanwhile sent envoys to study in Europe. These envoys, including pioneering figures such as Rifāʿah Rāfiʿ al-Tahtāwī (1801–1873), returned with fresh ideas of political reform and cultural revival. Such contact with Europe had a lasting impact on the Arab world, an impact represented and expressed by poetry, including that of al-Tahtāwī himself.

If, on the one hand, the Arab world was at the receiving end of the Ottoman Empire's decline, on the other it was waking up to the heavy spectre of colonialism. On both fronts of struggle, against the despotism of the Ottoman Empire and the ambitions of the Western empires, the Arab world represented itself and resisted in prose and poetry. Its nationalism and resistance vis-à-vis the Ottoman Empire in particular are the subject of this chapter, which opens by highlighting the historical context of the Ottoman Empire and Arab nationalism while giving an account of the intellectual currents of that time. I then turn to analysing poetic excerpts from renowned poets, from the inception of Mohammad Ali's rule in Egypt to the collapse of the Ottoman Empire, alongside the dynamics and repercussions of colonialism in the Arab world. The overall theme of this chapter is the concurrence of poetry with nationalist and cultural developments, using poetic extracts as ethnographic and aesthetic sources of prime importance in explaining the socio-political and emotional climate of the times when the poetry was composed.

The Ottoman Empire versus Arab renaissance

The predominant development concerning the Ottoman Empire and its rule over the Arab world throughout the nineteenth century was the Empire's gradual collapse in the face of Arab national consciousness in conjunction with Western powers bent on controlling the Arab world and its resources. French and British colonialism had already emerged in Arab territories, starting with the French campaign led by Napoleon in 1798. All the external powers that competed for authority over the Arab world left their mark on it in one way or another; culture is a key word in this context. The founding of literary and educational societies in Egypt as well as Syria sparked an Arab renaissance and a curiosity about Arabic cultural renewal and independence from foreign rulers.

Mohammad Ali of Egypt (though in fact of Albanian origin), and his son Ibrahim in particular, started an educational process in the Arab world that had enduring effects. Their opposition to the Ottoman Empire was premised on their ambition to establish an empire of their own with an Arab character and with Egypt at its heart.[2] They were fortunate that the Ottoman Empire was already weak, targeted by domestic, regional and other imperial powers. Mohammad Ali and Ibrahim sent educational convoys to Europe and to other centres of learning, such as Beirut, to acquire the best possible educational methods. They also established schools for translation and encouraged the emergence of cultural societies. Among the pioneers of these societies were intellectuals and poets from across the Arab world. All this coincided with missionary schools implanted for imperial, religious and political objectives, paving the ground for Western dominance, be it by France or Britain. By the end of the nineteenth century, nearly all the Arab countries, hitherto under the tutelage of the Ottoman Empire, were split between or competitively occupied by France or Britain, or Italy as in the case of Libya.

The Arab-inspired cultural societies had great local effect, however. In particular, two prominent scholars played a pivotal role in creating educational societies and spreading political consciousness through linguistic and literary means, namely the Lebanese educators Nasīf al-Yāzijī (1800–1871) and Butrus Bustānī (1819–1883). With time, their scholarly activities turned into ingredients of political and cultural consciousness that activated resistance to imperial powers and empowered people to think of Arab identity on a sovereign and prosperous cultural basis.

Both were great educationalists steeped in Arabic language, culture and literature. George Antonius, one of the first to write about the emergence of Arab national movements in his book *The Arab Awakening* in 1938, relays the story of the first poem that, according to him, signified a new era of nationalist awakening in the Arab world. His book opens with the first line from the poem written by Nasīf al-Yāzijī's son, Ibrahim al-Yāzijī (1847–1906), 'ayyuhā al-'Arab tanabahū wa-istafiqū', 'Awake, O Arabs, and arise!' Antonius' summary of the poem and its value widens the scope of the discussion with regard to the intellectual and poetic trends then defining the Arab world. Antonius writes of Ibrahim al-Yāzijī's poem and its immediate effects:

> It was at a secret gathering of certain members of the Syrian Scientific Society that the Arab national movement may be said to have uttered its first cry...in substance, the poem was an incitement to Arab insurgence. It sang of the achievements of the Arab race, of the glories of Arabic literature, and of the future that the Arabs might fashion for themselves by going to their own past for inspiration. It denounced the evils of sectarian dissensions, heaped abuse on the misgovernment to which the country was a prey, and called upon the Syrians to band together and shake off the Turkish yoke...such is the talent of Arabs for memorising poetry and for secret conspiracy that it was spread by word of mouth throughout the town and, later, throughout the country, without a hint to betray its origin...the poem did much to foster the national movement in its infancy.[3]

Political effects born of timely poetic creations recur quite often in the Arab world. What is striking about Antonius' summary of the poem is that its content was very much alive in the intellectual and political arenas of the Arab world at that time. The poem urges the Arabs to rise up, take the initiative, and be masters of their fate; it also asks them to wake up, no doubt meaning to tap into their cultural power and achieve their aspirations using their own resources. It stirs them against the Ottoman Empire and against other imperial powers. Against this background, Yasir Suleiman, highlighting Antonius' epigraph, writes that 'no account of Arab nationalism would be complete without understanding the contributions literature made, and still makes, to its articulation or to its role in group mobilisation.'[4] It is poetry in particular that best embodied national sentiments and cultural values in the history of the Arabs, permeating the public sphere with expressions of active meanings and values. The content of al-Yāzijī's poem maps out a variety of cultural and political setbacks in the Arab world, to which several intellectuals from the Arab world contributed explanations, criticising as well as suggesting solutions to recurrent flaws:

> *Awake, O Arabs, and arise!*
> *Such an overwhelmingly grievous predicament has stricken you*
> *Why take refuge in hopes that deceive you*
> *When you are torn apart by spearheads from all sides ...*[5]

The despotism of the Ottoman Empire was such that the poet in question, Ibrahīm al-Yāzijī, published his poem anonymously in 1868 out of fear of persecution. His decision demonstrates the corruption of the time in which he lived and is indicative of the dictatorial practice that has been familiar ever since. His poem is accented with attitudes of pan-Arabism, prevalent at the time among many Arab intellectuals and poets and certainly among the three Christian writers mentioned so far. His poem also registers the different powers by which the Arab world felt attacked and crushed, a condition that the poet suggests demands Arab unity. But this spirit of Arabism with which the poet opens his poem is paralleled by an Islamist streak of a different colour. The narrative of unity in the Arab world was grounded on the one hand in the Arabic language, shared history and culture,[6] and on the other in Islamic-oriented governance, as mapped out by different intellectuals and writers. These two foundations in fact went hand in hand in a manner that to an extent reflects today's tensions between Islamists and secularists.[7] Nevertheless, it is in the context of the Ottoman Empire and other imperial powers that this poetry, with its various intellectual and ideological underpinnings, emerged, in an attempt to direct the Arab world towards independence, unity, cultural vibrancy and socio-political awareness. A poem of the famous Lebanese poet Khalīl Muṭrān (1872–1949), known as 'the poet of the two countries' because he was born in Lebanon and lived in Egypt, aptly evokes the theme of awakening in Arab life, hence 'the Arab awakening'.[8] It is suffused with references to Arab origins, which are depicted as grounded in nobility and enriched with cultural and scientific vivacity:

> O noble company of Arabs, ye
> My pride and boast, over every company,
> Long have I reproached your carelessness and sloth,
> But candidly, as if to awake a friend
> Unconscious of vast perils that impend.
> Long night of intercession, and of pleas,
> Your slumber kept me wakeful with unease,
> Till I would cry, 'had ever nation kept
> Its bed such centuries, as you have slept...
> You are a folk whose chronicles abound
> With noble deeds, since valour was renowned,
> You from Qahtan found a hero's grave
> Even to Shaiban's Qais, and Antar brave,
> To the Quraishite orphan, who was lord
> Of wisdom marvellous, and mighty sword...
> Wise governors, that with accomplished skill
> Revolved the world's affairs upon their will;
> Scholars profound, who shed true learning's light

On human hearts, to guide mankind aright,' ...
'Now is the hour of peril come!' I said,
'That shall awake them! O my soul, be glad!
Danger's the thing to stir a frozen soul,
A people's bound-up virtue to unroll'⁹

Making the Arabic-Islamic past a relevant solution for the present is a major trope of the poetry written during the Arab awakening. This poem is a call for renaissance, with past Arab achievements and historic figures referenced as its sources of inspiration. It laments the current status quo, in which Arabs are not the upholders of their own fates. By contrast, as the first few lines suggest, Arab pride was once authentic, enlivened by Arab characteristics and actions. The poet wears the mantle of remembrance, reminding the Arabs of exalted aspects of their history before they lost agency and became subject to others' rule. The origins of the Arabs; the father figure of Qaḥtān, the epic characters of Qais and 'Antar, and then the Prophet Mohammad, as referred to by his tribe, Quraish; all are etched in the Arab imagination as symbols of the Arabs founding identity, dripping with psycho-sociological meanings and transformations. The last few lines ring the alarm bells, as the Arab world is now under foreign rule and further colonial dangers are looming. So the poet reverts to the psychological truth that danger encourages acts of survival, and survival breeds creativity and awakening; a nationalist message that echoed throughout the nineteenth century in intellectual as well as poetic discourses.

I now turn to the intellectual voices of the nineteenth and the beginning of the twentieth century; those who spearheaded the Arab renaissance and engineered the revival. These intellectuals and writers nurtured the poetry of the time and marked its identity with their various views on the issues of the day. Also worth noting are the poems written in praise and commemoration of these intellectuals, as they represent a long-standing tradition of panegyric poetry directed towards rulers and intellectuals, more often towards the former than the latter.[10] As will be seen, in the absence of a united and politically strong Arab world, the intellectuals in question served as leaders, as beacons to whom the Arab world looked for guidance in reaching a more promising future.

Intellectuals with a message

What has come to be popularised as 'speaking truth to power' in the twentieth century, an intellectual attitude championed by the Palestinian–American intellectual Edward Said (1935–2003), has deep roots in the Arabic tradition.

(Here, the Arabic tradition is defined as a canon of rituals, texts and oral culture that have all added texture to Arab life by endowing it with historicity, intellectual substance, and socio-political and linguistic traits of continuous relevance and accessibility). The questions of power, authority and regulation in the establishment of a just and morally sound society has been a nodal theme, debated and contested throughout the centuries. The Qur'an, the main scriptural wellspring of Arabic culture, emphasises how 'God reveres [literarily: fears] his scholars, among his servants'.[11] God is not supposed to fear anyone in Islamic culture, for He is the one whom all should fear and be in awe of. But this verse, no matter how it has come to be interpreted by Islamic scholars and pundits,[12] highlights the reverential position God takes towards scholars, those who are concerned with raising the consciousness of their people and guiding them, as well as revealing to them the secrets of God's wonders. Yet Islamic culture encourages both scholars and lay people to rebel against a corrupt leader or authority. One of the sayings of the Prophet Mohammad usually cited in this context is, 'whoever of you sees a wrongdoing should change it with his hands; but if he cannot, then by his tongue; and if he cannot, then by his heart; and this is the least of faith'. In short, the message of God as well as his Prophet is one of rejection and rebellion against despotism in particular, since the Prophet says, 'the best of you is he who says a just word in the face of a corrupt Sultan'.

There is, however, no straightforward basis in the Islamic canon for accounting for just rule, much as there are attitudes of governance underpinned by God's sanctions and the Prophet's vision of justice which are arguably not of enough uniformity or clarity to serve as an abiding legal system of timeless quality. Particular Islamists have sometimes even blocked rebellion against despotic rulers themselves. This was done on the basis that a Muslim ruler with claims to stability is superior to one clouded by uncertainty and liable to plant seeds of strife, or *fitna*, amongst Muslims, the harms of which would exceed any potential benefits. From the Islamic canon, there are influential sayings that either suggest or affirm that the 'Caliphate is the shadow of God on earth', and others that go so far as to command, 'whoever amongst you comes forward when all your hearts are on one man, and tries to split your group, kill him'. So long as the ruler does not prevent prayer, he should be obeyed, even if he *jallada ẓahraka wa-ṣalaba mālaka*, 'lashed your back and stole your money', say some Islamists.[13] The unity, *wiḥdah*, of the Islamic *umma* is indeed paramount in Islamic theology and the expressive realms of cultural practices. Any hint of its breach calls for rectification or retribution.

In short, governance based on Islamic ideology is an issue of such intense debate that no party could claim a total hegemonic understanding and ownership of it, as has been the case with many Islamists throughout the centuries, and is even more so today. One of the main reasons for this position is the malleability of language, which, given its uncalculated contextual deployment and development, could not, in any meaningful way, sustain fixed meanings of uncontested value and applicability, despite the fact that many Islamists advocate and desire this. And it is this malleability and diversity of language that manifests itself so abundantly in poetry.

Thus, in Islamic culture and theology as practised and perpetuated in the discourse of the public sphere, there are a variety of opinions which have either coexisted or developed into conflicts of interest and orientation, resulting over time in major changes in the power structures of the polity in question. This reality is evidenced in the case of the Ottoman Empire. Although its control over the Arab world led to relative cultural stagnation and political weakness, its offer of alleged stability and prosperity as a Caliphate with Islamic credentials made many Arabs prefer it to foreign or even other potential Arab rulers. In addition, many Arab notables were so deeply entrenched in the Ottoman Empire that they could not stop viewing it as a legitimate polity.[14] Here, broadly, we observe two camps: one assertively against the Ottoman Empire and its ambitions of domination over the Arab world; and another fiercely defending it as a paragon of Islamic guardianship. Both camps tapped into expressive cultural reservoirs to validate their views. The literary Arabic canon has been in use extensively throughout the centuries, constituting a historically rooted culture of communication.[15] To this end, for the Arab intellectual climate during the nineteenth century, literature vacillates between the restoration and establishment of an Islamic order which will inspire justice and prosperity on the one hand; and the construction of an Arab nation along the lines of its cultural and linguistic unity on the other. These are the major distinctions between the two groups in the Arab world in the nineteenth century. Others advocated a regional or national state, such as those in Egypt or Lebanon; this view had congruence with the discourse of nationalism, nation-state and national identity, widespread in Europe first and then in the Arab world.[16]

The intellectual ambience of the Arab world in the nineteenth and early twentieth centuries is, therefore, one that encompasses interpretations and options encased within a historical experience of revival beset by internal and external limits and uncertainties. The Arab world, as well as having its own

Arab power struggles, was also engaged with international power contests in which its very sovereignty and cultural integrity were at stake. Poetry embodied the tensions, struggles and aspirations of each age in a way that revealed the Arab intellectual as well as emotional identity. Before turning to the poetry of this time, and its expressions of political ideas and events, it is instructive to refer to some of the intellectual figures whose ideas pervaded the era in question and found expression in its poetry.

Three Arab intellectuals whose ideas endured besides those mentioned above are Mohammad 'Abduh (1849–1905) of Egypt, Jamāl ad-Dīn al-Afghānī (1838–1897) of Iran and Egypt, and Abdel Rahmān al-Kawākibī (1849–1902) of Syria. These three intellectuals were pioneers of culture and political awareness. Each of them engaged with serious issues concerning culture, governance and justice. Although they also all came from Islamic backgrounds of one kind or another, they had all been exposed to and therefore influenced by Western civilisation and schools of thought. They took seriously their mission as figures of renaissance operating amidst acute political challenges, whose echoes continue to reverberate today.

They are to some extent a product of Mohammad Ali's attitudes towards culture and the importance of its role in restoring a sense of intellectual viability to Arab life, one that would give the newly emerging nation-state the confidence it needed to face the challenges of an increasingly interdependent world. As mentioned before, Mohammad Ali and his son Ibrahim took the initiative to delegate educationalists to establish centres of translation and cultural restoration by making texts from the Arab tradition available. Experiencing the richness of their heritage, many Arabs awoke to the stultifying status quo in which they were living. Mohammad Ali's attitudes here resemble those of the Abbasid Caliphates (750–1258), who encouraged translation schools and aided the renaissance of Europe by making Greek and Roman sources of education and culture available to the Europeans through translation.[17] The Arab intellectual pioneers of the nineteenth century also tapped into rich sources of diverse quality and relevance, in addition to their encounter with European colonialism and civilisations. This context of colonialism, cultural awakening, resistance and despotism drove critical thinking about the course of the Islamic world and its future. The name of Mohammad Ali is associated with the inauguration of serious cultural and political developments in the Arab world, and he had great significance for the poetry of the time. One renowned Egyptian poet whose work illustrates Mohammad Ali's importance is Aḥmad Shawqī (1868–1932). Shawqī occupies a distinctly pioneering place in the history of modern Arab poetry, hence his reception of the esteemed appellation *Amīr al-Shuʻarā*, the Prince of Poets. He composed panegyric poems to Mohammad Ali and his sons, who ruled Egypt after him, and particularly to Khedive Tawfiq (1852–1892). In the poem that Shawqī dedicated to Mohammad Ali, he wrote:

> *What an outstanding pioneer you are in the East*
> *You are eternally remembered among the people*
> *How great a state and kingdom*
> *Whose basis you have founded, O Mohammad,*
> *You conquer the earth bit by bit*
> *The way people entered the realm of (Prophet) Mohammad*
> *He who conquers a state to exhaust it*
> *Is not the same as he who makes it happy,*
> *Egypt knew and so did Hijāz and the land of the Nūb (Sudan)*
> *And greater Syria that your reign is golden...*
> *They have claimed that the East is agitating about your deeds*
> *While I see it as stable and prosperous in your hands*
> *You came to it with life, light and civilisation*
> *With reason, wisdom and the protective sword...*[18]

Shawqī, the most famous Egyptian poet of his day, praises Mohammad Ali for the historical contributions he made to Egypt, the Arab world, and what he describes as the East in general. Along the way, Shawqī points out historical references and achievements that relate to Mohammad Ali's role, revealing the integrity of knowledge within poetry. The pioneer is one who enters a realm and changes or advances it. Shawqī is vindicated in pointing out the enduring legacy of Mohammad Ali, as it is with him that the Arab renaissance gains a political and cultural foothold. Thus, Mohammad Ali is portrayed as a guiding cultural and political figure whose reign witnessed a turning point of profound significance. Shawqī evokes monumental characters such as the Prophet Mohammad, creating an iconic connection impregnated with historical meaning. Indeed, Arab poets, even broadly secular ones like Shawqī, often related their political and social works to the first era of Islam as led by the most revelatory character in Islamic history, the Prophet Mohammad. In particular, Shawqī helped to resurrect a tradition of panegyrics by writing a long poem evoking the spirit of Mohammad and his mission and teachings, namely his 'Nahej al-Burda'. This portrayal of the Prophet affirms his political as well as his religious roles; and this is an aspect that even Christian socialist thinkers, such as Michel 'Aflaq (1910–1989), highlighted in their writings on the Prophet Mohammad and his historical position as the first unifying figure of the Arab *umma* (nation).[19]

Furthermore, the poem in question includes historical information that defined Mohammad Ali's rein. One of the first cracks to appear in the Ottoman Empire was the uprising in central Arabia in the early eighteenth century, when a religious figure, Muhammad ibn 'Abd al-Wahhab (1703–1792), led an uprising in the Hijāz area of the Arabian Peninsula against the Ottoman Caliph and called the Muslims to return to Islamic purity, meaning 'strict obedience to the Qur'an and Hadīth as they were interpreted by responsible scholars in each generation, and rejection of all that could be regarded as illegitimate innovations'.[20] At the behest of the Ottoman Caliph, Mohammad Ali crushed this rebellion and restored the Ottoman Empire's status as the seat of the Islamic Empire. Yet this was only temporary: Ali's sons led campaigns against the Ottoman Empire itself and ultimately contributed to its overall demise in 1923.[21] In this context the poetry of Shawqī, who wrote praising the Ottoman Empire and its order, is indicative of the pervasive intellectual climate of the time. In addition, Shawqī highlights another aspect of Muhammad Ali's role in cultivating intellectualism, encapsulated in 'reason, wisdom and the protective sword'. These dimensions made up what he called civilisation, a combination that hints at the influence of Europe on the Arab world that Ali himself encouraged through educational envoys and interactions. To this end, some of the Islamic intellectual pioneers who shone in the wake of Ali's dynastic rule included Jamal ad-Dīn al-Afghānī and Mohammad 'Abduh.

Jamal ad-Dīn al-Afghānī is usually mentioned as one of the first Islamic reformers. Though ethnically Iranian in origin, he spent most of his life occupied with the travails of the broader Islamic world and its status under the Ottoman Empire and in the wake of European colonialism. Jamāl ad-dīn al-Afghānī, who influenced Mohammad 'Abduh of Egypt, believed in the compatibility of Islam with law as crafted by human reason that took into consideration the spiritual presence of the divine in the world. Both men advocated a spiritual return to an Islam that welcomes vitality and dynamism. Their contribution was not only theological; it was grounded in the political context of their time. Soundly explicating al-Afghānī's view, Albert Hourani writes:

> There could be no real reform of Islam unless the *uluma* (scholars) returned to the truth of Islam, and the community as a whole accepted it and lived in accordance with it [...] He wishes to destroy the false views of Islam held by Muslims and criticisms of Islam made by Europeans. When he maintains that only by a return to Islam can the strength and civilization of Muslims be restored, he does so the more emphatically because it had become a commonplace of European thought that religion in general, and Islam specifically, sapped the will and restricted reason, and

progress was only possible by abandoning it, or at least by making a sharp separation between religion and secular life.[22]

This summary demonstrates the enduring effort of Islamic scholars in their attempts to ensure Islam a place in public life and law. While they opened themselves to Europe and its scientific and intellectual advancement, they advocated *ijtihād* (independent reasoning)[23] as a method of understanding the Islamic past and refitting it within the context of their time. Mohammad 'Abduh in particular was vocal in stressing the importance of *ijtihād* in Muslim life, in all areas that do not touch the fundamentals of Islam or those constituted in what is known as *'ibadāt*, abiding rituals and forms of worship directed towards God. In the other domain, however—those aspects of religion that regulate relations between people and afford human practical reasoning, respectful of God's revelation, called *al-mu'amalāt*,—'Abduh embraced *ijtihād*. Meanwhile, 'Abduh warned of ignorance; the ignorance of the rulers and their despotism, directing his criticism towards the Ottoman rulers in particular. In this context, we find al-Afghānī and 'Abduh inspired by the early community of Muslims and their descendants of interpreters and scholars, such as Ibn Taymiyya (1263–1328) and the *al-Mu'tazilat* school of thought. It was the opinion of earlier interpreters of the Islamic canon as constituted in the Qur'an and the Hadīth tradition that they should attempt to revive and explain in the Qu'ran within their historical contexts. Together they established the influential periodical *al-'urwa al-withqa* (The unbreakable bond) in 1884, and defended the Islamic *umma* against outside interventions, such as those instigated by European powers. Meanwhile, they were suspicious of the Ottoman sultans and called for an Arab Caliphate with Arab credentials. 'Abduh went further in inflecting his view with Egyptian nationalism, reflecting an emerging discourse of nationalism characteristic of that era. In explaining 'Abduh's thoughts and his attempt to wed Islam to modern ideals of democracy and freedom, Hourani writes:

> He carried farther a process which we have already seen at work in the thought of Tahtāwī, Khayr al-Dīn, and al-Afghānī: that of identifying certain traditional concepts of Islamic thought with the dominant ideas of modern Europe. In this line of thought, *maslaha* gradually turns into utility, *shura* into parliamentary democracy, *ijmā'* into public opinion; Islam itself becomes identical with civilization and activity, the norms of nineteenth-century social thought.[24]

Thus, whereas al-Afghānī and 'Abduh directed their attention to reforming Muslim life through reintegrating Islamic teachings and ensuring adaptability within modern systems of living, others focused their energy on reforming

Muslims from within and particularly in relation to condemning and resisting internal despotism. One such thinker who was also active and significant in the course of the second half of the nineteenth century was 'Abd al-Rahmān al-Kawākibī. Al-Kawākibī was one of the clearest thinkers of his age. His most significant work is *Tabāi' al-Istibdād wa-Masāri' al-Isti'bād*, 'The Nature of Despotism and the Harm of Enslavement'. In this book al-Kawākibī lays out the harms of despotism and the ways in which it can be resisted. His target in stressing the devastating effects of despotism is the Ottoman Empire, particularly under Sultan Abdulhamid II (r.1876–1909). Like al-Afghānī and 'Abduh, al-Kawakibi stands for the restoration of an Islamic *umma* on the basis of justice and development driven by human needs and will. Being the educationalist that he was, he lays emphasis on education and its virtues in nurturing aware citizens, making them conscious of their rights and obligations.[25]

The figures Hourani authoritatively delineates in his magisterial book *Arab Thought in the Liberal Age, 1798–1939*, and particularly al-Afghānī and 'Abduh, all project the multiple sources of struggles they were engaged in, as well as the heavy intellectual responsibility they felt towards their societies and the Muslim world at large. They were not alone. Poets were comrades in this path of struggle, intellectual responsibility, and attempts to adapt to modern times. To this end, these intellectuals were praised and commemorated in poetry by the great poets of their age and those who benefited or felt empowered by their intellectual heritage. Before the nineteenth century and Muhammad Ali, the Arab world was suffering from an increasing cultural decline, marked by naivety regarding their narrow understanding of their past and its relevance to the present moment. In particular, 'Abduh grappled with contradictions, privileging human reasoning and innovation over imitation and blind obedience; he was daring in suggesting practice-oriented approaches to social and legal problems, as well as in highlighting the virtue of learning from other civilisations, mainly Europe. With these figures on the scene, and especially given the sense of urgency with which they wrote, the Arab world felt enlivened and animated. And it is from this period onwards that Arabic poetry becomes an essential ingredient of Arab renaissance and nationalist awakening. With this in mind, I highlight three panegyric poems written in memory of the great thinkers by two notable poets, namely Ḥāfiẓ Ibrahīm (1868–1932) of Egypt and Mohammad Mahdī al-Jawāhīrī (1900–1997) of Iraq. These poems reflect the interactive nature of culture with politics and poetry as the prime form of expression and artistic representation in Arab lives.

Poets and intellectuals

The poems in question show how politics was reconstituted by the thinkers they commemorate, and thus how the poets responded to the political climate of their age, accenting their poetry appropriately. Political poetry of the type presented below suggests that politics is integrated into the cultural fabric of the Arab world. Even those who wrote what is known as 'pure poetry', the brainchild of the 'art for art's sake' literature with which the nineteenth-century cultural climate abounded, blended political ideals and concerns with their poetry.

One of the poetic streaks of the nineteenth-century Arab world is summed up in the striking political command 'Awake, O Arabs, and arise!', as discussed above. When al-Afghānī arrived in India in 1868, he gave a speech stirring his audience to rise against the British Empire, of which India was then the largest part. Al-Afghānī addressed his receptive audience as follows:

> O people of India, if God was to reincarnate all of you in your millions each as a turtle, and you seized the sea, and besieged the Island of Great Britain, you would have routed it to the bottom and returned to India free.[26]

Al-Afghānī's essential idea is that people are stripped of their will because of their ignorance, and that they are therefore incompetent and unable to challenge Britain effectively, despite the fact that British colonists were only a tiny fraction of India's population. It is the notion of power involved in the rhetorical slogan 'arise'—change and return to your roots—that al-Afghānī, 'Abduh and others adopt and emphasise. They preached and persuaded with both poetry and prose. Al-Afghānī arrived in Egypt in 1871 from Constantinople, the then seat of the Ottoman Empire, where he had been a guest of the Ottoman Sultan 'Abdul Azīz (1830–1876), and immediately noticed widespread ignorance, with myths and fables being treated as facts. He called to the Egyptian people:

> Arise from your slumber, wake up from your drunkenness, shed off the cloak of stupidity and tear apart the chests of the despots as you split your land with your ploughing machines; live like all nations, free and happy, and die rewarded as martyrs.[27]

Rhetorical though it is, al-Afghānī is employing a message of resistance in his poetic preachings. He calls for freedom and emancipation from injustice and despotic rule as it was then being meted out by the three centres of power: the Ottoman Empire; the Khedive Ismail Pasha of Egypt (1830–1895), grandson of Mohammad Ali; and the colonising countries of the West: France and

Britain. The speeches of al-Afghānī and others, and their intellectual and poetic leanings, served as materials for the poets who commemorated and celebrated these thinkers. Al-Afghānī is remembered for his active involvement in the affairs of the Arab world at political, cultural and religious levels. To this end, poets and writers continued to debate and write about the meaning, relevance and scope of his contributions, which found long-lasting echoes.

In his commemoration of al-Afghānī, the renowned Iraqi poet Mohammad Mahdī al-Jawāhīrī writes:

You have risen to stand by the bright righteousness
Had it not been for death, you would not have stopped...
O Jamal ad-Dīn, a soul in the height,
Who came with a message and then returned...
You did not succumb to the whims of a despot
Or give up on what you wanted for what he wanted.
There were two camps: one of pervasive oppression
And another of the oppressed, but you did not stand on the sideline.
O Jamāl ad-Dīn, you were and it was the East
And it was a boat loaded with Jihād...
It was a 'ruwa wuthqa' giving
To the divided: love and unity...
How many a wounded country in the East
Complaining not only of wounds but also the healing cloths...
The foreigner had got what he wanted, and assumed charge,
Seized authority, and raped the country...
Our lot were like dispersed plants, far apart,
But when you reined, you rained with abundance...![28]

Al-Jawāhīrī was born in Iraq in 1899 in Najaf in Iraq, two years after al-Afghānī passed away. The fact that al-Jawāhīrī wrote this poem in the 1930s indicates the living and lasting resonance of al-Afghānī's thoughts, on politics, himself and his generation, in the culture of the Arab world. Al-Jawāhīrī's other poetry is also concerned with protest and renewal in the Arab world, reflecting a widespread trend. Reference to two lines from his poem '*Sabīl al-jamahīr*', 'The way of the people', reveals this symbiotic connection between what cultural figures, such as al-Afghānī and 'Abduh, embodied, and poetry:

Had the affairs of the people been in my hands,
I would have led my countries on the path of rebellion
For I have known that there is no life for any nation
That strives to live without renewal.[29]

Al-Jawāhīrī lived a long life, filled with dramatic political events and incidents in his native Iraq and in the Arab world at large. It is pertinent to consider him as an important poetic witness to the landscape of Arab politics in the twentieth century. The above lines offer an entry-point for understanding his interest in al-Afghānī, evident from both the poem explicitly dedicated to him and 'The way of the people', which evokes the path of renewal that al-Afghānī, 'Abduh and others advocated. Al-Jawāhīrī projects al-Afghānī as a philosopher–king: a figure with intellect, courage and, most importantly, vision. The evocation of *al-haqq* in the first line of the poem is indicative of the return that al-Afghānī called for. This would be a return to *al-haqq* for Islam made possible by and instituted through a community of interpreters and scholars, a message that Islamists from all over the Arab world carried forward. We will see this message in the poetry of Sayyid Qutb (1906–1966), one of the principal figures of dogmatic Islamism in the twentieth century.

Al-Afghani's publication in collaboration with his disciple Mohammad 'Abduh, the *al-'ruwa al-wuthqa* (The Unbroken Bond) periodical, which ushered in a sense of cultural renaissance in the Arab world, was another of his enduring achievements. Most importantly, however, it was his fight (*Jihād*) against the colonisers and his message of unity that al-Jawāhīrī celebrates, emphasising the 'wound of the East' epitomised in iconic words such as 'colonialism', 'ignorance', 'disunity' and 'despotism'. Al-Afghānī's identification of these ideas, his reflections on them, and his preaching and struggles against them, have all made him significant, which explains the affection that al-Jawāhīrī heaps on him. Most importantly, the poem of al-Jawāhīrī contains a notion that became a commonplace in nineteenth century Arab poetry: he laments the state of the Arab world, lambasting its second-place status in relation to the West, and he is deeply mindful of reform and revival.

As above, al-Afghānī is often mentioned in association with Mohammad 'Abduh. They were long engaged in similar debates and struggles, even though the end of their relationship saw a noticeable cooling. 'Abduh became a figure of canonical importance; in addition to establishing his reputation as a moderniser and premier thinker in the Arab world, he occupied the position of Mufti of Egypt. One of the period's eminent Egyptian poets, Ḥāfiẓ Ibrāhīm known as the *Shā'ir an-Nīl*, the poet of the Nile, who is often mentioned in connection with *amīr al-shu'arā*, 'the Prince of Poets' Aḥmad Shawqī, celebrated the occasion of 'Abduh's appointment as Mufti in poetry. Ibrāhīm developed such affectionate admiration for 'Abduh that he called himself *fatā al-Imām*, 'the boy of the Imam'. To some extent, what 'Abduh advocated in prose, Ḥāfiẓ put down in poetry. Thus, the first few lines of the following poem by Ḥāfiẓ encode a conscious departure from the poetic tradition of the Arab past by direct allusion to the poet's intention to transcend it:

I have reached you without declaring loyalty or penning flattery
I did not flail between love and submission
Nor did I describe a cup of wine or weep over a house
Or adopt pride or nobility
There is no place in my heart untouched by praise for you
Where you wander between the memory of a beloved and one with high status...[30]

In short, the poet responds to the new age's need for clarity of thought and practical actions, as advocated by 'Abduh. This is done through a poem that from the outset vocally declares its severance from the poetic traditions of the past. Addressing 'Abduh directly, the poet states that he need not do what the pre-Islamic and medieval Arab poets did, adhering to set conventions in their poetry as represented in *Nasīb* (declaring allegiance to their tribe at the outset of the ode); *ghazzal* (flattery, a form of love poetry); or the praise and embracing of wine, characteristic of Abu Nawwās' poetry (756–814); or showing which nobility he hails from. He intentionally leaves the habitual tradition of beginning the classical Arabic *Qasīdah* with *Nasīb* behind, registering his rebellion and his immersion in the modernist hopes that 'Abduh came to represent. The poet invites the Imām to walk in his heart to see the high standing in which he holds him. It is not the convention that matters, but the content—here, sincerity and pride in 'Abduh. It is his merit that mattered most in forming Ḥāfiẓ's admiring attitudes towards him, not his origin as such. Ḥāfiẓ, like 'Abduh, came from a humble background himself; an affiliation that showed itself more in Ḥāfiẓ's solidarity with the disadvantaged and poor classes of Egypt. This is in contrast to Shawqī, whose panegyric poetry associates itself with the governing elites in Turkey and Egypt. Meanwhile, Ḥāfiẓ's poetry became a vehicle for the modernising 'Abduh's attitudes in the field of literature. He therefore starts his poem without the typical introduction found in classical poetry that can often impinge on the poet's subject matter.

But if Ḥāfiẓ claims to abandon poetic conventions so as to reach the heart of the matter, he does not do so completely. In the rest of the poem, aspects of the past—its figures, their deeds, and moments drawn from the history of Islam—become objects of praise whose return and inspired presence in the present lives of Muslims are projected as the salvation *par excellence*, as embodied by Imām 'Abduh. Ḥāfiẓ writes:

I have seen you surrounded by piously attentive eyes
So I said: is this Abū Ḥafs or Alī between your hands?
I downgraded my sadness over the glory of a nation
For whose sake you came, as problems were mounting...[31]

33

In the Islamic realm of expression, there is a popular saying attributed to Prophet Mohammad that runs as follows: 'God sends from amongst you someone to renew the affairs of your life every hundred years.' Evidently, not all the premises of culture are rational. Some are spiritual and mysterious, and when a prediction of mystery or spirituality is confirmed in one form or another, faith in that mystery is substantiated to the point where it is treated as fact. Ḥāfiẓ recalls the Prophet Mohammad's companions, Abū Hafs and the fourth Caliph of Islam, Alī, and views 'Abduh in that light, essentially as an exalted revivalist. Exaggerated as his praise sounds, it is evidence for an era when Islam began to be invited, in direct and literal fashion, to account for the events and travails of the day—this form of invitation persisted into the twentieth century, and particularly into the latter part of it. Arab history is poured into the powerful personalities who composed it. In this sense, institutions, the modern fundamentals of the nation-state, tend to take second place if they appear at all. Thus, praise poetry is often directed towards grand personalities, be they from political or intellectual realms. The example above shows 'Abduh as an important historic figure invested with a key spiritual and intellectual role, which he highlighted through writings that demonstrated attempts at reforms inspired by Islam but that at the same time were congruent with modernity, and particularly with its scientific aspects. Yet, the panegyric poetry of Shawqī as well as Ḥāfiẓ, two of the most important poets of their time, demonstrate their socio-political backgrounds: the first is bourgeois and more in tune with the powerful and governing elites like the Turkish premiers, while the second emerged from a less advantaged background and reflected those concerns and grievances. This can be seen further in their reflections on colonialism.

But before turning to the Arabic poetry that emerged within the context of Western colonialism, it is time to highlight Arab poetic interaction with the Ottoman Empire, with some of the poets mentioned above in mind.

The Arab world at a crossroads

The nineteenth-century history of Egypt and the Arab world in general is one of struggles, cultural revival and political uncertainty. No Arab country had an overall and firm grip on its territory. The crumbling Ottoman Empire, unpopular though it had been, had maintained a sense of stable rule over the Arab world for long and quite unproductive centuries, distancing the Arabs from their once rich and illuminated past. Mohammad Ali and his sons were influential figures in the nineteenth century. Not only did Ali breathe new life into a hitherto slow-moving Egypt; he also set it on a path of sovereignty and cultural evanescence with lasting consequences. But the fact that Egypt, which contested and rebelled against the Ottoman Empire, was unable to break away totally from it until 1882, when it was occupied by Britain, directed attention towards the symptoms of decline in the Empire. At this point, Egypt was unique in the Arab world, mainly for the political and cultural leadership it demonstrated.

When Mohammad Ali's rule came to an end, he was succeeded by his son Ibrahim Pasha. In all the places in which Ibrahim established a foothold, a new cultural orientation stamped with Arabic sensibility struck roots. Even when Ibrahim retreated, under the pressure of the Ottoman Empire and Western powers opposed to his father's ambition of founding a new Arab Empire, many notable cultural figures from Syria and elsewhere either followed him or kept an eye on Egypt as a pioneer of cultural and political revival, and Arab sovereignty. It is with Ali and his sons, particularly Ibrahim and Ismail, that we find the seeds of an epistemic shift, to use Foucault's term, one marked by new attitudes towards knowledge and politics in general. This shift in cultural attitudes and orientations came after a period of stagnation in which literature in the Ottoman Empire was not of high merit. It did not have the promise of the Umayyad period (632–750) nor the vivacity and depth of the Abbasid period (750–1258)—two eras that are often evoked with nostalgic appreciation. Muhammad Mustafa Badawi, a notable scholar of Arabic literature, characterises the Arabic poetry produced within the context of the Ottoman Empire as follows:

> This sort of verbal juggling could in no way be described as poetry in any meaningful sense of the word, and yet such acrobatic exercises met with much approbation of the time. The subject matter of these poems was confined to the narrow range of conventional empty panegyric addressed to local rulers and officials, commemoration of events in poems ending in chronograms, trivial social occasions like congratulations on a wedding or greetings to a friend. These were often in inflated and highfalutin terms, the Arabic being poor and stilted, the style generally turgid and the imagery merely conventional and lacking in original perception...[32]

While it is true that, on the one hand, the Ottoman Empire was marked by literary stagnation, it is equally true that the period of contested power explained above resulted in cultural and literary activities within the Ottoman Empire that showed promise in the long run. Hussein Kadhim contends that the relative decline of the traditional Arabic poem, *Qasīdah*, as recounted by

Badawi, is related to 'the dearth of the grand occasion which once provided poets with an apposite subject-matter (as opposed to the insignificant "occasion" decried by recent literary history)'. Thus, the modern *Qasīdah* does not merely recount an event, but 'very often it participates to varying degrees in the event while memorializing it'.[33] It was in this context that it became possible to recognise poets of distinguished quality, such as Barūdī, Shawqī, and Ḥāfiẓ among others, who engaged with a variety of social and political conditions while maintaining a distinct Egyptian and Arab national pride that also showed nuances in their loyalties and understanding. In particular, their works show no straightforward condemnation of the Ottoman Empire, nor is there uniform opinion on its viability, particularly in the face of Western colonial encroachment and political and cultural Arab revival engineered by different figures from diverse origins, including Turkey.

Instead, there are often multiple narratives and voices that reflect the landscape of an era in the process of serious transition. In several ways, this transition, political as well as cultural, has been strikingly visible in the Arab world throughout the twentieth century, and perhaps never more so than during the Arab uprisings that began in 2011. The connections between these uprisings and the politics and literature of the nineteenth century are notable, even if the medium of artistic expression has shifted and acquired new dimensions. For the poetic ideals of the nineteenth century, which vacillated between modernity and tradition, did not settle into one coherent shape that could then have matured and diversified. Political fragmentation within the Arab world was apparent in various poetic trends, most of which, like the idea of nationalism and nation-state in the first place, are touched by and react to Europe and its advances.

The condition of the modern nation-state in the Arab context did, therefore, in several important ways impede its own progress, due to its fundamental cultural, political and legal fragmentation. The value of contention in politics had been noted and welcomed,[34] but if contention is not solidified by a system of transparency and legal unity of substantial merit, then politics, culture and literature, all in their own and interrelated ways, appear fragmented and contradictory, reflecting almost unbridgeable sides of the Arab world. While some praised the Ottoman Empire and clung loyally to it, others bitterly attacked it. Badawi's statement reveals the situation clearly:

> Much poetry was written by the Egyptians Shawqī and Ḥāfiẓ Ibrahim in defence of the Ottoman Caliphate and against the enemies of the Ottoman Empire, while in countries like Iraq, which were still directly dependent upon Constantinople and therefore experienced the tyranny of Abdul Hamid II, poets like al-Zahāwī or

al-Ruṣāfī wrote bitter attacks on the Ottoman Sultan and his henchmen, although some of the best political poetry which lashed the Sultan's oppression was written by Waliyy al-Din Yakan in Egypt. Again the birth and development of nationalism resulted in a good deal of poetry, especially in Egypt, which attacked British imperialism and supported local movements of independence.[35]

The poets who stood by the Ottoman Empire and defended the old order it provided were looking at their immediate ancestors' past, not beyond it. The poets who condemned the Ottoman Empire were not sure-footed in their approach to modernity, thus incorporating classism and actually impeding full-fledged adoption of new ways that could have been inspired by European advancements as well as keen Arab reformers. Instead, we find the past being revisited not always in an inspiring fashion but rather in a nostalgic mood of lament and loss.

It is characteristic of transitions that they are ambiguous and split people into camps of enthusiasts, sceptics and opponents. We find these streaks, psycho-political in nature, in abundance in the poetry of the time.

Poetic contestation

The three well-known poets who sided with the Ottoman Empire were political and literary figures of immense influence in Egypt and the Arab world in general. They are the pioneers of the renowned school of poetry named *madrast al-Ihiyyā' wal-ba'ith*, 'the school of resurrection' or 'school of renaissance', signifying the period in which they lived and the wide-ranging attempts at revival that took place around them. All of them are identified as Egyptian and proud Arabs, but all have Turkish sides. Their main preoccupation in their committed poetry (that which entailed direct social or political message or representation) was with the Ottoman Empire and its conditions, the socio-cultural and educational problems their societies were facing, and finally the struggle against the colonial powers that occupied their countries. One of the first of these poets was the Egyptian poet Mahmūd Sāmī al-Bārūdī (1839–1904). Badawi identifies al-Bārūdī as:

> The true precursor of the modern poetic revival [...] in whose work is abundantly clear the conscious return to the classicism of early medieval Arabic poetry, especially the poetry of the Abbasid period. This neoclassicism, or return to the Arab heritage of the past, marks the first stage in the modern literary revival—a stage in which modern Arabs asserted their own cultural identity in a world threatened by alien forces [...] that is why Arab critics and historians of literature are generally agreed that it is with al-Barudi that the renaissance of modern Arabic poetry truly begins.[36]

Al-Barūdī is an example of a political–poetic figure that occupied political, military and literary positions and rendered his experiences into revealing poetry. The appellation *rabbu'l saif wa'l qalam* (master of the sword and the pen) ascribed to him reflects his political and literary stature. His political poetry describes his involvements in battles and debates. One of the first battles that he experienced was in Crete in modern Greece in 1865, where he fought in an Ottoman contingent against a rebellion aimed at the Empire. The rebellion was one amongst many in which the Empire was involved in the nineteenth century in order to protect itself from collapse. The poem echoes pre-Islamic poetry where the poet defended his 'tribe', its virtues, and its prowess, as we see in poems such as that of the poet 'Amrū Ibn Kulthūm, who describes the forty years' pre-Islamic battle between the tribe of Banū Bakr and his tribe Banū Taghlub.[37] In his poem, al-Barūdī writes:

Sleep had crept up the eyelashes
Walking quickly at night, stoked the knights
While the night struck darkness everywhere
Hills and slopes were imbued with obscurity,
Through which the eyes see nothing
Except the burning fire at the tips of arrows...
People whom the devil determined to lose
So they slipped off the Sultan's command.[38]

Al-Barūdī returned to Egypt after eight years' absence in Constantinople, where he learned Turkish and Persian and pursued his literary and political activities avidly. He wrote poems keenly admiring the Ottoman Empire and defending its fledgling orders; praising the rulers of Egypt; and targeting the colonisers of Egypt, calling for resistance. Yet, in the poem above there is more than description of the battle; there is a hidden political reality yet to emerge. It is the image of darkness that dominates the poem, darkness as opposed to confidence of victory. Though the battle was, materially speaking, won, in the long term it became clear that the Ottoman Empire was doomed. While several poets such as al-Barūdi, Shawqī and Ḥāfiẓ praised it, they also shrouded their poems with dim images of darkness that suggested troubles ahead for the Ottoman Empire, whose dominions were gradually prised out of its command as a result of Western colonial interest in its territories as well as internal unrest and decay.

Furthermore, the tone of the poem embodies, although unintentionally, a common theme in modern Arabic poetry. Prophecy is not always intended or even considered overtly but the poet's sensitive grasp of the most essential of the socio-political conditions of the time can result in visions of startling acuteness. Some of the main figures within what is known as the neo-classical school of poetry, particularly the Egyptian side as opposed to the Iraqi and Syrian sides, were generally supporters of the Ottoman Empire and its order. Yet, there exist in their poetry hints of anxiety at the increasingly weak Empire. This streak of poetic prophecy emerges over time, and particularly whenever what is known as the *Nakba* of Palestine in 1948 is hinted at; the 1967 *Naksa* defeat of the Arabs is also suggested by poetry prior to its occurrence. To fast-forward to the Arab Spring, there is even a linear line of prophecy whose content has been confirmed by the events of the Arab Spring, as we will see in the last chapter.

Another palpable theme in Arabic poetry is that of longing. In the same poem above, al-Barūdī expresses longing for Egypt:

I have remembered Egypt,
Where is the water of Egypt,
Who towers above all...[39]

Egypt becomes a subject of longing for its devoted son, who grieved for an Empire which was losing ground unabatedly to colonial Western powers and local Arab nationalist movements. We find in the poetry of al-Barūdī and others images of quiet despair, alongside feelings of longing for their individual countries and an evocation of socio-political problems from which the Arabs suffer, such as shades of ignorance and social weakness. All these problems are accounted for in the poetry of the nineteenth century, and are sometimes carried further and with greater urgency in the twentieth century. But the longing of the poet expressed in the poem above is contagious.

It is possible to read two dimensions into al-Barūdī's lines. They introduce sentiments of loyalty to the individual nation-state from which the poet hails, rather than treating the Ottoman Empire in its entirety as his home. Such longing suggests a degree of alienation that upgrades the political into the existential. The nation-state becomes central in the late nineteenth century, both in Egypt and elsewhere in the Arab world. Secondly, the longing of the poet, which sharpens in other contexts, develops into a major poetic theme in the lives of Arab poets of the nineteenth and twentieth centuries. Longing, a psychological state for absent or unfulfilled wishes, has indeed been the *modus operandi* of Arabic poetry. It is possible to read a deeper meaning into nationalist longing and equate it with an existential condition that connotes crisis or freedom at an ultimate level.

The most famous poet to write panegyric poems to the Ottoman Empire and express admiration for its order was Aḥmad Shawqī. He was another neo-classical poet; Egyptian, but of mixed background, including Turkish and Greek connections. Badawi described him as 'the best-known of the neo-classicists, if not the best-known of all modern Arabic poets'.[40] Here is another poet who was at the heart of politics, not only by virtue of the highly charged political times in which he lived, but also due to the positions he occupied in various Egyptian administrations and his involvement in the struggle against British colonialism in Egypt. His renown is of multiple poetic dimensions. Yet, it is worth highlighting one of the strands that his poetry exhibited: its praise of the Ottoman Empire, for this praise demonstrates that there were no uniform views on the Empire.

While we see opposition to Ottoman oppression of Syria and Iraq in other regions of western and northern Arabia, we find supportive voices in the east, in Egypt, then the leading cultural centre of the Arab world. One of the topics that Shawqī returns to, whether in the context of the Ottoman Empire, the Egyptian state under Mohammad Ali's dynasty or colonialism, is that of democracy and the rule of law. This is hardly surprising given that Shawqī studied law, and was sent in 1887 by Khedive Tawfiq to France to study at the University of Montpellier. Interestingly, he put this background to good use in his poetry, turning it into a haven of social and political invocations to enthusiastic popular approval. As Badawi wrote of Shawqī, 'what Shawqī managed to do, which is no mean service, was to make the traditional Abbasid idiom so relevant to the problems and concerns of modern Egypt. The banishment of Shawqī by the British authorities is in fact an eloquent testimony to the extent and significance of this force.'[41] Making the past so relevant that it appears to be the present is one aim of nationalism. For the past is never entirely past; it is often to be found inflecting the present and its travails. Shawqī emphasises the theme of exile in his poetry, which, although it is not an alien theme to classical Arabic poetry in general, is still associated with colonialism and modern nation-state imperatives: it is in Arab poetry a by-product of modern political developments. To this end, the exile of the poet at the hands of the British colonial occupation is another theme that gained significance in nineteenth- and twentieth-century Arabic poetry.

There are several poems by Shawqī in which he praises Sultan Abdulhamid II, whose reign was marred by corruption and unrest in Turkey and abroad. Shawqī writes under telling titles that do not necessarily reflect in serious terms the topic about which he speaks; but they show his fervent support for the Ottoman Empire and its Sultans as the Caliph of the Muslims, underwriting the importance of Muslim unity over justice in this case. In a poem entitled 'The Ottoman Constitution',[42] whose title reflects the influence of his legal education, Shawqī writes:

The state of the Bedouins roaming in its environs
And you are the torchbearer of care
... You have read the laws of heaven
And possessed the keys of the height...
How do you sleep, Abdulhamid
And winds have come to you, marching like a nation...
Your rule had settled after turbulence
As you embody the gifts of two Sultans: education and intelligence...
You have horses with luminous wings
The horses of Gabriel to stand by the Prophets...[43]

In these lines, Shawqī does not refer to the Ottoman Constitution in any significant detail, but instead celebrates its consequences and its sources. In this, he uses traditional and Islamist evocations, which are revealing when read within the context of the poem itself as well as in subsequent periods. Shawqī confirms the origins of the Arabs as Bedouins, nomads, who are 'not prone to settlement. But Sultan Abdulhamid united them on the basis 'of the laws of heaven', Islam. In being a staunch defender of the Ottoman Empire, Shawqī downgrades the emerging Arabian Peninsula (Saudi) claim to be the governing heart of the Arab world by referring to its upholders as Bedouins, not fit to govern in his parlance.[44] Instead, Shawqī resorts to what he evokes as the highest centre of loyalty for the Muslims, namely Islam, which eclipsed all other social affiliations, treating the unity of the Muslims under an Islamic, even if Ottoman, rule as supreme. It has been explained above how unity is paramount in the discourse of Islam in general; and how this message of unity has been used in various contexts, which are essentially political, in order to legitimise one particular rule over another. Such poetry is entangled in structures of knowledge and in historical claims, and is a facet of communication where political ideologies and positions can be hailed as objects of concrete materiality, integral to what Foucault calls a subjective regime of truth masquerading as an objective truth.[45] Poetry tends to stem from subjective sensibilities that, once politicised to the point of ideological representation, become a concrete object of knowledge mired in aesthetics of representation. To see this in action, it is instructive to highlight the context of the poem above and how it transmits the political ideology of the dominant party at the time into poetics of representation. In this context, Islam became important in the reign of Abdulhamid, who tried to keep legitimacy away from the rulers of the Ḥijāz area (now Saudi Arabia). Challenged by the Wahhabī movements in Saudi Arabia, which contributed to sowing the seeds of Islamist movements in the Arab world, particularly as represented by the orthodox Salafism, Abdulhamid claimed the honour of being the Caliph of all Muslims. Caroline Finkel clarified the consequences of this in her comprehensive book *Osman's Dream: The Story of the Ottoman Empire (1300–1923)*: 'the rule of the Ottoman Sultan as the chief benefactor of the Muslim Holy Places was more important than ever now that "Islamism" had replaced Ottomanism, and Abdulhamid's jealousy in respect of the Holy places had led him to feel threatened whenever other Islamic leaders offered gifts to these shrines: he forbade the practice, and also refused them permission to acquire property in the Hijaz.'[46]

Today's Islamism is infused with symbolism and evocations rooted in particular understandings of the Muslim past. The Qur'an is often invoked; its stories, style and vivid imagery used to bear witness, inspire and account for the lives of Muslims today. In his attempt to make Islam central to his claim to authority, Shawqī endows Abdulhamid with divine blessings: he has 'horses with luminous wings; the horses of Gabriel to stand by the Prophets...' This Qur'anic imagery, which originally refers to presumed angelic figures who descended from heaven to aid Prophet Mohammad in his first battle against his opponents of the Qurayish in the battle of Badr (624), is supposed to comfort Abdulhamid as well as honour him with a prophetic message and attributes, for such creatures could only come to chosen people. Abdulhamid was losing ground on his home turf to a newly emerging Turkish movement known as the Young Turks. They wanted to build a new state centred on Turkey, aided by Turkish culture, history and language, and inspired by the model of the constitutional and institutional European nation-state. Inviting a metaphysical image is poetic in essence, but making it literal and political is something else: it decorates political assertions rather than questioning them.

In the face of the decline of the Ottoman Empire, particularly within the course of the nineteenth century, alongside European ascendance and Arab nationalism and turbulence, poets responded with the acuteness that their medium of expression allowed. If Abdulhamid was supported by some poets for reasons already mentioned, others challenged him and the Ottoman Empire, such as the Iraqi poets Ma'rūf al-Raṣāfī and Ṣāddiq Jamīl al-Zahāwi. Both were accomplished poets who tackled a variety of themes in painstaking detail, one of which was the corrosive effects of politics.

In this context in particular it is worth focusing on Ma'rūf al-Raṣāfī, as he was consistent and poetically competent in his portrayal of the Ottoman Empire, as well as engaging in a critique of it and of Arab conditions in general. Al-Raṣāfī was born in 1875 in Baghdad. He came from a poor Iraqi family but nonetheless resisted the attractions of authority and its offerings. He chose to depict the suffering of the poor in Iraq and the oppression of his people at the hands of the reigning authority, later turning to colonialism. It is said that he was offered 10,000 dinars to compose a poem praising the governing family in Iraq but declined, walking away extremely poor. Al-Raṣāfī was not totally against the Ottoman Empire. He appreciated its Islamic background, particularly given that it was soon to be replaced by British colonialism in Iraq, a change about which he composed poems of unflinching condemnation. Meanwhile he yearned for an Arab realm with its heart in Saudi Arabia, rather than the new order of nation-state that divided the Arab world in his lifetime. To this end, he writes in one of his poems:

> Is it not time for the nation to have its Saudi reign
> So that people can be awakened from their deep sleep...
> I am fed up with free people whose nation is imbued with evil
> Imprisoned to rulers, whose chains are ferociously tight...
> I am surprised by people subservient to a nation,
> Whose ruler afflicts them with plagues...
> Indeed freedom in life is grace,
> The hope of every spirit and its origin and extensions...[47]

The poems of al-Raṣāfī demonstrate the continuous role of Arabic poetry in providing a central and complementary narrative to political discourses. If power is at the heart of politics, and power is often located within dominant as well as contested fields, the poem demonstrates this aptly. Yet, the poet shows preference for the Saudi realm, honouring it as the seat of Islamic governance, the Caliphate, rather than the Ottoman Empire. The latter's power in Islamic unification had progressively waned. Moreover, the poet admonishes the Arabs for lying asleep, in effect letting what amounts to an alien power rule them for so long for so little in return in terms of development, a sentiment with considerable resonance among educated circles in the Arab world. The poem is a call for an Arab awakening, for pan-Arabism with Islamic symbolism. It is not accidental that al-Raṣāfī chooses Saudi Arabia. The symbols of Islam, which Saudi Arabia houses as the cradle of Islam, continue to serve as the pivot around which the unity of the Arab world is sought and evoked.[48] Meanwhile, rather than being heavy with historical illusions, the poem is conceptual in the sense that it rejects oppression and subjection to indignities. It cries out for freedom with liberating powers.

The assured tone with which much of the poetry of the time is written demonstrates the urgency of messages that the poets attempted to convey.

Several Arab poets, including all those already mentioned, were in particular alarmed by the increasing subjugation of their people to unjust rule and rulers, whether from their midst or from outside powers. In an age when mass communication hardly existed, poetry dramatised events, effectively playing the role the visual media undertake today in publicising certain viewpoints and interests. In this case, poetry was an enlightening tool of engagement with political conditions; its direct language gave way to mobilised actions and historical memorialisation through poems that recorded events and interacted with them. As the eminent Palestinian writer Jabra Ibrahim Jabra put it:

> Poetry might be condemned as too weak a toy against guns, but in actual fact it was often as good as dynamite. It gave point to a whole nation's suffering and wrath. It crystallized political positions in telling lines which, memorized by old and young, stiffened popular resistance and provided rallying slogans, in an age when radio and television were still unknown.[49]

Other poets who condemned the status quo of the Ottoman Empire and its oppression from a pan-Arab (secular) perspective included the Lebanese poets Khalīl Muṭrān (1871–1949), Bishāra al-Khoury (1883–1969) and Anīs al-Maqdisī (1885–1977). These poets witnessed the last stages of degradation of the Ottoman Empire, while it failed to offer serious political reforms or basic human rights. At the beginning of the First World War (1914–1918), the fearsome Turkish leader Jamal Pasha and his henchmen massacred a group of Arab nationalists from the Levant area of Beirut and Damascus. These nationalists were protesting and resisting against the Turkish oppression that Jamal, known as *as-safāh* (the slaughterer), epitomised given his ambition to lead the nation-statist movement of the Young Turks in Turkey. The Iraqi poet Jamīl Ṣādiq al-Zahāwī (1863–1936), known for his critical stance and philosophical mind, commemorated the victims and highlighted the grief of the Arab world and its unity in a poem called '*al-nā'iha*', 'The lamenter':

> *On each branch, there is a friend and companion*
> *And in each house, there is an outcry and lament*
> *And in each eye, there is a streaming teardrop*
> *And in each bosom, there is regret and rancour...*
> *(But) what a tragedy that had afflicted a nation*
> *And struck people, indeed, it is so awful...*
> *This generation would wane with its sorrow*
> *And another happy and secure generation would come.*[50]

Al-Zahāwī invokes the collective Arab pain over those killed at the hands of Jamal and his men in Beirut and Damascus in particular, and shows how that pain spreads across the entire Arab world. These nationalists hanged on tree branches triggered scenes of overwhelming sorrow and rejection of the Turkish order, particularly its nationalistic side. Hence the poet refers to the *umma*, the collective Arab nation, forecasting that it will be the source of future progress that will deliver the next generation from present woes. Thus, the time of al-Zahāwī abounds with references to the importance of a united Arab nation that will shed the burden of imitating the past and liberate itself from the Turkish yoke. This can be found in the poetry of the Lebanese poet Anīs al-Maqdisī, who wrote a poem in 1910 responding to the newly drafted Ottoman Constitution of 1908, which Shawqī celebrated as we saw above.

Adopting a pan-Arab voice, al-Maqdisī called to the Arabs to unite and relinquish the past and the stale ways often used to evoke it, particularly by poets with Islamist (rather than Arab-centred) orientations:

> Stop weeping over the dead ruins
> It is not fate that keeps the nation down
> Wastefully we dwell on bygone traces
> While time calls to us to be the best for tomorrow...
> If faith sets us apart
> Our Arabic tongue is the valve of our unity...[51]

The first line of the poem is daring in its call for action, rather than dwelling on stagnation in the name of fate. It is an explicit turning against the past. It calls to Arabs to leave their ruins behind, not to stop by them, as was the entrenched custom in the classical Arabic *Qaṣīdah* (ode). Standing by their ruins was a constant delaying habit for classical Arab poets, such as the inventive pre-Islamic poet Imru' al-Qays (d. AD 540), who canonised this tradition in his famous poem '*mu'llaqat Imru al-Qays*', with its opening:

> Halt, you two companions, and let us weep for the memory of a beloved and an abode amid the sand-dunes between al-Dakhūl and Hawmal.[52]

Imru al-Qays's lines, which are widely echoed in the aesthetic realm of the Arab world, propose a state of transfixion in the face of what had happened in the past. Beholden to the memory of the beloved, Imru al-Qays orders the freezing of time in what once was. Unlike the shifting sand-dunes, he is motionless, he wants to weep in the place of his beloved. His golden age was when he was with his beloved and his sentiment is one of utter surrender to nostalgia. He evokes a moving object, most notably the sand dunes, rendered as the centre-ground where the transfixion would take place.

By contrast, in al-Maqdisī's poem the call is for movement, one triggered by human intention and action. Like Ḥāfiẓ Ibrahim's writing, as noted above, al-Maqdisī's poem is steeped in the potential directions of the future. It emphasises the Arabic language as the embodiment of Arab unity, not Islam as such, to which the Ottoman Empire increasingly clung in order to sustain its legitimacy over the Arab world. In particular, this aspect of the Arabic language underpinning Arab unity is echoed in the writings of Sāti' al-Husri (1882–1968).[53] This author was a Syrian educationalist who argued for Arab unity on the basis of its shared Arabic language as well as history. The echoing of these widely circulated ideas in poetry demonstrates the intimate connection between cultural and political knowledge and poetry as an accentuating and often mobilising force for it.

All of the above themes, including lamentation over the state of the Arab world, calls for unity and reform, resistance against colonialism, and Islamism and nationalism, became signature topics in the struggle against foreign colonialism from the French and British colonial powers, to which I devote the next chapter.

Conclusion

'In Arab life,' wrote the Syrian poet and critic Adonis (Ahmad Ali Said), 'the poetic has always been mixed up with the political and the religious, and indeed continues to be so.'[54] This statement is not entirely precise when applied to the modern period, particularly after the 1940s, when some poetic trends escaped or transcended political and religious strictures in innovative and consciously subversive ways. Hence it is possible to treat such poetry at a reasonable distance from immediate political and religious constraints and pressures, even if such poetry emerged as a reaction to such pressures. Yet, this statement is apt when one focuses on poetry with political or religious content, which has always been part of Arab culture and life, rather than on Arabic poetry in general. In particular, the poetry discussed in this chapter testifies to Adonis' thesis that political and religious structures and discourses permeated and underpinned Arabic poetry of the nineteenth and early twentieth centuries in a manner that shows how poetry was integrated into the political, religious and cultural difficulties of the time in immediate and often influential ways, as poetry served to mobilise, direct and educate.

The trends in Arabic poetry of the nineteenth century testify to this view, in the sense that, with Mohammad Ali's political reforms in Egypt and its reverberations elsewhere in the Arab world, poetry, the nerve of Arabic culture, witnessed structural and epistemological developments congruent with rising political awareness and activity. These developments were ground-breaking in the topics and styles they covered, even though they covered ground familiar since the classical age, such as lending support to the legitimacy of one political order rather than another. The 'epistemic shift' in knowledge was embedded in calls for Islamic reforms, Arab nationalism, political issues and resistance against colonialism. It is these aspects of the major shift in modes of knowledge on which the next chapter will focus. In particular, it will highlight the poetic Arab responses to and interactions with colonialism, and the results of this within the interconnected fields of Arabic poetry and politics.

2

POETRY IN THE SHADOW OF COLONIALISM

When Napoleon launched his conquest of Egypt in 1798, he knew that the Arab world was attached to an Islamic identity whose emblem was the Arabic language. He therefore addressed the Egyptians in what he assumed to be their emotional mode of thinking. He responded to many Egyptians' requests, using knowledge acquired through regular consultations with the group of experts he brought with him, and reassured the Egyptians that his own and his soldiers' behaviour would accord with Egyptian and Muslim culture. He went as far as saying to the people of Alexandria that '*nous sommes les vrais musulmans*'.[1] The historical record, however, indicates that his discourse was motivated by considerations of power, rooted in colonial competition with England and the Ottoman Empire and in his desire to expand the commercial base of France. He revealed this clearly to his soldiers in Malta on their way to Egypt: 'Soldiers, you are about to undertake a conquest, the effects of which on the civilization and commerce of the world are immeasurable. You shall inflict on England the surest and most palpable blow, while awaiting the opportunity to administer the *coup de grâce*.'[2]

Napoleon's campaign established colonial patterns in the Arab world that included cultural, political and economic control and representation. Britain followed suit in the Arab world by conquering Egypt in 1882, on the basis that it was restoring the authority of the incumbent Khedive Tawfiq (1852–1892), which was challenged by a nationalist army officer, Aḥmad 'Urabī (1839–1911). Albert Hourani writes of this conquest:

> The pretext for the British invasion was the claim that the government was in revolt against legitimate authority, and that order had broken down; most contemporary

witnesses do not support this claim. The real reason was the instinct for power that states have in a period of expansion, reinforced by the spokesmen of European financial interests.[3]

Britain, as France before, presented itself as the guarding moderniser of such nations as Egypt, whereas in practice modernity, in whichever form it appeared, was an accident in the expanding enterprise of colonialism rather than its main concern, as many poets highlight in their engaging takes on colonialism. To this end, Edward Said effectively pioneered the analysis of how the West portrayed the Arab and Islamic world in its cultural and political productions using a set of reductive and misrepresentative cultural misunderstandings.[4] And yet there is something to be said for Napoleon evoking Islamic symbolism at the beginning of a colonial campaign of conquest impregnated with violence and exploitation. Napoleon knew that language in all its aspects plays a role in the construction of reality and that a pretence of cultural sensitivity to the addressee can help to authenticate the most deceitful projects. His use of the Arabic language and his purported respect for Muslim customs was meant to ease his campaign of conquest.[5] But the fact of the matter is that the Arabic language belongs to the Arab people and it is they, steeped in its cultural fabric, who used it to resist the campaign of Napoleon and colonialism in general. In this context, the Arabs waged their resistance in their own language as much as on the battlefield, particularly in poetry. Poetry in the nineteenth century was still the uncontested mode of artistic creation. It was not only an exalted medium of expression—it was one of effective mobilisation and defiance. Such mobilisation became an important right of passage as the discourse of Arab nationalism developed and became further entrenched in the struggle against colonialism.

Furthermore, colonialism showed that exploitative power breeds only ambition for more. Poetry, in its outspoken exposition and opposition, highlights the limits of such material power. In other words, poetry of the sort discussed in this chapter embodies spirits and values which, in the souls of those they inhabit, represent a different and opposing kind of power; it is an essential element in the imaginative power of revolt and resistance. Unlike the disciplinarian, this was institutional power those such as the French philosopher Michel Foucault focused on and saw as essential to and reflective of the human condition in different historical eras.[6] The Arab world's powers have been politically diffused as well as historically and culturally grounded in a language that carried within it powerful connotations and memories continuously evoked through poetry. Even though the power of the poetic word is unquantifiable, it can break through the limits of the material world of crude power with its sheer spiritual force. Impelled by such poetry, people feel that they cannot allow their land and resources to be taken from them and therefore act accordingly. After all, much of classical Arabic poetry is grounded in the invocation of loyalty to land and ancestors, and the defence of honour and traditional values.[7] Arabic poetry written in the context of resistance against colonial powers abounds with references to Arab roots in the land, to pride, dignity and confidence in the future. It was clear that colonialism stood in stark contrast to the historically accumulated Arab identity and indeed threatened to undermine it psychologically. Hence the power of resistance is at its zenith in poetry. Unlike other forms of discourse, poetry tends to articulate emotions with an open-hearted directness. And since this is political poetry written at a time of vociferous nationalism, it resonates with national pride and nostalgia for the past.

Primarily, the Arabs realised that colonial conquest entailed a basic violation of their traditional values, which were being disrupted and forced into defensive modes of resistance. Barbara Harlow writes that 'these traditions constitute in an important way their means of identifying themselves as a group, as a people, no less than as a nation, with a historicity of their own and a claim to an autonomous, self-determining role on the contemporary staging grounds of history'.[8] Even those who saw and acknowledged Western progress and its benefits could not submit to their land being ruled by people other than themselves. This distrust of colonialism materialised as an all-out rejection as the colonial powers committed massacres, created zones of exploitation, and expropriated resources from the Arab countries. As is manifest in the history of colonialism, the colonial powers exercised their control in stages, the first being an attempt to justify and consolidate their presence. Often this stage subsided quickly; people found themselves being ruled by powers with economic and political interests that clashed with their own interests and cultural values. Such powers were bent on maintaining their superiority and ensuring their grip on the country in question through a variety of methods, including the creation of a subject bourgeoisie facilitating the colonialists' desire for effective control.[9] Uprisings multiplied and the violence of colonialism became further manifest in extreme suppression of these revolutions. This suppression is vividly depicted in Arabic poetry designed to mobilise resistance.

Poets against colonialism: violation and corruption

Two factors dominated the intellectual milieu of the Arab world as the Ottoman Empire collapsed in 1923. Firstly, the cultural identity of the Arab world as consisting of the Arabic language and a shared history became more pronounced in the discourse of Arab intellectuals and the politically aware.[10] Secondly, the Arab world shares an identity rooted in salient elements of nationalist ethnicity, in which Islam is an integral element.[11] The debate therefore oscillated between those who wanted to focus on their nation-state— Egypt for the Egyptians and Lebanon for the Lebanese and so forth—and those who advocated a united Arab nation, with an Arab political leadership. Partisan politics eventually led to an emphasis on the nation-state, with local Arab rulers invoking their rootedness and right to rule within their own specific geographical area. This localised nationalist attitude naturally bred competition for control among the Arab countries. In return, this made them seek 'clientele' alliances with international powers, namely France and Great Britain. Meanwhile, these powers harboured political designs of their own, which were often in stark contrast to Arab leaders' ambitions for sovereignty. To this end, France and Britain divided the Arab world between them into zones of influence through various agreements, most notably the Sykes–Picot Accord in 1916. The accord violated the spirit of the correspondence between the Sharif of Mecca, Husayn Ben Ali of the Hashemite family (in office 1908–1924), and the High Commissioner in Egypt, Henry McMahon (the McMahon–Husayn correspondence, 1915–16). The correspondence promised to assist Arab independence once the Ottoman rule was brought to an end. Sykes–Picot and subsequent agreements mandated Iraq and Palestine to Britain, while France was made responsible for Syria and Lebanon. Once the Arab world came under colonial powers and people became conscious of the secret negotiations between ambitious Arab leaders, such as Husayn Ben Ali, and the colonial rulers who had betrayed them, the cultural ambience gave way to angry poetry that denounced those leaders. Some poets saw them as traitors who had betrayed the nationalist Arab cause. This is particularly true of the poets who had hoped for a pan-Arab nation or who had felt secure within the old Ottoman order with Islam at its heart.

The Arab world therefore continued to resist the new forms of colonial domination. This resistance, as mentioned above, harks back to the Napoleonic invasion of Egypt and, later, to the French occupation of Algeria in 1830, Tunisia in 1881, Morocco in 1912, and to the British occupation of Egypt in 1882 and the Italian invasion of Libya in 1934. In all these Arab countries, and in others, nationalist movements sprang up and fought colonialism politically and culturally. They all gave rise to influential poets who inscribed in poetry the struggles of their people against colonialism. While they focused on the conditions of their nation-state, they also attended to the collective fate of the Arab world. Thus, the cultural identity of the Arab world, as enshrined in its language, continued to function as the pivot of Arab pride and nationalism, which often went beyond the borders of the nation-state. Cultural identity never ceased to play a role in rallying the Arab world around common purposes in the face of the 'other', in this case the colonial powers.

Against this backdrop, one aspect of colonialism highlighted in Arabic poetry is the division of Arab land between the imperial powers. Such division is lamented and viewed as being in stark contradiction to Arab hopes of independence and unity, hopes which proliferated after the collapse of the Ottoman Empire and the rise of 'culturally-minded' Arab nationalist movements. One of the first poets giving voice to Arab nationalism is the Iraqi poet Ma'rūf al-Raṣāfī (1875–1945). 'With him,' as Jayyusi wrote, 'the role of the poet as a national fighter for his people's cause became well established.'[12] In another instance, Jayyusi wrote of al-Raṣāfī that 'he brought poetry to the heat of life around him, exemplifying the aspirations of all Arabs'.[13]

There are several themes that run throughout the nationalist poetry of al-Raṣāfī.[14] One clear theme is his denunciation of colonialism, and British colonialism in particular. Ma'rūf al-Raṣāfī wrote in his poem, 'The English in their colonial policies':[15]

> How much they have devoured in their colonies
> Dark oppressions that constituted the worst of ploughs
> And how many people in their homes they have awakened from their sleep
> Where they bred strife, like crossbreeds, writhing in their dirt
> They eat butter from its products and throw leftovers to the natives
> Visit India, if you travelled among nations, how much you would see
> There of dust and hardships

One of the central themes in this poem is the exploitation on which much of colonialism is based. The natives are immediately put at a disadvantage by the colonisers, who rob them of their resources. The disparity in power relations is vividly depicted in this poem. And India, then the epitome of British colonialism, is shown as the prime example of colonial domination. Interestingly, the poem is integrated into the historical experience of colonialism as underpinned by economic expansionism. Most of the Arab countries, such as Egypt and Tunisia, were catapulted into colonial economic schemes and ended up saddled with debts that they could not pay back; they were therefore both conquered and pillaged in the process. It is pillage that al-Raṣāfī highlights. He draws on two sources of inspiration in this poem: one is the Arabic linguistic tradition, enshrined in the Qur'an, and the other is the political and economic Marxist tradition. As for the Qur'anic inspiration, it relates to the verse, 'And when he [the hypocrite] goes away, he strives throughout the land to cause corruption therein and destroy crops and offspring. And Allah does not like corruption.'[16]

Colonialism expropriates the land from the people, which violates the primary principle of respecting the rights of others, whoever they are. Moreover, colonialism devours the land it takes for resources that it uses to magnify its own wealth and power, whilst leaving others to languish in poverty and destitution. Thus, colonialism is born with violation and corruption at its heart. The language of al-Raṣāfī is not specifically religious. It is political, but it draws on images from the Qur'an that castigate the wrongdoers for violating others' rights and for continuing on a course which leads to utter corruption. In addition, Marxism can be felt in al-Raṣāfī's poem where he mentions India as a prime example of British colonialism. India is taken as an example to show how relations should be based on solidarity between nations, not on colonialism. The poet's opening words are 'How much they have devoured in their colonies...' His indictment of colonialism is based on personal as well as collective experiences. In his vision, al-Raṣāfī wants to see coexistence between nations and cooperation between their workers. He wants to tear down barriers between peoples; in this, Marxism has clearly marked his thinking:

> The civility of people is but
> In their cooperation to achieve the best
> Their corruption would not be repaired
> Except by money earned by their own collective hands
> With which shelters are built for the orphaned
> And restaurants are frequented by the hungry (poor)[17]

Al-Raṣāfī's Marxism is even clearer when he lambasts the English in the wake of their occupation of his country, Iraq, and seeks a solution in the socialist revolution of the Bolsheviks:

> The English have ambitions in your country
> They will not be evaded unless you are Bolshevised

When Baghdad fell to the British (1920–1932), al-Raṣāfī lamented this with characteristic passion:

How can I not weep tears, and my pride
Is gripped by humiliation, bred by destructive conquest
The hands of time had landed me an awful blow
The night had no morning.[18]

The principle of cooperation and unity between the workers of the world as enshrined at the end of Marx's Communist Manifesto is evoked in the opening lines above: 'the civility of people is but in their cooperation to achieve the best'. The superstructure (economy) must be made sound by just political schemes so that equality is established and the poor are justly accommodated. To achieve equality, workers must be active agents, not objects of their own oppression through capitalist systems that alienate them from their products and themselves, exactly as Marx envisaged.[19] In such a world, where powerful players accumulate undeserved wealth and disregard the rights and wishes of others, a revolution in the style of the Bolshevik revolution, engineered by the workers, must take place. Al-Raṣāfī suggests mass mobilisation and revolution as a way to overturn the status quo. Then, in the final lines quoted above, al-Raṣāfī appears engulfed by sorrow over the state of his homeland: it has been violated and corrupted to such an extent that morning cannot emerge from the shades of night.

Al-Raṣāfī was not alone in condemning colonialism, but he was an outstandingly uncompromising and effective figure. He personally suffered under it and the leaders who served under its aegis. He felt forced to leave Iraq for Beirut in 1931, where he wrote one of his most famous poems, which resounded widely in the Arab world, 'After exile'. Once the British (in the person of Winston Churchill) declared their favourite, Faysal, as King of Iraq (1883–1933, r. 1921–1933), many Iraqi nationalists suffered marginalisation. Al-Raṣāfī's position dwindled in Iraq, because he had opposed Faysal's father, Sharif Husayn Ben Ali, when the latter led the Arab revolt against the Turks on 10 June 1916 at the behest of the British. Al-Raṣāfī found himself lamenting the state of his country and bemoaning the fact that people of lesser ability were being promoted to prominent cultural positions at his expense. Loyalty to the colonialists, as shown by Faysal and his father before him, entailed servility and subservience, albeit cloaked in noble terms. Thus, in 'After exile', the poet wrote:

They are the homelands that I draw near while they drive me away
Like adversities that I addressed while they afflict me
Long have I complained against an age I endure;
Will I ever find a freeborn man to redress my grievance?...

Is it part of virtue that the ignorant man is held in high esteem there,
While I dwell in degradation's grip...
I made a vow to myself; the days are my witness
Not to acquiesce in the inequity of Sultans,
Nor to befriend an imposter even if he be a king
Nor to associate with the brethren of Satan.[20]

For someone so emotionally bound to his homeland and aware of its cultural pulses, colonialism and dictatorship are personal afflictions. They undermine the very basis of one's security, linked to one's rootedness in the land. Highlighting the pathologies of colonialism and dictatorship were perennial themes in the Arabic poetry of the twentieth century and al-Raṣāfi was a committed commentator on and against them. Though he was not forced into exile, the psychological pressure to take the opportunity to live in dignity elsewhere, away from his homeland, was irresistible. These pressures are the primal degradations that the Martinique-born psychiatrist Frantz Fanon refers to in his great 1963 book *The Wretched of the Earth*, in the context of colonialism and its wholesale injustice and degraded morality. Al-Raṣāfi is on the side of his people, as Fanon would have liked. The people are a source of power, no matter how taxing one's relations with them might be. It is this insight into the power of solidarity that arms the poet, particularly in circumstances of colonialism, where the collective identity is being suppressed. Fanon calls on poets to draw their inspiration from the predicament of their people: 'let there be no mistake about it; it is to this zone of occult instability where the people dwell that we must come; and it is there that our souls are crystallized and that our perceptions and our lives are transfused with light'.[21] Under colonialism and dictatorship—both premised on basic injustices of an interrelated nature—many people of conscience like al-Raṣāfi felt displaced within their own country: 'is it part of virtue that the ignorant man is held in high esteem there, while I dwell in degradation's grip...' His poem echoes some of the thoughts expressed by the important Egyptian intellectual and nationalist Ahmad Lutfi al-Sayyid (1872–1963), whose image of society entailed 'a vision of what the really free man would be and what the good life is: the free man is he who, spontaneously and without external impediments, fulfils his function in society, and in so doing fulfils his human capacities...'[22] Thus, al-Raṣāfi refuses to be subservient to unjust powers, whether they are local or international, referred to here pejoratively by the term 'brethren of Satan'. Yet the latter reference is the kind of negative phrase that dictatorial regimes such as that of the late Saddam Hussein or Ruhollah Khomeini used against international powers such as the US. It is redolent of negative and unproductive anger. The phrase has been used in various contexts in the twentieth century to tarnish other countries and their societies, sometimes in a way that weds religious fanaticism to narrow nationalism. But lest al-Raṣāfī be accused of extremism, he refutes this at the outset of another poem, 'The government of the mandate':

Of government and politics, I know
Should I be blamed for refuting them and be subjected to violence
I will talk about whatever I like without fear of them
Saying that 'he is an extremist poet'[23]

In the previous poem, as well as this one, al-Raṣāfī uses the language of the colonisers against them. He starts by setting the basic premise that he has knowledge of politics and government; those skills which the colonisers often alleged the colonised do not possess, or practise inadequately, are refuted with a clear 'Of government and politics, I know'. There are enough people in the country who know about politics and governance to represent their own people; and al-Raṣāfī counts himself as one of them. Al-Raṣāfī also suggests that he is not an extremist for defending basic rights, such as freedom of expression. Essentially, al-Raṣāfī addresses the imbalance in the power relations between the coloniser and the colonised by stating that the latter also has knowledge and experience and that his attempts to obtain his rights are not extreme. In this respect, al-Raṣāfī is one of the pioneering figures in the field of poetry that talks back to the empire and refutes its claims. At such an early point in modern history, an Arab poet of significant stature addressed the same question of orientalism that the Palestinian–American philosopher Edward Said opened up in his 1978 masterpiece *Orientalism*, which reveals how colonialists, through a cabal of cultural, political and literary personnel, denigrated 'the other'.[24] In other words, for al-Raṣāfī and others, resistance to power is inbuilt in power relations. Although hegemonic power can be and often is overwhelming, the fact that there are those who see it and do so critically, even if they are on the receiving end of its oppression, means that power is only really overpowering to those who totally submit to its grip, without awareness or resistance.

Furthermore, al-Raṣāfī was not only against the government of the British mandate in Iraq and colonialism in general, viewing it as a violation of principle that should be resisted: 'man is a principle first and foremost'.[25] He also volunteered alternatives. He was a firm believer in freedom of thought and expression as a guarantor of cultural prosperity. In a celebration organised by the Egyptian government for the (Arab) coronation of the Egyptian poet Ahmad Shawqī in 1927 as the prince of poets, al-Raṣāfī castigated the Egyptian government for undermining and attacking the works of two pioneering Egyptian intellectuals, namely 'Alī 'Abd al-Rāziq (1882–1947) and Taha Hussein (1889–1974). Both intellectuals had published books challenging orthodox views—views that had influenced the political field in the Arab and Islamic worlds with theological claims about Islam and its centrality to practical politics. The writers instead affirmed the secular basis and responsibility for the organisation of societies along just rules by modern political means that take into consideration the changing nature of societies. In particular, 'Abd al-Rāziq affirmed the spiritual message of Prophet Mohammad rather than his political role, and in this respect suggested separation between the practical world of politics and the spiritual and metaphysical milieu of religion. As Albert Hourani wrote of 'Abd al-Rāziq and his 1925 book, *Islam and the Foundations of Governance*: 'it is, quite simply, that Muhammad had no function except the essential prophetic function of preaching the truth; he was not sent to exercise political authority, and he did not do so'.[26] Ironically, as we will see later, the celebrated Aḥmad Shawqī made the Prophet Mohammad a political figure *par excellence* in some of the more than twenty panegyric poems he devoted to him. But as for al-Raṣāfī, he described the persecution of these authors by the state as follows:

> *If Egypt had celebrated Shawqī, so why is it*
> *Blocking the free from the pursuit of their educational vocation?*
> *It has roared mightily and struck*
> *Ali and Taha with such a flying thunder*
> *What is it to Egypt considering this possible*
> *And what is it to lampooning that as infidel*
> *If ideas in Egypt were not freely expressed*
> *Then Egypt is not qualified to honour a poet*
> *The crowning of the godfather of poetry is not an honour*
> *From those who block the freedom of thought...*[27]

In another poem, al-Raṣāfī writes about freedom:

> *If man is not living in his country free*
> *Then name him dead and his country a tomb*[28]

There is an intense desire for freedom in this poem. Al-Raṣāfī rejects the abuse and the state oppression of two intellectual giants in Egypt and the Arab world. The harsh treatment of 'Ali and Taha,[29] as well as the populist labelling of them as infidels, created dangerous rifts in society, based on the manipulation of religious sentiments that cheapened cultural freedom and diversity of opinions. Though the occasion on which the above lines were read was to honour Shawqī, al-Raṣāfī shows the hypocritical face of a state and culture that honour an important poet while shunning some of its best intellectuals because they voice ideas contrary to its populist orthodoxies. In this, al-Raṣāfī shows himself to be the committed poet that he was, placing human principles above valueless loyalties that undermine people's capacities for change and freedom and lessen the respect of people for each other. In addition, al-Raṣāfī contributes significantly to a culture of critical engagement rather than blind loyalties. Unlike other panegyrics, overflowing with unqualified praise and focused single-mindedly on their objects, like some of Shawqī's poems in his praise of the Ottoman sultans, al-Raṣāfī both gives praise where it is due and incorporates constructive criticism. Thus, freedom of thought, resistance to domination, nationalism, social justice and equality were all signal themes in the poetry of the important Arab poets at the beginning of the twentieth century. Yet they were tackled in a variety of ways that reflect very different ideologies, personal orientations and conditions, as will be further explained below. What al-Raṣāfī opens up is revealing in the sense that his poetry, while being embedded in Arabic and Islamic traditions, also accommodates modern ideas and influences. Hence, the above themes bear further exploration and elaboration.

Contesting the roots of knowledge

Ideas about freedom were commonplace at the time of al-Raṣāfī. Some of these ideas originated in the Islamic and Arabic traditions. Most famously, the second Caliph of Islam, 'Umar Ibn al-Khaṭṭāb (579–644), is believed to have wondered: 'When did you enslave people while their mothers have given birth to them free?' Another famous Arab poet, lover and warrior, 'Antara Bin Shaddād (525–608), exhorted his son, 'Run away and be free',[30] in response to the enslavement of his tribe—an exhortation which is still expressed in the Arab culture of today. Many poets were of the opinion that colonialism was enslaving the Arab people. Thus, the defence of Arab values and ideas, and their rootedness in history, became a way of claiming historical originality. And concepts such as socialism, freedom and nationalism, common in al-Raṣāfī's poetry, were taken to be of an Arab or Islamic nature, and to have contributed throughout the centuries to the formation of the Arab and Muslim human subject. Several Arab poets, particularly from the neo-classical school of poetry, found themselves appropriating clearly modern concepts and situating them within the Islamic tradition.

The famous Egyptian poet Ahmad Shawqī is one such poet, who in his famous panegyric poem dedicated to the Prophet of Islam, Muhammad, '*al-Hamza al-Nabawiyyah*', 'The Prophetic initiation', writes:

> *Your message was founded on monotheism and it is the truth*
> *Which Socrates and the ancients called for...*
> *And you shaped a government for others after you*
> *Free of nepotism or emirs*
> *God alone is above all creatures*
> *Under His reign, all are equal*
> *Religion is not a burden, and the Caliphate is through allegiance*
> *And consultation is fundamental and rights are arbitrated by law*
> *As for the socialists, you are their Imām*
> *Had it not been for the false claims of the people and extremism...*
> *You have been fair to the poor through taking from the rich*
> *All are equal in their right to life...*[31]

Here Shawqī defends the present and tries to validate it by exalted references to the past. He presents the revelation of the Prophet as complete, containing the timeless seeds for good governance, echoing along the way widely popular conceptions of Islam as grounded in ease rather than difficulty. The present is only the last manifestation of a long and laborious process of birth. But the present in which Shawqī wrote was one dominated by colonial claims of superiority over the culture and ways of the Arabs. In this context, Shawqī fits the description of Frantz Fanon, who highlights the condition of the native poet taking refuge in the past to authenticate and validate his present against external threats: 'The artist who has decided to illustrate the truths of the nation turns paradoxically towards the past and away from actual events. What he ultimately intends to embrace are in fact the cast-offs of thought, its shells and corpses, a knowledge which has been stabilized once and for all.'[32] Fanon is critical of poets who barricade themselves in the past and locate the travails and thoughts of the present in it. Yet Shawqī is extreme in using modern terminologies and concepts and situating them within Islamic frames of reference in peculiar and appropriative ways that are echoed widely in the Islamist discourses of today. He attributes monotheism to Socrates, rather than to the Abrahamic religions as conventionally known, starting with Judaism through Christianity. He then highlights an Islamic government with an inbuilt basis of equality. The poet does not shy away from using a word such as *Ishtirākiyya* (socialism) and lodging it within an entirely Islamic context, describing the Prophet as 'the Imām of the socialists'. ('Imām' is normally a term reserved for the leader of prayer in Islam.) Such cross-breeding of ideas and human experiences testifies to the fact that under colonialism Arabic culture sees itself as vast, encompassing a range of ideas, both traditional and at the same time eternally up-to-date. For the *Amīr al-Shu'arā'* (the Prince of Poets) himself to go so far as to view socialism, consultation (democracy) and the rule of law as an integral part of the Islamic heritage suggests that Shawqī is impervious to external influences and pressures, as well as being frozen in alleged times of former glory, which is what today's Islamist discourses also tend to do.

By comparison, the Iraqi poet al-Raṣāfī is more forthright in his condemnation of colonialism. His views are clearly articulated and are true to the historical experiences and the evolution of human consciousness as far as socialism is concerned. Socialism first entered the Arab scene through a Lebanese physician who lived in Egypt, Shiblī al-Shumayyil (1860–1917), who called for socialism, secularism and progress, treating them as derivative concepts of one another. In particular, his ideas stoked controversy among Islamic-orientated thinkers, such as Mohammad 'Abduh and Rashīd Riḍa (1865–1935). And it was the Egyptian thinker Salama Musa (1887–1958) who furthered the cause of socialism by publishing a book on it, in the hope that 'it would ferment in the minds of the people until the country is prepared for socialism'.[33] Subsequently, several Arab parties named themselves after socialism, such as 'the Egyptian Communist Party' founded in Egypt by Salama Musa in 1922. Later such parties became widespread in the Arab world and socialism became incorporated into its educational syllabus; countries such as Syria and Iraq adopted socialism as a creed. In particular, it was the Syrian Christian educationalist Michel 'Aflaq (1910–1989) who expressed a sense of Arab socialism inspired by love and unity of the Arab world, and founded the Arab socialist Ba'ath Party in the 1940s. He believed in the unity of the Arab world and referred to the Prophet Mohammad as the founder of the first Arab nation.[34]

Against this backdrop, the appeal of socialism to the Arab world and its invocation in their favoured medium of expression deserves further reflection. Later renowned Arab poets who came of age in the 1950s and 60s, such as the Iraqi poets Badr Shākir al-Sayyāb (1926–1964) and 'Abd al-Wahhāb al-Bayātī (1926–1999), produced a wealth of socialist poetry.

Poetically, the word socialism became very common in the vocabulary of poets from several Arab countries throughout the twentieth century, often competing with Islamism and other forms of nationalism. There may be several reasons why socialism gained such attention. Firstly, it is an international template of economic, political and cultural organisation that aims to eradicate exploitation and institute social justice. Secondly, it lays emphasis on the workers as the vanguard of progress and equality and as the spiritual backbone of society. Thirdly, it is seen as productive and reproductive in a way that honours the essence of humankind, rather than placing merit and competition at the heart of the economic system, as capitalism does. Socialism trusts the state to distribute resources fairly and to accommodate the poor in a dignified manner. Socialism as an ideal was viewed as rejecting deprivation and a colossal disparity in wealth, such as we see across the world today and particularly in the capitalist West. Socialism ensures a sense of emotional security in a state obliged to care for its people. It does not leave them to their own devices to struggle and compete if they are not born in the 'right' economic and social category. Moreover, socialism promotes the virtues of attachment to one's work, which the system creates by virtue of its distributive and benevolent nature. Socialist ideals resonate with some well-established Arab values embodied in Islamic culture, perhaps most notably that 'justice is the very basis of authority', *Al-'adl asās al-mulk*, as well as commitment to understanding and engagement with the dynamics of the material life, which includes literature. At the heart of socialism is the idea of economic justice. Traditionally, the economic basis of the Arab world has been grounded in the cultivation and produce of the land. The land is therefore impregnated with historical and cultural significance which socialism celebrates in its emphasis on labour as a productive human force. Much poetry, unsurprisingly, inscribes a meaningful topography to the land and its evocative centrality to Arab life. Perhaps one of the most memorable lines celebrating the intimate connection of the Arab people to their land was that sung by the iconic Egyptian singer Sayed Mikāwy (1926–1997). It was originally written by the Lebanese–Egyptian poet Fouād Haddād (1928–1985) in colloquial Egyptian Arabic, at a time when colloquial Egyptian Arabic had acquired Arab universality in so far as it relayed Arab nationalism through songs charged with symbolism and historical sensationalism:

The land speaks Arabic[35]

In this simple line, which runs as a refrain throughout the poem, the poet combines two enduring aspects of Arab pride and imaginary unity, namely land and language. The land is endowed with an aura of authenticity communicated and continuously affirmed through the Arabic language.

Colonialism, however, reinforced capitalist elitism in the Arab world, which reduced the emotional value of the land. This elitism looked down on or merely paid lip service to the poor and disadvantaged members of society, such as the workers and peasants, and literally reaped the fruits of their labour by spawning bourgeois leaders in the newly independent states. Colonialism valued convenience rather than a transparent and nationally accepted democracy, propping up particular figures on the basis of their loyalty to its system so that it could function with alleged native support and legitimacy. The prospect of bottom-up justice that the concept of socialism imparted to the Arab world therefore appealed to several poets who felt the anguish of ordinary and marginalised people. The latter were the engine of revolutions against colonialism in a way that made committed poets such as al-Raṣāfī, in particular, stand with them and honour the workers and the ethos of labour in their poetry. Socialism never trumped nationalism politically, however. Even the states that adopted socialism into their discourses in the 1950s and 60s, such as Syria and Iraq, remained, first and foremost, narrowly nationalist. Their elites promoted their own interests and often oppressed whoever opposed their rule. Equally, while poets celebrated the ideal of universal camaraderie, economic justice, the virtue of work and the honour of workers, most poets defended their own brand of nationalism, the sovereignty of their homelands, and the Arab world in general as one unit consisting of an authentic and expansive culture. These include the poets mentioned above, as well as others. In what follows, I highlight the nationalist poetry of some important poets, particularly within the context of colonialism.

Poetic nationalism against colonialism

Arab nationalism arose in reaction to the increasing weakness of the Ottoman Empire as well as to European colonialism in the Arab lands. With the internal rivalry within the Ottoman Empire being challenged by the Young Turks and the European powers expanding at its expense in the Arab world, the Arab peoples realised that they had to carve their own nationalist destiny amidst colonial dangers. Colonialism heightened these fears. In the poetry of Arabic nationalism, there are several features that reflect these aspects and it is not possible to examine them all here. But there are two notable dimensions to Arab nationalism in the context of colonialism that deserve special attention. The first belongs to the local nationalism of each Arab nation-state and the admiration or otherwise with which its own poets viewed it; the second relates to the collective Arab nationalist fate in the face of colonialism. Often, there are mixtures of both, namely the nation-statist and the collective, culturally-grounded Arab nationalism. Not every country had poets of pan-Arab standing who could render the important events of their day. Famous Arab poets tended to be pan-Arabist by nature, except for a few who utilised the 'glories' of their own particular nation for the purpose of authenticating it above other nations. The Algerian poet Zakariyā Mufdī (b.1908), for example, focuses on Algeria and its colonialisation by France, and on the resistance that the Algerians exerted against France, particularly from 1952 to1962, in which the poet himself played a key part.

What often appears in anti-colonial Arabic poetry is the might of the colonial powers, unleashed nakedly against popular resistance. One incident that embodied the dialectic of established colonial power and native resistance occurred in the Egyptian village of Dinshawai in 1906. The incident took place against a background of rising anger among the Egyptians against the departure of the British governor of Egypt, Lord Cromer, in 1907. Cromer had been a British colonial governor since Britain colonised Egypt in 1882, ending the nationalist movement as led by Ahmad Orābī (1841–1911). Hourani told the story of Dinshawai as follows:

> In 1906 a fight broke out between the villagers of Dinshawai, near Tanta in the delta, and a group of British officers who were shooting pigeons in the neighbourhood. Several officers were injured, and one died of shock and sunstroke; a peasant was beaten to death by the British soldier who found the dead officer...a special court was set up, a number of peasants were condemned to be hanged, others to be flogged, and the sentences were carried out with barbarous publicity. This event had a profound effect on public sentiment.[36]

The incident revealed the extent of colonial injustice; it sparked poetic reactions from several Egyptian poets throughout the twentieth century. Dinshawai seared itself into the memories of the Egyptians. It showed them that they were not governed benignly and for their own good by a colonial power, as some Egyptians had been made to believe. A contemporary of the incident, Ḥāfiẓ Ibrahīm (1872–1932), 'The poet of the Nile' and 'The poet of the people', addressed the Dinshawai incident as follows:

O you who are ruling us
Have you forgotten our loyalty and appreciation...?
We and the pigeons are the same
Chains have been tightened around our waists...
Kill well if you doubted forgiveness
Are you attacking human beings or sterile objects?

O my poetry, what is this: are they medieval courts (the inquisition),
Returning, or is it the era of Nero, coming back?
How could the strong take revenge
On a weak man who entrusted him with his fate
This is an example of vindictive jealousy,
And we are opponents of your jealousy
Take pity on us in our land where you are
For the generous honour the generous...
You are our torturer, so do not forget
That we have worn mourning at your hands.[37]

Though the poet Ḥāfiẓ Ibrahīm came from a poor background, like many Egyptians he worked as an officer in the colonial administration itself. But he never lost sight of the fact that his country was occupied and remained subject to a rule which contradicted the value-system and nationalist desires of Egyptians, even while some Egyptian figures such as Ahmad Lutfi al-Sayyed recognised that certain phases of British colonialism had brought a semblance of economic stability to the country after the rule of Khedive Ismail (r.1863–1879). Though Ismail facilitated cultural renaissance and infrastructural development, he saddled Egypt with debts to Britain, which led to the country's colonisation. Ḥāfiẓ Ibrahīm was an officer in the army who took part in the Egyptian–British military campaign in Sudan in 1899 to end the rule of the Islamist government set up by Muhammad Ahmad (1844–1885), known as the *Mahdī*. Ḥāfiẓ noticed (and experienced) that Egyptian officers, like himself, were not highly regarded. He protested alongside some other Egyptian officers against the British commanders but he was taken to court and made to retire early. His nationalist poetry is therefore marked with an insider's awareness of how colonialism functions. Revenge underpinned by arrogance is one of its cruel methods of rule, starkly manifest in the case of Dinshawai. Ḥāfiẓ was committed to Egypt being ruled by its people but, having served in the Egyptian army under the broader tutelage of British colonialism, he addresses the British as if they have forgotten that the Egyptian people showed loyalty and wanted to advance their country even while under colonialism. Instead, they received punishment so severe that it evoked the Dark Ages or the reign of Nero, an image that recurs often in modern Arabic poetry treating similar conditions. It is the absence of justice and mercy that Ḥāfiẓ bemoans, as well as the failure of the powerful to protect the weak: 'How could the strong take revenge on a weak man who entrusted his fate to him?' The harsh sentences that were meted out to the villagers in Dinshawai suggest that the humanity of the Egyptians involved was betrayed. Ḥāfiẓ's message in the poem is one of humanism grounded in the observation of basic human norms, so that the rights of people in their own country are respected rather than violated. The Dinshawai incident is revealing in the sense that it was a critical moment when the colonial British authority could have shown compassion. Instead, it chose excessive cruelty, unmasking its corruption through its actions. Interestingly, the poet's tone is similar to that of the famous Irish writer George Bernard Shaw who wrote in the preface to his play *John Bull's Other Island*, describing the situation at Dinshawai and its implications:

> They had room for only one man on the gallows, and had to leave him hanging half an hour to make sure [he was dead] and give his family plenty of time to watch him swinging, thus having two hours to kill as well as four men, they kept the entertainment going by flogging eight men with fifty lashes each... If her [England's] empire means ruling the world as Dinshawai has been ruled in 1906—and that, I am afraid, is what the Empire does mean to the main body of our aristocratic–military caste and to our Jingo plutocrats—then there can be no more sacred and urgent political duty on earth than the disruption, defeat, and suppression of the Empire, and, incidentally, the humanization of its supporters...[38]

The message in Ḥāfiẓ's lines as well as Shaw's is that unjust powers are blind in their suppression of their opponents. They need to reform themselves before they go about reforming others. Unlike nationalist political discourse, which tends to focus on the causes and consequences of the incident and openly reprimands the colonials, poetry in Ḥāfiẓ's hands takes the issue to its root: the violation of the humanity of the other represents an ultimate low in anyone who commits it. In this sense, within the neo-classical school of poetry of which Ḥāfiẓ is a pioneer, the values of humanism and reasoned poetics clearly enter the fray. It is the negative attitudes and feelings that Ḥāfiẓ registers as inappropriate in the conduct of governance, such as jealousy, vindictive anger and contempt, that lead to gross injustices. Thus, Ḥāfiẓ ends the poem by highlighting how Egypt is gripped by mourning because its fate is not in its own hands but in hands that treat it harshly.

Furthermore, Ḥāfiẓ was not only critical of the British occupation of his country, particularly since colonials occupied positions that Egyptians were not allowed to hold. He was also concerned about the rights of women and their condition in Egypt and the wider Arab world. His ideas coincided with and seemed inspired by Qāsim Amīn (1865–1908)'s book *The Emancipation of Women, Taḥrīr al-mar'ah*, which had gained significant popularity. Amīn is widely credited with advocating the rights of women at a time when Egyptian society and the Arab world were rife with masculine patriarchy, although there were several other important figures who joined the struggle for female emancipation. One of Amīn's key emphases regarding women was the importance of education in giving them the confidence to earn a living and to gain access to the public sphere. As Hourani wrote of Amīn, 'education would end the tyranny, and in doing so it would also end the veiling and seclusion of women'.[39] For his part, Ḥāfiẓ Ibrāhīm stresses the same point in poetry as Amīn:

> *Who can I trust with the education of women?*
> *For indeed the main pitfall of the East is in this field*
> *A mother is a school, should you groom well*
> *You would have groomed an authentic people.*[40]

The use of the word 'East' in such sweeping terms was quite common in the vocabularies of Arab poets in the nineteenth century. It demonstrates an awareness that the West was more advanced in terms of women's rights. Such a view is not sufficiently nuanced, however. Women in both the East and West were still struggling to attain basic rights, such as the right to vote and equal pay. It could generally be said that poets such as Ḥāfiẓ Ibrāhīm assumed Western superiority in certain fields such as the sciences and bureaucracy; and he called on the Arabs to catch up with these aspects. But the fact that the situation of women was visibly bad made Ḥāfiẓ stress education as a panacea. In this context, the degraded position of women is critically situated at the heart of society's ills. The lack of equality or a proper public space for women represented a stain on Eastern societies, and indeed it is still considered a crucial issue. In a line widely quoted in the Arab world even today, Ḥāfiẓ emphasises that education is the solution to the endemic problem of ignorance among women, enforced through men's domination and control over society, a problem that is deeply concerning, *'illat*.

Ḥāfiẓ does remain paternalistic in the way he constructs his poetics. He uses the masculine form to highlight that women need to be educated, presumably by men, in order to be equal partners in society; and he specifies motherhood as a source of national well-being. Yet in his poetic vocation he is clearly influenced by European ideas, paying conscientious attention to his society's ills in a way that still tallies with the traditions and Islamic basis of his society. In this respect, the poets played an important role in the education of their societies, by translating political developments into poetry that resonated with emotional attitudes to enlightening effect.[41]

With the above in mind, it is still the condition of Egypt and the Arab world under colonialism that most exercises the Arab poetic imagination. In fact, some poets, such as Ahmad Shawqī, as will be seen below, painted an idyllic picture of Egypt before colonialism as a prosperous country that colonialism then robbed of its past, distorting its image. The conditions of Egypt under colonialism are further depicted in another poem by Ahmad Shawqī, which he wrote in the wake of Lord Cromer's departure from Egypt in 1907. Shawqī laments the state of Egypt and refutes as well as satirises the argument of Lord Cromer that Egypt was made secure and more developed under colonialism in comparison with previous periods.[42] Under colonialism, Egypt suffered discrimination in favour of the colonial population, social deprivation, and the tainting of its culture and identity. In the famous poem 'Farewell to Lord Cromer', Shawqī writes:

> *Your days or those of Ismail?*
> *Or are you the Pharaoh reigning over the Nile?*
> *Or are you governing the land of Egypt at the behest of the Pharaoh*
> *Never either accountable or held to stand for any charges...*
> *When you left the country, she sighed with relief*[43]
> *As if you are the disease of which recovery is in your leaving*
> *In the day of your farewell, you filled us with humiliation*
> *Such manners which are unlike any others whatsoever...*
> *They said that you brought prosperity and wealth to Egypt*
> *They have dishonoured God, His creations and the Nile*
> *And the life of Egypt under Mohammad Ali*
> *And its renaissance at the time of Ismail*
> *He built schools for generations to come*
> *In which the share of the poor was great*
> *And he established ineradicable shelters*
> *And there are the armies of Ibrahim and the fleet...*
> *Cities and roads were planned*
> *They were sadly derelict but became like fertile valleys*
> *Cotton was planted due to Mohammad [Ali]*
> *By which Egypt was embroidered and interwoven....*
> *In every report, you say that I have created you:*
> *Do you see revealed holiness in your report?*
> *Is it part of your bounty for the schools*
> *To leave science behind and take up 'football'*
> *Or is it of your care over the court in Egypt*
> *To make the judge of Dinshawai a supreme judge*
> *Or is it due to you that you left*
> *An army like that of India, in tatters...*
> *You have deprived them of reaching high ranks*
> *And you have elevated your people above them as a matter of superior preference...*
> *So leave with the Almighty God's protection, whose design is the best,*
> *By your own accord if you want or be forced...*
> *Whoever lashes out at the religion of Mohammad*
> *Mohammad is confirmed by God as His prophet*[44]

The poem above demonstrates that the colonial discourse of superiority and innate ability in governance was challenged strongly: colonial discourses have never been a one-way street. It draws on native cultural references, here most evocatively represented in the Pharaoh, who gives an almost spiritual legitimacy to Egyptian rulers, which the colonial rulers inevitably lack. The Pharaoh in Egyptian culture is known both as a tyrannical figure as well as a founder and protector of Egyptian civilisation. In the underlying discourse of the poet, colonialism is masquerading as a successor to Pharaoh, practising tyranny in the name of spreading order and civilisation, as the speech of Cromer affirmed.[45] In addition, with a culture as proudly rooted and as vast as that of the Arab world, fused with an ancient Egyptian heritage and rituals, colonial officials could not have escaped the eye and conscience of Arab poets who were aware of widespread colonial intimidation and violations. Poets have been at the forefront of defiance and refutation in the face of colonialism, offering other alternatives and visions. Lord Cromer, one of the chief orientalists referred to in Edward Said's *Orientalism*,[46] is essentially depicted as a fabricator of falsehoods. Typical of a poet rooted in the past of the Arabs, Shawqī delineates the identity of modern Egypt in this poem as already established by Mohammad Ali and his dynasty, implying that the British came too late to Egypt to be able to claim, as Cromer did, that they had created modern Egypt. The poem projects three levels of identity in relation to modern Egypt: firstly as led by Mohammad Ali, secondly as affected by colonisation, and thirdly as situated in Islam as an integral part of its outlook; and all these modern aspects of identity are inflected by an ancient Egyptian civilisation. But what the poem above highlights most is the distortion that Egyptian history and life sustained under colonialism.

The assumed superiority of the West to the East is encapsulated in far-fetched claims, such as 'I have created you'. Shawqī satirically suggests that such discourse cannot be accepted as holy writ, or *munazal*. He implies through his religious idioms, *khalaqtukum* (created you) and *munazal* (revealed), which he culls from the language of Cromer and other colonials, that Britain could not assume the role of God. The underlying premise which Shawqī establishes at the beginning of the poem is that Egypt has a very ancient civilisation, and that since the time of Mohammad Ali and his sons, Ismail and Ibrahim, it had been set on a path of development and cultural revival, which colonialism manipulated and derailed. Cromer's claims of superior governance and economic prosperity are met with a nationalist Egyptian discourse. Shawqī showed that colonialism was not sensitive to the culture and nationalism of others, and imposed its templates of governance that left widespread material and psychological problems for the native population to deal with. Colonialism produces a clash of values, attitudes and representation, in various spheres of life. Basic areas of government, such as education, the legal system and the army, are all depicted as badly managed and unjustly run by colonials who denigrated the locals and their ability to govern. It is the aspect of discrimination and disparity that the poetry in question focuses on.

In addition, the political poetry grounds itself in a detailed knowledge of colonial rule like that of the British in India, the largest British colony. The poet asserts that arrogant colonialism, buttressed by a sense of entitlement, is bound to produce unjust effects on the people in question, as demonstrated by the Dinshawai incident. Moreover, the poet defends the Islamic faith against Cromer's demeaning disregard towards the Prophet of Islam Mohammad and the associative connotations of such denigration. Shawqī, who as we have shown above is steeped in the Islamic traditions and their supreme figure, the Prophet Mohammad, seals his poem with a religious note that Mohammad cannot be downgraded by someone like Cromer, a mere mortal; the Prophet's status is part of a belief system that should be respected, not demeaned. Violent colonial incidents, such as Dinshawai, formed an important milestone in Egyptian nationalism: they gave rise to the reinforcement of political parties in Egypt led by nationalist figures, such as Mustafa Kamel's National Party and Muhammad Sulayman Pasha's Umma Party. In particular Mustafa Kamel (1874–1908), who is described by Hourani as the 'first popular politician of modern Egypt',[47] benefited from the rising national feelings at the expense of the presiding Khedive 'Abbās Ḥilmī, who 'cared more for his own power than Egypt's independence'.[48] These nationalist developments triggered the 1919 revolution in Egypt against the British, forcing the latter to recognise the former's independence in 1922, which was more fully attained in 1952.

Furthermore, Ḥāfiẓ Ibrāhīm and Ahmad Shawqī were not only concerned with Egypt. They extended their portrayal and condemnation of colonialism to other parts of the Arab world. One notable uprising in Syria, which was harshly suppressed by the French mandate between 1925 and 1927, shows an example where pan-Arab and Islamic values were deployed to demonstrate cultural and political bonds across the Arab world and the role of poetry in memorialising signal events. Even though the colonial powers abetted the division of the Arab world into nation-states, which with time produced particular independent narratives related to their own past, the Arab world never ceased to be one cultural unit, manifesting itself mostly at times of calamities perpetrated by outside powers. Therefore, Shawqī's poem '*Nakbat Dimashq*', 'The catastrophe of Damascus', which focused on the shelling of Damascus in July 1926, gained widespread Arab recognition.[49] Hussein Kadhim, who studied the poem and its background thoroughly, contextualised it as follows:

> The series of events that occasioned this qasīdah are what came to be known as the Great Syrian Revolt of 1925–1927, in the course of which Damascus was subjected to bombardment by the French army of occupation. The Revolt broke out on the twentieth of July 1925, against a backdrop of mounting discontent with French domination.[50]

The bombardment of Damascus had grave consequences. As one account, quoted in Kadhim, put it:

> In less than 12 hours the French Army struck with more intensity than it had done in October or in February. The number of houses and shops destroyed during the aerial bombardment or as a result of incendiaries was estimated at well over 1,000. The death toll was equally staggering, between 600 and 1,000. The vast majority of casualties were unarmed civilians, including a large number of women and children....[51]

In his elegiac and panegyric Qaṣīdah ode 'The catastrophe of Damascus', Shawqī writes:

> *Peace to you gentler than the east breeze [blowing from the river] Baradā*
> *And tears that cannot be held back, O Damascus.*
> *The pen and the rhymes entreat [your] forgiveness*
> *The enormity of the affliction eludes a [proper] description....*
> *A memory, when recalled, my heart*
> *To you ever turns, throbbing.*
> *I too endure what the nights have visited upon you,*
> *Wounds deep in the heart...*
> *They said: the monuments of history have been levelled;*
> *They said: ruin and burning struck them.*
> *Have you not, O Damascus, suckled Islam?*
> *The wet nurse of paternity not to be disobeyed!*
> *Salāh al-Dīn is your crown, nought more beauteous*
> *Or more graceful has adorned a head.*
> *Every civilisation that ever flourished on earth*
> *Had a root from your lofty tree...*
> *In a night beyond whose sky*
> *Shells and fates [of death] were flashing, stupefying...*
> *Ask him who filled your maidens with terror in the deep of the night,*
> *Is there a difference between his heart and rock?*

The colonisers—although they may feign tenderness—
Have hearts like stone that feel no pity.
He struck you, as he did France, heedlessly
A warlike man, full of vainglory and folly...
The blood of the revolutionaries is known to France;
She knows that it is light and truth...
Sons of Syria, lay aside wishes,
Cast away dreams, cast [them] away.
For it is a political trick
That you are deceived by titles of Emirdom—which are nothing but enslavement...
Red liberty has a gate
Upon which every blood-soaked hand must knock...
The Druzes are not an evil clan
Even though they are undeservedly held to blame.
No, they are warriors, magnanimous to the guest,
Like al-Safā spring, they are hard and soft...[52]

The mourning of Damascus in these extracts fuses the past with the present to highlight the gravity of what has befallen that historic city. The attack on Damascus resonates with the poet deeply, as if it is a personal affliction that he is struggling to describe. Language, which is a fundamental tool in the hands of the poet, challenges him to seize it at a moment of profound psychological disturbance born of collective calamity in Damascus. Lamenting the destruction of cities in the Middle East is an old and recurrent poetic theme. The poet packs intense collective and personal anguish into evocative poetic constructions, affirming an unbroken allegiance to the place that so imprinted itself on the psyche of its inhabitants. Like in amorous situations, at the moment of loss the preciousness of the lost city gains exclusive and uncompromising attention, as the example of Palestine and its loss would later vividly demonstrate.[53] Characteristically, Shawqī draws on the rich history of the city to encompass the disaster. Grounded in the classical tradition, Shawqī evokes the historical significance of Damascus as the former seat of the Umayyad power (661–750), a timeless political capital filled with precious treasures. All the symbolic and material weight of history is described as having been targeted by this French assault: 'the monuments of history have been levelled'. In this context, historical evocation is a powerful trope laden with literary, spiritual and political connotations, all combining in a lamentation over Damascus, with which the poet is deeply acquainted. The romanticism of Damascus is contrasted with the savagery of colonialism; as Kadhim writes, 'the imagery derives much of its intensity from the way it is contrasted in the ode with the inclemency and violence of a war visited upon a once peaceful city'.[54] In addition, as is characteristic of Shawqī, Islam is invoked to demonstrate Damascus' centrality to it, in embracing, nursing and spreading it. Salāh al-Dīn who defeated the crusaders in the battle of Ḥittīn in 1198 is also mentioned as a milestone figure of courage in the history of Damascus, which suggests that the city is protected by the memory of its history. Therefore, it is the historical dimensions, even in the structural organisation of the poem, that make the bombardment of Damascus and the suppression of its revolt a destructive act carried out by inhuman perpetrators: 'Ask him who filled your maidens with terror in the deep of the night, Is there a difference between his heart and rock?' This anger makes Shawqī strip 'the other', the perpetrator, of his humanity. Yet ironically Shawqī draws on the historical experience of France and its revolution (1789–1799), which established the concept of the nation-state according to democratic and republican principles; he wonders how such a country could deny another people a revolution grounded in a claim to nationhood. Kadhim notes that 'from a postcolonial perspective, the irony is that the colonized (Arabs) have co-opted the enlightenment rhetoric of the colonizer'.[55] This argument finds considerable echoes in the work of important Arab poets of the time who, while condemning colonialism, refer to the experiences of the colonial countries and their discourse of enlightenment in favourable terms. Shawqī, therefore, is a historical, polemical and political aesthetician with profound rhetorical gifts. His rhetoric when he describes Damascus as having been once a cradle of idyllic peace could be dubbed romantic, paying little heed to the facts of history. Yet Shawqī is in thrall to Damascus as an historic, symbolic capital, and what irks him most is that it is colonised and occupied by an 'other' who is not even aware of its historical value. Thus, any colonial act, including making King Faysal the Emir of Damascus, is rejected: it is utterly at odds with what Damascus, and for that matter the Arab world, needs. The monarchical status imposed on Damascus is described as enslavement, as King Faysal was appointed the Emir of Damascus by the British. Furthermore, as was shown in the previous chapter, Shawqī was passionate about the Ottoman Empire, which was undermined by revolutions and ambitious rulers in the Arabian Peninsula, birthplace of Faysal. Damascus could not therefore be under such rule, when the French came to control the country.

The road to freedom for Shawqī can only be reached through resistance. Hence his panegyric and elegiac poem abounds with diverse references, evoking history and political ideals, bitterly lamenting the destruction of Damascus, and treating the French assault as an act of destruction of the first order. In particular, Shawqī pays homage to the Syrian resistance, drawing on the fact that the Syrian revolution started in the mountains and was led by the Druze before it reached Damascus. The Druze leader Sulṭān al-Aṭrash (1891– 1982), who is credited with leading the revolution, hailed from this particular Muslim community, which was linked 'to the Arab/Muslim populace of Syria'.[56] The Druze could not be blamed for sparking the revolution, since Shawqī views this as a natural response to colonialism and its assaults on the native population.

Lamentation and national commemoration in modern Arabic poetry are widespread in the context of colonialism in the Arab world. In particular, two other countries that witnessed notable colonial deprivation and destruction spurned their native poets, who portrayed the state of their countries in a committed and compassionate manner; namely Algeria and Palestine. These countries (alongside other victims of colonialism such as Libya, Yemen, Iraq and Egypt) witnessed an outpouring of poetic creativity by local as well as pan-Arab poets, who saw in their calamities an attack on Arab identity and its future trajectory. The following section is devoted to treating the thematic poetics of Algeria and Palestine in the context of British and French colonialism, through writers whose poetry has enduring historical and national values.

Algeria and Palestine: loss and reclamation

Several poetic schools and trends emerged in the first half of the twentieth century, particularly after the First World War. The new schools did not replace the old ones; the Arabic poetic tradition has more often operated by elaboration and innovation in styles and themes than erasure. There have always been different orientations in Arabic poetry, expressed in various forms and modes. The newly added forms dispense with the rule-bound two-hemistich odes, whereby a line of poetry is divided into two parts, often equal in foot and rhyme.[57] The expansion of the form constituted a novelty with wideranging consequences for Arabic poetry. As the range of poetic forms expanded, so did the consciousness and scope of poetic vision. This is particularly true with regard to the rise of the individual voice and the ascendance of various romantic and introspective trends in Arabic poetry, which took off from the 1920s onwards. Nonetheless, the Arabic poetry that dealt with political issues remained relatively formally conservative until later decades, when the free verse movement incorporated politics into its poetic innovations, as in the remarkable works of the Iraqi poet Badir Shākir al-Sayyāb

(1926–1964) and others. Still, the classical form remained important for some poets for its expression and assertion of tradition. Often a combination of stylistic, poetic and political reasons determined the poetics of each poet. The fact that political Arabic poetry written under colonial rule in countries such as Palestine and Algeria was a poetry of reclamation, combined with mobilisation, meant that it carried echoes of traditional Arab values whether at the formulaic or epistemological level. This is particularly true of the generation of Arab poets before the 1950s. That generation was educated in the classical and neo-classical styles, and was influenced by poets such as Aḥmad Shawqī of Egypt and Khalīl Muṭrān of Lebanon and others. Yet even after the 1950s, there were poets who subscribed to the neo-classical form, using it as a way to assert the Arab roots and identity of their country.

The rhythmic nature of such stirring and purpose-driven poetry facilitated its oral spread among the people. The collective predicament and the morale of the nation was captured by some poets through expressive lines that became part of the staple of resistance within an intense period of anti-colonial struggle with national, pan-Arab and even international resonances. Most of the poets considered below were published after they were successful with one or two poems—or even fragments from poems—that reached the public orally and were enacted continuously through memorisation and recitation. The orality of poetry in its compositional, thematic and performative aspects never ceased to be significant for attracting popular momentum. Most poets were teachers who used the schools, universities and places of social gatherings as public stages, highlighting the plight of their people. Therefore, their poems embodied the spirit of the struggle at an acute moment in the life of the nation, after one major incident or another by which the nation was mobilised to respond. This was the case for many of the Algerian and Palestinian poets who played an indispensable role in their peoples' struggles for freedom. Some of these poets were imprisoned or harshly treated and their poetry stemmed from such experiences. Most portrayed the suffering of their people: the palpable injustice underlying such suffering as well as their determination, hopes and aspirations for liberation and unity, whether among themselves or through a wider Arab unity.

One such poet who adhered to the neo-classical form with some innovations and who is significant to his country and its colonial history is the Algerian poet Mufdī Zakariyā bin Suleiman (henceforth, Mufdī Zakariyā). Mufdī was born in 1908 in the village of Banī Yasjin and passed away in Tunis in 1977. His importance is related to the tumultuous events that his country underwent under French colonialism, which require some explication.

Algeria endured the longest colonial occupation in the Arab world. After France occupied it in 1830 for its commercial and geographical significance, Algeria gradually became a bastion of French colonial power, to the extent that it was described as a *département de France*. Giving such an appellation to an obviously Arab country says much about the colonial attitudes of France, which consolidated its colonialisation through the imposition of linguistic and cultural norms as well as through economic and political control. Nevertheless, Fanon's "Wretched of the Earth"—in this case the colonised, with their own histories in mind and their own understanding of them-selves—retain a sense of power. This is often expressed in their poetry, which demonstrates the power of rootedness in the land and the spirit of its history, which refuses to admit defeat and values long-term, principled resistance. Such values were perhaps nowhere more passionately expressed than in the poetry of Mufdī Zakariyā, known as the poet of the Algerian revolution. He studied the Qur'an and learned grammar and other elements of literary Arabic heritage, essential to his vocation. He is also an heir to an important tradition of nationalist poetry written by prominent figures, nationalist Algerian and North African poets. The iconic leader Abdelkādir al-Jazāirī (1808–1883), who led resistance campaigns in the nineteenth century against French colo-nialism is one; Mohammad al-Fitūrī, who celebrated Africa and the heroism of its people in the face of colonialism, is another. To this end, many of the poets were also freedom fighters, combining revolutionary words with revo-lutionary actions.[58] Mufdī Zakariya joined the major resistance movement, the Algerian National Liberation Front (FLN), when it was first formed in 1954, and was imprisoned on several occasions until he escaped from prison to Morocco in 1959. He wrote several poems, and some while in prison, such as the one quoted first below, which he composed in cell 69 in the prison of Barbarossa in 1955. Some of his important poems, including the ones quoted below, were used for various nationalist purposes within what can be described as practices of 'canonising nationalism', in the sense of perpetuating national-ism through oral poetic rituals that invoke the homeland and depict its defence as sacred. Most of his directly nationalist and revolutionary poetry appeared in a *diwān* (collection) called *al-lahab al-muqaddas, The Holy Flame*, which was published in Beirut in 1961. He also produced another impressive anthology called *The Iliad of Algeria* that he composed in 1972, invoking the history of Algeria and its resistance to various foreign occupations. Yet it is the first set of poems that Mufdī composed, at the height of the revolution, which made his poetry a viscerally emotive call for mobilisation. In one poem, which became the anthem of the National Liberation Army, called 'In the name of the descending destroyers', Mufdī writes:

In the name of the descending destroyers...and the precious gushing blood
And the shining orders in the horizon...from the high proud mountains
We have revolted, so either life or death
We have strengthened our resolve...that Algeria will live
So bear witness...
We are soldiers; we revolted in the name of righteousness...
Towards our independence, we marched
It [the coloniser] *was not listening to us when we talked...*
So we put up the sound of our ringing rifles
And we played the music of the machine gun and produced a melody...
We have strengthened our resolve...that Algeria will live
So bear witness...

In another poem, later to become the 'The anthem of the Algerian martyrs', the poet writes:

O mountains, shake,
O thunders, shoot,
O wounds, expand,
O shackles, loosen,
We are a strong nation
There is no coward among us
We are fed up with living
In destitution and humiliation
We do not give up on struggle
We do not give up on Jihad
For the sake of the country
They have forced us into prisons
They have made us drink death
But there are no traitors among us
No one would bend or be humiliated
Lash out...torture us...
Hang us...crucify us...
Burn...and destroy
We never terrorise
We never give up on struggle
We never give up on Jihad
For the sake of the country.

Both poems had important sentimental associations and significance for the Algerian revolutionaries, the second in particular. In 1956 the FLN issued an order asking those sentenced to execution to chant it before they went to the guillotine. The poems are shot through with a spirit of flat rejection, defiance and bellicosity. The main message of the first one is that Algeria will live independently on its own soil, and France will be forced to withdraw. As France refuses to respond to negotiation or entreaty, Algeria will march forward with its revolution; and there is no turning back until total liberation is achieved. Poetry in the hands of Mufdī is a declaration of defiance, a familiarly intransigent theme in anti-colonial poetry. The second poem has similar nationalist themes. No matter how aggrieved Algeria is, how savagely targeted by the colonials, it will not give up on struggle. Its resistance is its dignity, and its dignity is its identity, and its identity is in its independence; whatever France does to suppress it and break its spirit of resolve, Algeria never gives up on its 'Jihad' and struggle, words that combine Arab traditionalism with international principles of resistance to foreign occupation. The ingredients of resistance include patience, sacrifice, endurance and the strength of vision to see the country free of its occupiers, despite all the odds. Various metaphors express resistance through images of national resolve. For example, Mufdī evokes the mountains of Algeria where fighters sought refuge and emerged for a struggle that ultimately yielded independence in 1962, once the urban centres of Algeria had been roused to violent resistance. The image of Algerian mountains was used as a common sign of strength by other Arab poets in solidarity with Algeria, such as in the poem of the Iraqi poet Badr Shākir al-Sayyāb, 'In the Arab Maghreb', and in the work of the Egyptian poet Ahmad 'Abd al-Mu'tī Hijāzī, one of whose evocative poems is named after the Aurès mountains in Algeria and Tunisia.[59] Thus, as France under President Charles de Gaulle deployed several tactics, including massive suppression as well as hints of diplomatic accommodation and compromise with the revolutionaries, Mufdī wrote another long poem under the declarative title 'There is no dignity until Algeria is liberated', where he made the position of the Algerian revolutionaries clear:

> I am a revolutionary
> There is no dignity until Algeria is liberated
> That's how the sons of Algeria act...
>
> And we are the sons of nobles, Arabs, whose customs
> Are holy, we do not bear treachery or betrayal,
> France... let go of delusions, for the delusion is fatal
> We do not even give an ounce of our Algeria
> France...let go of ambitions, for the pursuit is futile
> We would not sell the desert (for all France)

If resources in its belly obsess you and you get all the riches
We will dig a tomb for you in the womb of our desert.

To situate the poem above within its political context, it is worth paying close attention to the political developments in Algeria before its independence in 1962. Prior to 1959, when de Gaulle was elected as the new President of the Fifth Republic, the main French tactic used in Algeria was military pressure: namely, attacks against military as well as civilian bases of the Algerian National Liberation Front (FLN), a traditional Socialist party with deep nationalist inclinations. What is today known as the Battle of Algiers began on 30 September 1956, when three women placed bombs at three sites, including the downtown office of Air France. It remains the battle signal that ultimately led to Algerian independence. The women who took an active part in the Algerian struggle (including the iconic Jamīlah Bouhired (b.1935), who was badly tortured by the French) are memorialised in Arabic poetry.[60] The battle entailed severe military clashes that resulted in many Algerian deaths and caused heavy damage to the urban infrastructure of the capital, Algiers. Such damage was particularly common in areas where the native population of Algeria resided, not the white areas or those of the Algerian elite subservient to them, whom the revolutionaries also targeted. For his part, de Gaulle made attempts to contain the resistance, visiting the iconic Algerian city of Constantine (Qasanṭīna) in October 1959 and offering to divide the rule of Algeria between France and Arab Algerian Muslims. The offer was met with adamant refusal by the FLN. The Algerian resistance continued with nationwide strikes and incessant attacks, leading up to the Evian Accords on 1 July 1962, which called for a referendum on independence that was approved unanimously by the Algerians. The independence of Algeria was officially confirmed on 5 July 1962.

The poem above gives emotional reasons as to why any offer other than that of full independence was rejected. It operates on the level of principle, historical memory and defiance. Mufdī asserts the Arab character of Algeria, and explains what 'being an Arab' means. While the Arab reality and their right to the land is self-evidently true and historically sacred, the French insistence on military pressure as a way to preserve and arrogate Algeria for itself is regarded as delusional; France has no place in the Arab reality of Algeria—that is the crux of the poet's vision. Mufdī places an idea and an ideal above the reality of France that, when the poem was written in 1961, was still oppressing Algeria and targeting its resistance; France's power was real, but its claim that Algeria was one of its dominions was not. Such poetry is endowed with faith: faith that injustice does not last forever, that it is futile, even though its propagators might look powerful and appear to hold all the cards. One aspect of the injustice of colonialism was the expropriation of resources of the colonised country, which formed the main motive for colonialism. In the last line of the extract quoted above, Mufdī asserts that the resources of Algeria belong to it; they are its sacred property. The poet acts as a judge in the last line, issuing the verdict of death for anyone who takes the resources of his country. The language is unmistakably harsh. Digging graves to bury people alive, whatever the context, is savagely inhumane. Yet, such an image of turning the invaded areas into graves for their invaders is not uncommon in Arabic political poetry and populist political discourse. Violent resistance tends to give rise to violent language, where primary human values, such as mercy, seem to have become irrelevant. Violence, whether at the level of discourse or even desire, is reciprocal between the powerful coloniser and those who resist. There is nothing more expendable than humanity in a tangled web of violence. Algeria is known in the Arab world as the country of a million martyrs. Incessant French military attacks against Algerians steeped the country in fiery rhetoric, reprisals and a legacy of violence. This inspired the great Martinique–Algerian psychiatrist Frantz Fanon to expose the face of colonial violence in Algeria and its dire consequences for its people in searing and surgical terms in *The Wretched of the Earth*. Fanon condemns colonialism for its degraded methods of control, pays homage to organised resistance and principled nationalism, and ultimately asserted humanism as the basis of life and coexistence.

Several North African poets joined the struggle and wrote poems lauding Algerian resistance and calling for unity between the North African countries, since the borders between these countries were seen as imperially imposed rather than of native origin. Such poets include the Tunisian poet Muṣṭafā Kharīf,[61] the Libyan poet ʿAlī al-Riqāʿī and the Moroccan poet Aḥmad ʿAbd al-Salām al-Baqālī, who wrote a famous poem while in Cairo in 1953 called 'The Arab Maghreb revolt'. Echoing the message of other North African poets, al-Baqālī calls to the North Africans to unite and resist their occupiers and invokes the diverse ethnicities that constitute North Africa as bound by one destiny of liberation and coexistence:

> *I am Berber, I am an Arab,*
> *And Andalucian and I am Moroccan*
> *North Africa has revolted*
> *Burning the wings of the night with its fire...*
> *Tunisia, do not surrender,*

Your day is inevitably coming
And our neighbour, Algeria,
Why are you unmoved when the night had gone?
And O the valiant people of Marrakesh
May God protect your revolutionary leaders...[62]

Such poems as the above were written when the countries in question were on the verge of launching systematic resistance against their colonisers, particularly in Algeria. They invoke the common bonds of the people of these countries and ethnicities in North Africa to authenticate the call for unity and solidarity. Indeed, solidarity was one of the methods that the FLN advocated, and it was multifaceted. Increasingly, Algeria gained wide Arab attention as it fought for its independence, which occurred whilst the Arab world was still reeling from colonisation in the 1950s and 60s. Mufdī's confident language was not built on quicksand; it stemmed from favourable international attention and the increasingly tarnished reputation of France as an aggressive colonial power. Meanwhile, the discourse of pan-Arab unity, most notably as articulated by President Jamal Abd al-Nassir (1918–1970) of Egypt, was in full swing. Thus, in the poetry of Mufdī, pan-Arabism is alive in a way that invokes the most important symbol of its time, Palestine. The Palestinian national cause became integrated into the nationalist discourse of the Arab world both culturally and politically. While the independence of Algeria brought immediate Arab relief and jubilation given the ferocity of the battles that had preceded it, the colonisation of Palestine in 1948 at the hands of the Zionist movement and the formation of Israel at the expense of the Palestinians made the cause of Palestine a cause of the entire Arab world, wounding Arab pride to the core. Despite the military weakness and fragmentation of the Arabs in the face of Zionism and its Western supporters, Palestine was etched in the memories of the Arabs as a land with long-standing spiritual and historic values for the Arabs in general. Such values were no better expressed than in Arabic poetry and cultural discourse. At the level of official political discourse, Palestine was evoked in dubious terms as well as sincere. But poetically Palestine was a sister or brother, forced into harsh separation from her family members. Thus, in the same poem above, in the eighth section in particular, Mufdī shows the territorial affinities that bind Palestine and Algeria and metaphorically knit the rest of the Arab world together:

O an Arab in a sisterly country
Our Arabism, who can deny it...??
Indeed, our war is only an extension for a revolution

That whoever wanted to betray us desired our loss,
The resurrection of Palestine is in the land of Algeria,
So extend a hand that safeguards the fortresses and frontiers...
There is no dignity till Algeria is liberated
And till we make the greater unity...

Structurally, not all the conceptual bonds of the poem are organically linked; but the underlying theme is clear enough: it derives its power from the rhetoric of the time. The poem reiterates the discourse of pan-Arabism on the basis of shared language and history and similar political and cultural inclinations, as is clear in the writings of many Arab thinkers and ideologues of the time. Arabism is a given in this poem; its elements are clear and need not be mentioned. It is as if there is a shared Arab sensibility around which the poet could construct a political discourse. The poet conflates the problems of the time and the issue of greater unity between the Arabs that many pan-Arab figures called for. The concept was popular, particularly with the ascendant socialist parties in the Arab world, in countries such as Egypt, Iraq, Syria and Southern Yemen. In reference to Palestine, the poet draws on the image of resurrection, *inbiʿāth*, an image that abounds in political, and even existential, Arabic poetry as a way for the Arabs to re-emerge after a calamity, whether it be individual or collective. The resurrection of Palestine is situated in Algeria in the sense that the latter can serve as a model of resistance and steadfastness; this in return will guarantee liberation and freedom for Palestine. Algeria proves that resistance is a means to resurrection, even for cities and countries that are geographically yet not spiritually distant, since they possess a similar language and cultural attitudes and are suffering a similar political plight. The poem asserts the shared cultural identity of the Arab world that transcends the physical borders of the nation-state, particularly at times of disaster or triumph. But while Algeria attained liberation and the dignity of independence, Palestine has remained occupied to this day. Its occupation shaped the poetics of many an Arab poet and writer. As the great Palestinian writer Jabra Ibrahim Jabra put it, 'the Arabs were suddenly on their own: independent in most cases, but beset by a world that seemed to make a travesty of their independence, with the added trauma of having most of Palestine hacked up into an illogical Zionist state. A supreme agony, a crucifixion. The poet's response was severe and radical.'[63] The following section continues to highlight the Palestinian problem as memorialised in poetry.

One Palestinian poet, Rashīd Hussain (1936–1977), linked the Palestinian struggle with that of Algeria, showing widespread Arab, and indeed Third

World, support. His poem demonstrates how the Algerian struggle inspired Palestinians by evoking natural objects as sites of intimacy and resistance that respond to the desires of the colonised natives for liberation and freedom, whether in Algeria or Palestine:

> *We will make the rock understand if humans do not*
> *That if people erupted, they would be victorious*
> *Whatever fire you ignite, we will put out*
> *Do not you see that we are dark-skinned because we grow up with such fire*
> *If you have obliterated all the revolutionaries*
> *The Sheikh, the stick and the stone will rebel against you.*[64]

All these objects, the rock, the stick and the stones, are neutral objects, but they are familiarly used for various purposes of life in a way that endows them with agency, even if one activated by people, in the context at hand, the revolutionaries. The Palestinian national movement began as the Algerian ended with independence; and it is the former that continued to acquire significance in the Arab world as the principal site of struggle against the last major occupation in the Arab world.

To this end, it could safely be said that Palestine gave rise to a number of important poets of a quality and depth hitherto unseen in the Arab world in the twentieth century. If there is any medium that expressed the uniqueness of the Palestinian experience and its Arab and international scope, it was poetry. From the outset, once Palestine ceased to be part of the Ottoman Empire in 1917 and Britain assumed official mandate over it from the League of Nations in 1922, Palestine became a battleground for diverse narratives and was catapulted into violent traps that culminated in the formation of Israel on 14 May 1948. Israel represented a challenge that has never ceased to haunt the Arab world. After that state was established, Palestinian historians and many conscientious writers went on to confirm that Palestine had always belonged to the Palestinian Arabs, refuting the Zionist claim that it was theirs by historical tradition that harks back more than 2,000 years. The fact of the matter is that the Jews were part of the diverse population of Palestine and had their share of the ebb and flow of ethnic political power as much as others. In addition, the Zionist conquerors were initially and mainly European Jews (Ashkenazim) who could not possibly be the inheritors of those who lived in that land thousands of years ago as individuals, let alone as a nation. Therefore, Zionism was a colonial movement of an aggressive kind fed by the broader colonialism of Europe in the nineteenth century, as many scholars of the European colonial empires have demonstrated.[65] In the political literature on

Palestine, there are two major political narratives that Palestinian Arabs put forward with regard to Palestine: firstly, Palestine was part of a broader Arab area including Syria and Lebanon (Greater Syria); and secondly, Palestine consisted of a diverse, multi-ethnic population which more often than not lived together in peace for many centuries.[66] So there could not be a state in Palestine other than that of Palestine itself. The strongest Arab discourse with regard to Palestine has been that Palestine is an Arab land and that its conquest by the British and then the Zionists in 1948 was morally and legally dubious;[67] therefore it has to be exposed and resisted.

Palestine, however, like most of the nations of the world, was integrated into a worldwide system in which power played a key role in the formation of historical trajectories. Once Israel was established in 1948, and despite the anguish, displacement and terrible injustices that the Palestinians have continued to endure, many world powers, such as Britain, France, Russia and the United States, recognised Israel and gave it legitimacy and support. As Edward Said highlighted in his 1979 book *The Question of Palestine*, the Palestinians ceased to be seriously considered or represented by the Western powers as a people with a long-standing political identity, with rights and emotional ties to their land.[68] It was Britain that first promoted the discourse of underestimation and denial vis-à-vis the Palestinians and their rights, through the Balfour Declaration in 1917. This infamous declaration gave the Zionist Jews the right to have a 'national home' in Palestine, a country which was not Britain's gift to give and to which the Zionists were not entitled. Later, Britain supported the Zionist movement through colonial practices that favoured the Jewish settlers in Palestine over the native Palestinians. Palestinian poets were confronted with the daunting prospect of their land and resources being taken away from them, entailing unending psychological traumas whose marks are still visible throughout the Palestinian refugee camps in Palestine and abroad. Resistance against the colonial power that had facilitated the establishment of Israel, namely Britain, began in earnest through revolts in 1929 and 1936, which included nationwide strikes and confrontations that resulted in Palestinian fatalities and losses on various fronts. Later, through well-trained militias, the Zionists perpetrated massacres against the Palestinians which paved the way for the colonisation of Palestine; and these found expression in acts of resistant reclamation enshrined in Palestinian poetry; thus, as Barbara Harlow wrote, 'the massacres of Dayr Yasīn and Kafr Qāsim, the disaster of 1948, the defeat of June 1967, which serve as nodal points within the poetic configurations and commemorate significant events in recent Palestinian history, betray as well an elegiac nostalgia for the idylls of a time past.'[69] Palestinian poetry is therefore the offspring of terrible experiences of dispossession, pain, estrangement, struggle and an unyielding desire for freedom from an occupation that has robbed the Palestinian people of their source of stability and pride—their land—and violently disrupted their political development.

At the same time, it cannot be overlooked that Palestine under the Ottoman Empire, particularly towards the end of the latter's rule, suffered terrible tribulations. The massacre in Jerusalem at the beginning of the First World War at the hands of Jamal Pasha, who attempted to suppress any rising Arab nationalist sentiments, prompted many people to welcome the British initially, as liberators rather than colonisers. One poet, among others, described the situation clearly in 1918: this was one of the rare moments when a native poet welcomes his invaders, using their discourse of enlightenment— in which colonialism was embedded and justified. Sheikh 'Alī al-Rimāwī (1860–1919) wrote that the victory of the British army brought happiness to the inhabitants, because it ended the darkness and replaced oppression of Jamal Pasha with justice:

> *Justice has superseded oppression, and after the dark we have begun to see the dawn. Thus every heart is bathed in pleasure, and every pen has freedom to write.*[70]

Justice, freedom and pleasure: all these lofty concepts are drawn from an internalised sense of enlightenment which Britain was seen to have brought to Palestine; and some poets reiterated and elaborated approvingly on these sentiments.[71] In fact, the political scene at the time when Britain conquered Jerusalem in 1918 was one that engendered mixed feelings. On the one hand, the Palestinians of Jerusalem generally welcomed Britain as better than the oppressive Ottoman Empire in its dying days; on the other, Britain, from the outset, showed that it was neither on the side of the local population politically nor was it sensitive enough to their nationalist aspirations and traditional narratives. Any positive image the Palestinian Arabs might have had of Britain at the beginning was dissipated. One stark example is evident in the speech of General Allenby, who led the British contingent that entered Jerusalem. At the end of a short speech, General Allenby made a remark that clearly offended the Muslim Arabs listening to him: 'This is the end of the Crusaders' wars.'[72] The Crusaders who pillaged Jerusalem between 1099 and 1291 had always been portrayed in Arab and Muslim discourses as hateful conquerors that had committed massacres and ransacked the city of Jerusalem.[73] In the same vein, this 'pleasant image of Britain', as Khalid Sulaiman wrote in his

1984 book *Palestine and Modern Arabic Poetry*, 'did not last for long, however, especially after the British policy of facilitating the transformation of the country into a "Jewish National Home" was pursued openly'.[74]

Against this backdrop, Sulaiman mentions three features that characterised Palestinian poetry before 1948; it is worth quoting him fully here:

> Firstly, these poets had been living in the country concerned and had witnessed the threat in close-up, and their poetry therefore expressed the emotions, feelings and reactions of the Palestinian Arabs who were directly affected by these events. Secondly, a great deal of their poetry concentrated on particular themes, such as the sale of land to the Jews and the nature of the Palestinian leadership of the time, which were not voiced in the poetry of the Arab poets living in Arab countr[ies?]. Thirdly, as one part of their role was to widen the struggle against the Mandate and the Zionists inside Palestine, so the other part of the role was to draw the attention of the Arabs outside Palestine to the vital danger threatening the future of the Arab land which had a special religious importance for them.[75]

These three features can be highlighted through the poetry of Ibrahīm Touqān, whose visionary voice, deeply engaged in the developments leading up to 1948, is informative as well as representative. Touqān, whose younger sister was the great Palestinian poet Fadwa Touqān (1917–2003), was born in the Palestinian city of Nablus in 1905. He lived in Jerusalem and Beirut and later worked in Nablus as a teacher before succumbing to stomach ulcers at the young age of thirty-six in 1941. Ibrahim was deeply affected by the events that accelerated the colonisation of Palestine. In particular, he focused on the British mandate and its policies. Initially, Ibrahīm, like other Palestinian poets, had a favourable view of the British, but it faded for the reasons given before: Britain aided the Zionist colonisation of Palestine and harshly suppressed the nationalist aspirations of the Palestinians. Regretting his earlier support of the British, he wrote:

O my homeland! it was my fault that I loved them;
Here is my heart, I offer it to you to stab.[76]

It was the broken promises to the Arabs that angered Ibrahīm and other Arab poets, starting with those made to Sharīf Husayn Bin Alī by the British in 1915, namely that the Arab desire for independence would be supported if they fought the Ottoman Empire and stood by Britain in its war against the Germans. Though the Zionist movement instigated the first wave of emigration to Palestine, starting in 1882 and later reinforced in Basel in 1897 by the selection of Palestine as the national home for the Jews, it was Britain through the Balfour Declaration in 1917 that aided the Zionists in establishing a

Jewish homeland in Palestine. The Balfour Declaration has therefore always been condemned and remembered with anguish by the Palestinians and the Arabs. The Iraqi poet Jamīl Ṣāddiq al-Zahāwī (1862–1936) summed up the Declaration in two lines:

> Seventy million with an Arab ancestry are
> Furious at you in the East, O Balfour.[77]

It was during uprisings such as that of 1929 that poets and writers high-lighted the Declaration as a milestone in the dispossession of the Palestinians. The uprisings of 1929 and 1936 were aimed at the British, mainly for the increasing visibility of its role in facilitating Jewish immigration to Palestine and the fear that this would lead to a Jewish state at the expense of the Palestinians. The uprising of 1929 took place as Britain gave Jews access to the Burāq Wall (geographically, the Western Wall), known to the Jews as the Wailing Wall, which had hitherto been part of the Islamic complex in the city of Jerusalem. The access added to the anxiety of the Arabs, who were already aware of increasing immigration to the country. As Ilan Pappé wrote, 'the 1929 outbreak was caused not only by the events in Jerusalem but also by larger circumstances. Some 90,000 Jews immigrated to Palestine between 1921 and 1929. Though the influx ebbed from 1926 to 1928, the presence of so many new immigrants in the labour market and the efforts of the Zionist organisations to purchase land for them made Zionism into a tangible factor in the lives of many ordinary Palestinians.'[78] The outbreak resulted in deaths on both sides, Jews and Arabs. Against this background, Touqān wrote a poem under the title 'al-balad al-ka'īb', 'The bleak (literally: depressed) country', where he stated:

> My sorrow over the bleak country, whose markets have ceased to function...
> This is your enemy and its morals...
> Balfour, that in your glass is not wine, but the martyrs' blood...
> Damn your promise, for it would not perturb
> People who had decided to revolt...
> Could you be lost, O my homeland?
> And the vein of Arabism is alive in you,
> I would go for the sake of my country
> Towards the streams of death...
> Until you live, O my homeland, in the shadow of dignity and peace...[79]

The expression of attachment to the land and sacrifice for its sake are common themes in Palestinian poetry. They recur throughout the twentieth century in various forms. In the above extract, the poet stresses that his country has been deeply afflicted; hence, it is 'depressed'. The psychological term suggests that the poet senses that his country is undergoing trauma. One element of this traumatic affliction that beset Palestine was due to the Balfour Declaration, the consequences of which had been paid for by the blood of the Palestinians fighting both the colonisation of their country and the Zionist threat to it. The poet also asserts the Arab identity of the land and his willingness to sacrifice himself for it. This is a sentiment that we encounter in all the poetry of Arab poets whose countries were undergoing colonisation, as in the case of Mufdī Zakariyā of Algeria. Though certain of its Arab identity, the poet fears that his country might nevertheless be lost, sensing the impending danger of Zionist encroachment. There is intuitive understanding of colonial power and its tendencies, which suggests that the 'truthful' sensibility of poets, while unconscious at times, has some merit. The poet enmeshed in the discourse of struggle advocates sacrifice as a means of liberation and protection. In fact, the theme of sacrifice is wide-spread in Palestinian poetry; and one of the iconic poets who evocatively expressed it and whose words in this field resonate to this day is 'Abd al-Raḥīm Maḥmūd (1913–1948):

> In my hand, I will bear my soul, ready to throw it into the abyss of death.
> A man should live with honour and dignity, otherwise he should die gloriously,
> The soul of the noble man has but two aims: either to die or to attain glory.
> I swear I can see my fate, but I quicken my steps towards it.
> The only desire I have is to fall defending my usurped rights, and my country.[80]

The words of 'Abd al-Raḥīm Maḥmūd are widely memorised by Palestinians. They stand for personal and collective principles and affirm that death is noble where the defence of the country is involved, a theme common to most, if not all, nationalist discourse. The country and its dignity are the source of life, without which life ceases to be worthwhile. Between Touqān and Mahmoud, we witness a primordial connection to the homeland: the poet is rooted in its soil; its life and his are indistinguishable and fused. Thus, much of the poetry that was discussed above, whether it is in relation to Palestine, Egypt, Algeria or other Arab countries in general, operates at the level of principles. These principles turn into values, which become what politicised poetry itself expresses: political positions. Touqān and Mahmoud give voice to a trauma-tised nation, defending its pride in the face of impending loss. The poets know that their country and its people are victims but this victimhood is not wasted; it is a sacrifice that the poet takes pride in invoking and celebrating. The life of his country is depicted as worthy of his own life, if his country is denied dig-nity and honour. The poets confirm al-Raṣāfī's earlier point that 'man is a principle first and foremost'; values outweigh interest-driven power which makes people submit and internalise its consequences as irreversible. In other words, Arabic poetry of the type discussed here inspires people with the belief that they can draw power from their principles to realise their individuality and personhood. All this confirms that the Arabic language, and indeed language in general, is part of the materiality of life; its historicity cannot be eroded by socio-economic and political shifts, important as they are. Colonialism therefore threatens the history of a people in their land—a history and land so dear to them that they are ready to sacrifice themselves in its defence. All these aforementioned dimensions make the poetry in question one of both defence and revolution.

One key moment relating to the nationalist commemoration of martyrs was crystallised in 1930, mobilising the entire Palestinian nation against their colonisers. Remembering that the Palestinian national identity in its later stages is steeped in nationalist commemoration,[81] one famous poem could be described as a milestone for the Palestinians. Ibrahīm Touqān's 'al-Thulathā' al-Hamra' ('Bloody Tuesday') foreshadows the bleak future facing Palestine at the time. The poem is an elegy in response to the hanging of three Palestinians in Acre during the 1929 outbreak. They were accused of murdering Jewish settlers in the clashes that took place between the Arabs and Jews in several Palestinian cities. The poem, as is explained by Sulaiman, is elaborate; it consists of three parts and eight stanzas, each depicting three hours of the fateful Tuesday on which the three Palestinians were executed by the British authorities, namely Fouād Hijāzī from Safad, and Mohammad Jamjūm and 'Attā al-Zayr from Hebron. Of the event, Touqān writes:

When your evil star appeared and heads swayed in the nooses,
The adhān wailed and the bells tolled.
The night was an ill one and the day grim.
Fury and fierce emotions were rampant...
Past nights disown this Tuesday and stare in perplexity...
Their bodies are in the soil of their homeland. Their souls are in Paradise...
Forgiveness should be sought only from God,
Only from Him whose hand possesses dignity and honour...
His omnipotence is greater than the power of those who are vain
Because of their power on land and sea.
This is your road to life so do not deviate from it
Al-Qassam has walked it before.[82]

The poem opens with contradictory images of harshness on the one hand, as in the method of execution, and peace on the other, epitomised in the

Islamic *adhān* (call to prayer) and the church bells. The opening of the poem shows how colonialism demeans and undermines traditions. For the colonised, therefore, the preservation of traditions constitutes an act of resistance. One peaceful tradition is mentioned here, namely that when someone dies, the mosque or the church or both signal his departure from this world. Here there are symbols of violence, 'the nooses', and those of peace, the *adhān* and the church bells; violence, whether it be physical or psychological, disrupts peace. Death here is cruel; it darkens the atmosphere and ignites fury. In addition, the poet draws on history, as is typical of many Arab poets of that time and indeed later. He alludes to past massacres, such as those committed by Jamal Pasha in 1915 against Arab nationalists, and suggests that even they did not match this level of brutality. But the poem reassures the martyrs that they are buried in their homeland and that their sacrifice is rewarded with paradise. In Islamic culture, reference to the power of God and his omnipotence in all spheres is common in moments of despair, as we saw above in the case of Shawqī as well. Thus, faith and principles are at work here as sources of resistance. Islamic references are common in Palestinian revolutionary writing,[83] often reinforcing confidence in the struggle and its righteousness, and the belief that no sacrifice is in vain. The iconic character who is invited to bear witness to the struggle is 'Izz ad-Dīn al-Qassām (1882–1935), a Syrian Islamic cleric who fought against the French in his native Syria before going to Palestine and mobilising its leaders, particularly Hāj Amīn al-Ḥusaynī (1897–1974) to fight the British and the Zionists. Al-Qassām launched his Jihad campaign from Nablus in 1935, and was killed by the British in that same year. Islamic references of the type included in the extract above were common then; and while some stand for canonical traditional Islamic themes, such as the promise of paradise, others are imbued with modern political meanings. The name of al-Qassām survives today in the naming of the military brigade of the Islamist movement, Hamas, suggesting durability and a continuity of ideas that stem from similar ideological backgrounds.

The Palestinian struggle against British colonialism and Zionism took various forms and was directed at different targets, including Palestinians who engaged in shady deals, such as selling their land to Zionists. In a poem written in 1929, under the title 'To the sellers of the country', Ibrahīm writes:

They have sold the country to their enemy in greed
For money, but they have sold their homelands instead
They would be excused if hunger forced them
But they have never been thirsty or hungry...

O the seller of the land, would not you be punished
Had you learnt that the opponent is a deceiver
Indeed, you have done badly by the ancestors...
Think of your death in a land where you grew up
And leave for your land the length of a tomb[84]

The poem, like others by Touqān, laments the phenomenon of selling land to the Zionists, showing fissures in the body of the Palestinian national movement of the time; others include rivalry among various notable Palestinian families who spearheaded the Palestinian movement before 1948.[85] The Jewish buyers were acting on behalf of the organisation that funded the Zionist project, namely the Jewish National Fund (JNF), which was set up in 1901 by the founder of Zionism, Theodor Herzl, to facilitate the Jewish colonisation of Palestine. The Zionists employed a variety of methods to expand their territorial base in historic Palestine, even though they never became a majority in terms of territory or people before their decisive conquest in 1948. Yet, the phenomenon of some Palestinians selling their land to obvious enemies bent on colonisation is such a shameful episode in the history of the Palestinian national movement that Touqān strongly decries it. He emphasises the deceptive character of the Zionist movement and the methods it uses to entice Palestinians into selling their land on lucrative terms. Most evocatively, he exhorts them to think of their death, implying that if they continue to sell their land in this way, they will end up with no place for their own graves. He reminds the sellers of their ancestors and their spirits, attached to the land, and points out that those selling the land are not driven by economic necessity to do so. Touqān's critique tallies with the discourse of mainstream Palestinian nationalism, which saw the selling of land to colonisers as an act of betrayal of the very national identity of the Palestinians and their historical rootedness in the land. It should be noted that most of the nationalist movements, whether in Egypt, Algeria or Palestine, had to struggle against doubtful colonial practices that included native collusion with the colonisers. Touqān's deep concern over the deteriorating conditions of his country accentuated his vision regarding its future trajectory to the point of luminous prophecy:

You people, your foes are not such as to be gentle and merciful.
You people, before you is nothing but exile, so get ready.[86]

Nevertheless, the struggle against colonialism in all the countries mentioned above galvanised and focused the Arab populations. Except for Palestine, all the Arab countries gained independence. Therefore, the voice of Touqān and that of other important Palestinian poets emphasise struggle over collusion or compromise. For this, they call for heroism and heroes who would fight for the land, not sell it. The lines of the famous Palestinian poet known as Abu Salma ('Abd al-Karīm al-Karmī, 1911–1981), 'Lahab al-Qasīd' ('The flame of the poem'), castigate those who ask the Palestinian peasants and revolutionaries to end the strike of 1936 instead of supporting it:

> Arise, hear the martyr's blood crying out on every side.
> Arise, see al-Qassām's light shining on the top of mountains, revealing to this world the secrets of immortality...[87]

Abu Salma, like Touqān and Mufdī, elevates the image of the hero or martyr, here typified in the national and religious leader, al-Qassām. The immortalisation of martyrs is interesting because the life of the nation is perpetuated through it; it represents a case of the collectivisation of the individual through principles, values and a shared national destiny. The celebration of martyrdom for the sake of the homeland represents a powerful theme that recurs in the poetry of the Palestinian national movement, whether in its secular or Islamist aspects. Ibrahīm Touqān and other Palestinian poets emphasised the heroism of martyrs as redeemers, an image visible in the nationalist poetry of Mahmoud Darwish and other Palestinian poets. Before 1948, the image of the hero defending the land and safeguarding its honour and dignity prevails, but after 1948 and with the spectre of defeat engulfing the Palestinians, Palestinian poetry and indeed Arabic poetry in general take other paths. As Jabra Ibrahim Jabra put it, 'it was no accident, therefore, that the great change in Arabic poetry started more or less with the Palestine disaster. In the decade that followed, from 1948 to 1958, what happened to Arabic writing was cataclysmic...'[88] Thus, following independence in the 1950s in particular, Arabic poetry branched out into radical innovations in form and content. Before explicating these innovations in the next chapter, it is time to give an overview of the issues covered in this present chapter.

Conclusion

This chapter opened with general remarks on colonialism and its context and ramifications in the Arab world. It focused on the cultural identity of the Arab world and showed how colonialism challenged it and how that identity was used against colonialism in poetry. The chapter gave examples from the poetry of various parts of the Arab world, mainly Iraq, Egypt, Syria and Palestine, and explained them in their contexts. Three main points can be drawn from the poetry studied in this chapter. Firstly, it tends to relate to specific Arab nations, emanating from particular contexts, as well as speaking to the conditions of the Arab world at large. Secondly, the poetry emphasises principles, and draws on both international and traditional and Islamic sources of inspiration, to affirm its identity and convictions. Thirdly, poetry brims with faith in the future of the Arab world. Despite the bleakness of the moment in which the poetry in question was written, it affirms and celebrates Arab identity and its virtues and memories, whether they are embodied in specific historic figures and places or memories in general. Political Arabic poetry enters a new stage once it frees itself of the formulaic approach to poetry at the end of the 1940s. It explodes in expression, in imagery and emotion. Although there is no clear division between one type of poetry and another, the context of the Arab cultural renaissance, entailing contact with European culture and the Arab soul-searching that ensued as a result of political setbacks, particularly in Palestine, led to poetic compositions that construct and deconstruct Arab identity rather than reproducing it, as will be highlighted in the next chapter.

3

POLITICS IN THE AESTHETICS OF MODERN ARABIC POETRY

The first thing I have to rethink is the question of the Arab thinker, whether he is a poet, painter, musician, philosopher or a writer. In the last twenty years, Arab thinkers created a Babylonian life par excellence. They made machines of our generations, which they slavishly used to imitate the West or to imitate the regressive tradition or to perpetuate ignorance. They helped positively or negatively with silence or with language to put people and their resources and heritage into the service of the ruler and his system. They elevated the party above the homeland and the people; the political doctrine became nobler than the truth and man. They turned the schools into cells for parrots, babbling, screaming and gesturing; they turned the universities into moulds that turn the illiterates and half illiterates into geniuses and leaders of countries. Of writers, they made a corpse, and of words, they made a mummy.[1]

Adonis, Ahmad 'Ali Said, 1980

Translating the words of the great Syrian poet and thinker Ahmad 'Ali Said, who adopted the name Adonis (b.1929), I am struck by how deeply he despairs of the conditions of the Arab world and its topsy-turvy structures, and how consistently his despair is maintained. The Arab world looks like a broken mirror that nothing can piece together except a new beginning, a second coming, a rebirth and resurrection. The poetry of Adonis is steeped in the idea of beginning, and so is the poetry of the 1950s generation that he influenced. It is worth highlighting the titles of two of his books, *A Beginning to the End of the Century: Pamphlets for the Sake of a New Arab Culture* and *The Language of Beginnings*. In both books, Adonis' seminal idea is that the

Arab world needs to treat its cultural and political ailments by itself from the roots upwards, not the other way around. It needs to begin a process of economic, political and cultural development to save it from its intricate reliance on others and also the cheapening of itself in the market of others. To this end, the idea of beginnings is illuminating at several levels, not least for the rationale that the human spirit is and can be innovative and critical; it is now and always; it does not need to be bound by authorities or time; it can begin itself anew. The regenerative capacity of language can give way to productive meanings that echo a diversity of human realities; and it is language that provides the enabling factor for the Arab world to start a process of regeneration, as Adonis and other Arab poets of similar attitudes have advocated.

To this end, Adonis' singular concern has been with the Arabic tradition and the question of modernity and how these—tradition and modernity—operate in Arab life; and how they can enable new beginnings. In three significant volumes published between 1974 and 1978, *al-Thābit wa 'l-Mutahawwil* (The Fixed and the Changing [in Arabic Culture]), Adonis decried the persistence of tradition which he saw as an archaic and unproductive form in modern Arabic life, impeding inclusive, creative and confident modern attitudes and methods. Accordingly, he saw Arab political and literary discourses as being afflicted with particular orthodox attitudes, which are divested of the dynamism of the past and its evolving nature. As Edward Said wrote of him, 'he has almost single-handedly been challenging the persistence of what he regards as the ossified, tradition-bound Arab–Islamic heritage, stuck not only in the past but in rigid and authoritarian rereading of that past'.[2]

Adonis explains that the early Arab Caliphs did not tolerate dissent and attempted to institute cultural homogeneity to facilitate their rule. This control runs counter to the Qur'anic ethos and certain notable strands within the literary tradition. These strands include subversive and innovative elements that ensured vibrancy and vitality within the medieval culture of the Arab and Islamic world. Adonis reconstructs Arabic culture as follows:

> Those in power designated everyone who did not think according to the culture of the caliphate as 'the people of innovation' (*ahl al-ihdāth*), excluding them with this indictment of heresy from their Islamic affiliation. This explains how the terms *ihdāth* (innovation) and *muhdath* (modern, new), used to characterize the poetry that violated the ancient poetic principles, came originally from the religious lexicon. Consequently we can see that the modern in poetry appeared to the ruling establishment as a political or intellectual attack on the culture of the regime and a rejection of the idealized standards of the ancient, and how, therefore, in Arab life

the poetic has always been mixed up with the political and the religious, and indeed continues to be so.[3]

Adonis pits the traditionalists against the modernists in dichotomous terms. The modernists refused to be bound by established norms from pre-Islamic times, when oral poetic traditions reigned at the expense of more introspective and existential modes of expression with timeless universal truths. Those who were truly modern in poetry, according to Adonis, were poetic figures such as Abū Nuwās (756–814) and Abū Tammām (788–845), and thinkers such as Ibn al-Rāwandī (d.910), al-Rāzī (d.1210) and the visionary mystics, who highlighted new concepts and added to rather than being bound by the past. For Adonis, modernity entails a constant search within an aesthetic of revelation and openness that transcends any fixed roots and remains open to conflict and tension. Accordingly, Arab modernity has been largely imitative rather than innovative, even that of the nineteenth century. Such imitation is selective and misapplied, in the sense that 'modernity in Arab society has continued to be something imported from abroad, a modernity which adopts the new things but not the intellectual attitude and method which produced them, whereas true modernity is a way of seeing before it is production'.[4] Therefore, in his poetry, Adonis set out to incorporate tension and contradictions as well as assert human agency.[5]

In his poem 'The beginning of poetry', Adonis lays seeds of tension and ambiguity in the very heart of language. He turns against classicism of the type discussed in the earlier chapters, which relies on stable structure, visible meanings, common motives and familiar sounds. Nothing is fixed; anything can be used, built on, modified or destroyed. The poet activates the creative possibilities of language as its most creative user. There is continuity, tension, conflict and contradictions in the very being of the people and their inter-relations that poetry should manifest rather than conceal or suppress. Continuity is inbuilt in the very structure of language. In this sense, Adonis is an enabler of modernity as an open project of exploration and revelation through language. He writes:

> *You are at your best when you disturb Space*
> *And the others: some think you are the call*
> *Some think you are the echo.*
> *You are at your best when you are the evidence*
> *For the light and darkness*
> *Where the end of language is its beginning in you*
> *And others: some view you as foam,*

Some see you as a creator.
You are at your best when you are an end in itself
A crossroad
For silence and language.[6]

The poet agitates the existing order rather than settling into it. There is always a sense of beginning, with all the risks involved, in the creation of poetry. Ideals of beginnings, continuity and creativity are therefore recurrent in Adonis' writings. This is not unique to Adonis, but he is a systematic poet/ thinker who revitalised their importance in modern Arabic poetry. Ideas about fluidity of expression and being, which ushered in European modernity, particularly from the eighteenth century onwards, are to be found in works such as those of the Marxist writer Marshall Berman, as the telling title of his book suggests, *All that Solid Melts into Thin Air: The Experience of Modernity.*[7] In addition, the idea of beginnings marked the scholarship of the Palestinian thinker Edward Said through his second book, published in 1975, *Beginnings: Intention and Method.* Congruently with Said, many of Adonis' poems put forward the notion of beginning as a way of questioning and secularising unimpeachable origins, mainly religious ones; a way of opening vistas within language that expand the scope of the often circumscribed and politically-streamed reality and identity. Inspired by the seventeenth-century Italian philologist Giambattista Vico (1668–1744), who traced the origins of European literary writings and religions to their shifting historical circumstances which gradually acquired a sacred status, Said puts forward views that situate the European tradition within its multiple earth-bound contexts. In Said, beginning is pitted against origin; and the former is definitively favoured over the latter. Beginning is secular and worldly; origins are religious and ideological, limited by their own hermetic authorities and authorisations.

Beginnings are beginnings because they are actions of will that add to the process of earthly regeneration, continuity and openness.[8] The political discourses of the Arab world, in Adonis' view, have been mired in bygone glories that force and manipulate the present reality into stagnant repetition, resulting in the mummification of life rather than its practical and creative reproduction at the cultural as well as political levels. Unless creativity is widespread, facilitated by state systems and grounded in the individual through education and free culture, life is entangled in oppressive and imposed ways of living. Metaphorically put, the past, with all its vast hold on the Arab imagination, is not a cage for the present to be locked behind it, but a field to be continuously tilled for the present and the future, and for the illumination of the past itself.

That is the crux of Adonis' conception of modernity. It does not exclude tradition, but it widens its employability and utility for the present. As Muhsin al-Muswai put it, 'modern poetry, with its postmodernist or postcolonial manifestations, offers many examples of engagements between modernity and tradition.'[9] While Adonis' modernity in poetry can appear apolitical and often is projected as such, it has deep political connotations: its spirituality encrusts its materiality. At the heart of his poetic vision and vocation is freedom that language gives flesh, spirit and sound. Such freedom supports subject formations unencumbered by unchecked loyalties to roots, ones that are open to rational affiliations and actions within the realm of human agency with all its conscious and unconscious ramifications. In this sense, Adonis' poetic–philosophical oeuvre is one that speaks to—indeed provokes—the individual, the smallest atom in any society, in the Arab world. In the mass of collective identification and collectivisation of identity in which the social formation of the Arab world is submerged, the beginning of reformation and rebirth can begin by an individual whose social ties are not psychological shackles but keys to her/his individuality, in the innermost of which resides the agency and will to productivity, creativity as well as critique. Adonis' poetry, therefore, offers an opening to a world beset with problems of expression as much as of relational liberation, which a more plausible socio-political basis could provide for the Arab individual and society at large. Generically, Adonis writes:

> Where is the distortion in the prevalent culture, and in the culture of the opposition? It is in the politicisation of language, i.e. it is in placing the linguistic action at the same level of judgement as the material action: whoever violates the 'law of the society' and steals, his hands get cut off. Whoever violates the thought of 'the prevalent regime' or the thought of the 'oppositional' regime, his tongue gets cut off...this prevalent Arab thinking, whether it stems from the regime or the opposition, does not only distort the reality and truth alone, but it also distorts language and logic.[10]

Adonis' conception of poetry is multifaceted in that it projects naturalistic tendencies and is equated with instinctual, sexual desires.[11] Yet latently, his poetry carries political values connected to the Arab individual and her/his spaces and capacities for freedom within the socio-political weight of belonging in the Arab world. In short, at the literary as well as the political level, Adonis is a pamphleteer of Arab enlightenment, which perhaps most closely finds resemblance in the work of the seventeenth-century Dutch philosopher Baruch Spinoza (1632–1677) and French existentialists, most notably Albert Camus (1913–1960).[12] Spinoza's emphasis on freedom as an individual right and his attitudes towards liberalist cultivation of reason and spirituality within a legally bound civil society represent an ethos of freedom to which Adonis subscribes:

> According to Spinoza, the state of nature is characterized by the primacy of the individual. Civil society arises when men recognize the advantages of society with respect to the enhancement of their power as individuals. Spinoza emphasizes that the individual retains his natural right when he enters civil society.[13]

To this end, Adonis' contribution to the intellectual culture of the Arab world is revolutionary. Due, however, to its patriarchal hegemonic infrastructure of knowledge and discourse, the Arab world is not sufficiently furnished with political equality and cultural openness to consider Adonis' ideas practically, and as a result his project of modernity and rationalism has been marginalised. Notwithstanding, this most mature as well as radical tradition of critique and transcendence that Adonis reiteratively put forward resonated widely in the poetics of the 1950s, even if not in the way that Adonis elaborated and pursued this course. Meanwhile, a holistic conclusion with regard to the works and attitudes employed in poetry would suggest that Adonis has a systematic and daring approach to modernity, which is deeply informed and aware of the Arabic tradition and is at an ultimate level politically transformative. Yet other poets tended to advocate a partial, sentimental or ideological view of modernity, often veering into periods of populism, and at times articulating this through fine poetic aesthetics.

Adonis' context nurtured various poetic sensibilities; it is possible to detect four poetic patterns borne out by the conditions described above. The first two were poetry that either disturbed the reality of the Arab world or glorified it without critique: it was the former that promoted profound political and cultural changes. Thirdly, there was poetry that sought to engage with the travails of political ideologies in the Arab world, and invoked the ideas of socialism, nationalism and Islamism. Fourthly, there was poetry that subscribed to the doctrine of rhetorical and authoritarian regimes that attempted to mummify the present through the past and its present idols.

Parallel to the general poetic trends discerned above are political and cultural developments. These are the latest in a series of political events that accentuated the need for revisionism in Arabic poetry. Such revisionism dates back to the beginning of the twentieth century, as manifested in the writings and poetry of the Lebanese writer Gibran Khalil Gibran (1883–1931); 'without his contribution,' as Jayyusi writes, 'the story of modern Arabic poetry would have been a very different one'.[14] In addition, there is a notable romantic streak in Arabic poetry, which abounds with the necessity of revolutionary change in the culture and politics of the Arab world, perhaps the most passionate representative of which is the Tunisian poet Abū al-Qāsim al-Shābbī (1909–1934). To this end, if one considers the political and economic basis of society to be at the heart of cultural change, as was demonstrated through the first chapter, then the case should be similar in this period. The call for new beginnings is grounded in the serious political changes and developments that happened to the Arab world after the Second World War, the clearest of which was the Zionist conquest of Palestine in 1948 and later the defeat of the Arabs by Israel in 1967. Meanwhile, Palestine was a relatively late development, preceded by new streams of Arabic poetry that advocated political and cultural change and bemoaned the slumbering state of the Arab world. Such calls for cultural and political revolutions are represented strongly in the writings of Gibran Khalil Gibran and Abū al-Qāsim al-Shābbī. I examine these poets in this chapter rather than the previous one because they exuded modernist attitudes, more so than other contemporaries such as Ahmad Shawqī and Ḥāfiẓ Ibrahīm.

Both poets have idealistic sensibilities combined with a despairing view of the reality of the Arab world, which they effectively saw as suffering from decadence. In this context, Adonis' strident modernity and critique of Arab culture can be better understood by taking stock of the ideas and sentiments of the two aforementioned poets, who hailed from significant poetic experiences in the first three decades of the twentieth century.

With the above in mind, this chapter begins by arguing against strict categorisation of poetic trends in modern Arabic poetry and for a more fluid and discursive understanding, which sees the multifaceted nature of each moment and broadens the meaning of the political in poetry. The politico-poetic dimensions in the writings of Gibran and al-Shābbī exemplify this, as representative of the modernist and romantic trend in poetry, and bear comparison with Adonis as an elaborator in modernist advances, particularly in relation to ideas of freedom, 'cultural' revolution and socially protected individualism and individuation.[15] This chapter also explores the poetry of Iraqi, Egyptian, Palestinian and other poets, such as Badr Shākir al-Sayyāb, Nāzik al-Malā'ika, 'Abd al-Mu'ṭī Hijāzī and Amal Donqol, who entrenched themselves in the aesthetics and ideologies of the 1950s, 60s and 70s. I conclude this chapter by evoking Adonis once more, this time as a universalist whose poetry expresses the zenith of Arab modernity as embedded in various poetic trends of the twentieth century.

Adonis and the Palestinian poet Mahmoud Darwish are two influential Arab poets who reflect diverse faces of modernity through their accomplished poetry and philosophically grounded prose. Adonis crafts his poetry with the chemical motion of poetry in mind, reaching towards a poetics that attempt to discern what he describes as 'the metaphysics of human existence'.[16] Darwish fuses several political, cultural and philosophical currents which the present moment and the aesthetic imperatives of poetry require, thus representing most expansively what several Arab poets of his generation grappled with; hence the collective appeal of his illustrative poetics, to which the subsequent chapter is entirely devoted.

The politics of the romantics

In her great 1977 work *Trends and Movements in Modern Arabic Poetry*, the Palestinian critic Salma Khadra Jayyusi writes, 'in fact a close scrutiny of the relationship of poetry to political strife in the Arab world will reveal that wherever the latter was constantly present, a factual realistic trend showed itself in poetry'.[17] In the classification of Arabic poetry in general, there is a tendency among literary critics to label periods as poetic trends that seem to bear little relationship to each other in terms of the content of poetry.[18] Accordingly, modern Arabic poetry evolves from neo-classical poetry to romantic to mythic, symbolist, surrealist and existential poetry, etc.[19] What is often missing from such accounts is a broader understanding of what counts as political. In this chapter, I take the view that some of those counted as romantic poets, including Gibran Khalil Gibran and Abū al-Qāsim al-Shābbī, are individuals with heightened political sensitivities which formed their very characters and imbued them with a hybrid understanding of political and social formations; and therefore the classification of them as mere romantics is not entirely inclusive of what they represented. While they sound introspectively individualistic and give elaborate space to the substances of their own emotions, they project an Arab subjecthood, at the same time deeply marked by politics. And there is perhaps no other century as crowded with political occurrences in the life of the Arab world as the twentieth century. It is difficult to think of any one time in the life of the Arab world in the twentieth century during which poets did not convey political concerns and anxieties, which, while veiled by individualistic impulses at times, reflect a sense of collective Arab identity with its emotional as well as its political ingredients at play.

What happened more generally in the twentieth century is more a case of broadening the political, social and existential conception of life in the practice of some poetic figures in the Arab world, particularly in the increasing interaction with the European literary tradition, an interaction that expanded beyond anything known before. This is unlike the neo-classical poets, whose formation is collectivist in the sense of its adherence to the Arabic tradition, particularly in its formulaic poetic characteristics which they reproduced, some of which could be described as strictly romantic when compared to those who are generally classified as champions of the romantic movement in Arabic poetry. Yet, one major difference that took place pertains to the fact that the latter poets freed themselves of the poetic hemistich form (pilliard, or *shi'ir 'amūdī*) towards an explosive experimentalism of expressionism in stanzic or poetic narrative forms which encapsulate several layers of meanings and evocations, personal as well as collective. In addition, the Romantics treated politics as a field of ideas as well as practices, giving voice to their personal attitudes and concerns as shaped and influenced by socio-political currents. This is despite the neo-classical poets tending to favour one existing political order or another, reflecting traditional Arab values and norms without questioning them or relating them to a wider human experience in the systematic and radical ways of the Romantics or later radical poets.[20] To this end, besides celebrating beauty, human love and the power and possibilities of imagination and language, some of the socio-political issues the romantic poets critically invoked in their poetry included the patriarchal structures of the Arab world, the lack of freedom, the inadequacy of education, gender inequality, religious dogmatism and the reproduction of the Arabic language and literature in sterile and conformist ways that tally with the discourses of authoritarian and patriarchal regimes.

In contrast to the social and political issues the poets criticised, they celebrated the power of language and the freedom to reflect deep human problems and possibilities. Take, for example, the emphasis on language as depicted in Gibran Khalil Gibran's essay, 'The Future of the Arabic Language'. The central thesis of the essay is that language is a key engine of invention and progress and that it falls on the shoulders of the poets to demonstrate and revitalise its inventiveness: 'I say the life of the language, its unification, its propagation, and all that has any relationship to it have been and will always be the product of the poets' imaginations.' Connected to the idea of invention and poetry is that of freedom. Gibran has a generous definition of 'poet' as 'every inventor, be he big or small, every discoverer, be he strong or weak, every creator...'[21] Gibran's broader premise is that the Arab world (which he includes under the then ubiquitous term 'the East') is imitative rather than inventive.

Unless it can create, by exploring and expanding on ideas that reveal and enrich its humanity with all its complexities and ambiguities, it will effectively stay languishing behind the ascendant West. One important right that Gibran decries as absent in the Arab world is that of liberty and freedom, an absence which Adonis regards as detrimental to the future of the Arab individual and world. One of Gibran's poems invokes the issue even in its title, 'From a speech by Khalil the Heretic':

> From the depths of these depths
> We call you, O Liberty—hear us!
> From the corners of this darkness
> We raise our hands in supplication—turn your gaze towards us!
> On the expanse of these snows
> We lay prostrate before you, have compassion upon us!
>
> From the sources of the Nile to the estuary of the Euphrates
> The wailing of souls surging with the scream of the abyss rises;
> From the frontiers of the peninsula to the mountains of Lebanon
> Hands are outstretched to you, trembling in the agony of death;
>
> From the coast of the gulf to the ends of the desert
> Eyes are uplifted to you with pining hearts
> Turn, O liberty, and look upon us....
> In our narrow streets
> The merchant barters his days only to pay the thieves from the West,
> And no one is there to advise him!...
>
> In order to secure their power and to rest at heart's ease they have armed the Durzi to fight the Arab;
> Have instigated the Shi'i against the Sunni;
> Have incited the Kurd to slaughter the Bedouin;
> Have encouraged the Mohammadan to fight the Christian—
> How long is a brother to fight his brother on the breast of the mother?
> How long is a neighbour to threaten his neighbour near the tomb of the beloved?
> How long are the Cross and the Crescent to remain apart before the eyes of God?
>
> Listen, O liberty, and harken unto us...[22]

It is often the utter failure of a system that prompts people to desert it. In this case, the poet identifies himself as a heretic, suggesting severance from the existing religious dogmatism engulfing the Arab world. The incessant and evocative call for liberty with which the poem opens or closes each stanza brings to mind the opening words of a song by the iconic Egyptian singer Umm Kulthum (1904–1971), to which the Arab audience responded rapturously: 'give me my liberty; let my hands be free; I have given all and left nothing for myself'. The level of despotic degradation to which the Arab world has sunk, whether under the Ottoman Empire, colonial powers or dictatorial Arab regimes, made the call for liberty ring with existential urgency. The American influence on Gibran, who was born in the village of Bshirri in Lebanon and emigrated to the United States, is clear in his reiterative repetition of the word 'liberty', one of the constitutive concepts of the American political system, and also the French, which Gibran experienced in Lebanon. The émigré poets (*shu'arā' al-mahjar*) who injected Arabic poetry with new sensibilities and refined libertarian attitudes, such as the Lebanese writer Mikhail Na'ima (1889–1988), had a clear-sighted view of the necessity of systemic socio-political change in the Arab world. Adonis singles out Gibran as a visionary, whose inventive language rebelled against all forms of oppressive authorities and thus played a pioneering role in the construction of an Arab poetics of modernity with the value of liberty at its heart.[23]

In the second stanza, the poet suggests that in the absence of liberty there is death: voices that cannot be heard, souls shackled with societal and political chains unable to manifest their desires—in short, individuals unaware of themselves and their potential, as they have no access to free political or social systems that inspire the realisation of their depths. Uncritical submission to authorities is a cause of fundamental psychological distortion. The poets, whose power of vision Gibran extols, can hear the collective pain and articulate it, both enlivening it and despairing against it. Gibran's poems here operate at the level of sense and spirit, with which the state of mind is inevitably inflected. Thus politics is very personal. Limits are being placed on the very personality of the Arab individual. Even when this individual is exploited by the colonial West, he cannot find someone in his midst to remedy the situation; he is besieged by his own society with its rigid rules as well as by the international powers that dictate the undercurrents of his society. There are multiple systems of exploitation, reducing the Arab individual to a mere ideologue within a field of contested faiths and ideologies that violently re-enact themselves for domination. The gruesome violence in Syria, and before that in Lebanon, Iraq, Palestine, Sudan, Yemen, Bahrain, Egypt and Libya, provides an accurate mirror to what Gibran describes in his visionary poem with regard to civil wars that have abetted one faith or streak of faith or ideology against another. The former colonial West continues to tear the Arab world apart with exploitative politics and economics: the West provides arms for one party to fight another, while ensuring the continuous superiority of its military industry. Yet that is only part of the story—there are forces in the Arab world that benefit from this exploitation and perpetuate it. The outcome is that the Arab world remains effectively enslaved to the West, and the West keeps advancing at lesser powers' expense. Meanwhile, in the absence of liberty, the Arab world lacks a sense of initiative to carve meaningful spaces for its own security and prosperity. Thus exploitation is cyclical, and something that an individual lacking societal means for resistance and protection cannot effectively under-mine. More pointedly, the value of liberty lies in the fact that it is a harbinger for a plurality of faiths and ideologies that can peacefully coexist alongside each other. In this sense, the poet declares heresy and the poem cries out for liberty and plurality as keys for justice and peace, which monotheism, whether religious or political, impedes. The sharpness of the poetic voice shines a light on the severe effects of corruption and injustice, and on the way in which they deform the life of an entire nation.

Such calls for individual liberty and societal responsibility can also be found in the poetry of the Tunisian poet Abū al-Qāsim al-Shābbī; an they have persisted in Arabic poetry, particularly among the poets of the Apollo group that he joined.[24] Despite the notable brevity of his life, having lived for only twenty-five years, Abū al-Qāsim al-Shābbī possessed a natural and devel-oped aptitude for the sublime and truthful in life and nature. He was born in a village called al-Shābbah in the south of Tunisia and was educated into the Arabic tradition and in French literature; he also obtained a degree in law from the Zaytuna College in 1928. His poems are passionately vivid and lumi-nous with tender spirituality. In addition to suffering tormented love, the passing of his father at a young age and his own affliction with fatal disease, al-Shābbī's poetic genius was not recognised in his lifetime. His society shunned him, particularly after he gave a lecture under the title 'The poetic imagination of the Arabs', in which he called for literary renewal and for sever-ance from the Arab past and its archaic reiterations, along the lines described by Adonis and Gibran above. At one point in his lecture and publication, al-Shābbī compares the Arab literary scene with the Western in the following terms: 'the Western sound is stronger in resonance; it represents a double melody (contrapuntal) at the same time; one aspect of it is connected to the deepest in the spirit and another to the content of the matter and its essence. As for the Arab sound, its source is not the spirit or the essence of the thing, but the form, colour and position, and what a difference between the shell and the gem inside.'[25] Al-Shābbī emphasises the need for a new literary and cul-tural beginning in the Arab world, which puts the substance of matter before its formulaic embellishment. In one poem with the title 'The obscure prophet', al-Shabbī evocatively showcases his poetic brilliance on the one hand and lashes against the state of his own people on the other, attacking the Tunis of his day as well as the entire Arab world:

> O people, I wish that I was a woodcutter
> I would have gone down to the roots with my axe...
> O my people, I wish that I had the power of storms
> I would have descended on you with the revolution of my spirit...
> You are a stupid soul, hating the light and spending eons in utter darkness...
> O my people, I am heading to the forests to spend my life there, alone, and in despair...
> Do you know the meaning of life, the glory of a people is in the awakening of their spirit...
> O people, you are a little child, playing with dust in a night of severe darkness...
> In the universe you have power, chained with the darkness of ages, from one past to another...[26]

In general, al-Shābbī's poems are made tender with images of sweet love, innocence, compassion, and evoke a broad sense of humanity, enlivened with beauty, mercy and justice. His penchant for prophecy is abetted by the powerful voice of his imagination and an overwhelming energy of emotional embodiment that his poetry communicates with effortless fluidity. Yet while, in the extract under consideration, al-Shābbī writes and coins images with acute expressive versatility, its content echoes destructive impulses bred from severe subjective discomforts. Be that as it may, his damning critique of his society should be considered for what it is. The image that runs through the poem is one of darkness and rotten roots that need to be literally eradicated and replaced by a new beginning. It is a case of creative destruction with Marxist undertones, in the sense that one order of life has to be replaced by another. The heightened sensitivity of the poet cannot bear the corrupt state of his people. So he seeks the forest, a place of symbolic estrangement as well as divine inspiration, accentuating the delusion of prophecy and the need for a revolution. Taking refuge in the forest and estrangement from society in the face of unbearable social corruption is not uncommon among the Romantics; it is vividly exemplified in Nietzsche's *Thus Spoke Zarathustra* as well as Gibran Khalil Gibran's *The Storms*. It shows the influence of Western literary Romanticism on al-Shābbī, an influence which manifests itself further on Arabic poetry in later periods, as will be discussed. The prophecy of the poet rests on the message that the Arab world has arrived at a stage where the manipulated deployment of the past darkens its present and blocks its progress into the future; and therefore the Arab world needs to remould its past towards a new beginning that nurtures it into material and spiritual re-creation, unencumbered by the superstitious weight of the religious past.

Al-Shābbī portrays his people as children, lacking the ability to decide what is good for them, whilst he portrays himself as possessing luminous and sensitive faculties that qualify him to be 'the prophet'. It is curious that al-Shābbī, who wrote poems against dictatorship and stirred the poetic and political will of the Arab world with his great poem 'The will to life', which is still recited passionately today, could also be so damning of his people.[27] The poem in question also displays notable epistemological merits in reflecting the customary populist reliance on the past: its use in the political discourses of the Arabs, and its lack of social and political progress that could protect the individual and enhance his social and political consciousness and responsibilities. The poet criticises his people for ignoring his inspired messages, as they continue to pay heed to useless traditions. It is clear that the poet was enraged by the reliance on tradition in the Tunisian society in which he lived, particularly since his country was a French protectorate (1881–1956), perpetuated by local subservience and languishing under a succession of uninspiring rulers. The Tunisia of his day was not attentive enough to the talents of its people, as al-Shābbī argues. Individuals did not feel recognised or valued at the social or political level, while traditional leaders with archaic discourses unfit for the modern period were elevated by colonial powers and in effect given platforms to preach corruption, as he also makes clear in another poem called 'Tunisia the beautiful'.[28] What al-Shābbī protests against is what amounts to the psychological displacement of individuals, which we also saw in the case of al-Raṣāfī in Iraq in the previous chapter. Yet the voice of al-Shābbī remains strongly individual, sharpened by the social and political frustrations to which he advocated radical solutions. Furthermore, introspective poetry acquires further dimensions with poets such as al-Sayyāb, where political and personal emotions intertwine in poems with expansively fluid conceptual and musical unity.

The expanded poetics of the political

It is clear that the generation of al-Shābbī and other Arab poets, whether they were émigrés or remained in their communities, inspired further revisionism and development in Arabic poetry in terms of form as well as content. The voice of the individual became as important as that of society in poetry; and this acquired genuine substance as a result of interaction with European poetic traditions. As Albert Hourani wrote:

Now the new poets tried to break with the subjectivism of the Romantics, while preserving something that they had learned from them. Poetry should express the reality of things, but reality could not be learnt by the intellect alone; it had to be apprehended by the total personality of the poet, by his imagination as well as his mind. Individual poets differed in their emphasis on various aspects of the many-sided reality.[29]

In the 1950s and 1960s, the many-sidedness of the Arab world appeared stark. It was an era of independence, beckoning modernist promises, as happened in Tunisia under the encouragement of its secular President Habib Bourguiba (r.1957–1987), particularly after the 1956 Personal Status Code gave women equal rights. More widely, the ascendant power of Jamal Abd al-Nassir of Egypt (r.1954–1970), whose rhetoric stirred ambitions for an independent pan-Arab nation reliant on its own resources and its proud people for progress and unity, seemed to open up new cultural and political avenues. Yet, although the Arab world felt empowered by its independence from the colonial powers in the 1960s, it was also still hurt by the Zionist conquest of Palestine, whose occupation in 1948 continued to cause widespread Arab frustrations. In addition, the 1960s witnessed the birth of the Palestinian national movement and its most prominent group, the Palestine Liberation Organisation (PLO). The Palestinian issue, which Nassir dramatised in his speeches as a quintessentially Arab cause, haunted Arabs further after Israel inflicted a sudden defeat on them in 1967, occupying more Arab land and controlling more Arab people.

In the face of several Arab setbacks, as well as cultural expansion born of advances in fields such as journalism, media, Arabic music and other forms of avant-garde and popular expressions, the vanguards of Arabic poetry developed modernist views with regard to the question of poetry itself, from epistemological as well as technical perspectives. Two poets and thinkers deserve special attention, namely the Iraqi poets Nāzik al-Malāika (1923–2007) and Badir Shākir al-Sayyāb (1926–1964). Both poets were exposed to European poetic forms, while also being well versed in the Arabic tradition. In particular, the basic thrust of al-Malāika's view was that there is an emotional and philosophical expansiveness to the human agent which includes ambiguities and depths; and that restrictive poetry in which the (classical) form guides the poetic outcome is not enough to manifest them fully: 'in general, the human spirit is not clear; it is encrusted with a thousand veils', as she put it.[30] Though traditional Arabic poetry with its historic metric character had throughout the centuries expressed an impressive range of human and natural concerns and phenomena, it needed to stretch into free exploration that many people could experience and express in a developed language without the obtrusive authority of tradition. As Hourani explains:

> A new world needed a new language...the basic unit of poetic language should not be the line composed of a fixed number of feet, but the single foot; the accepted systems of rhymes—and rhyme itself—could be abandoned; strict syntactical relations between words could give way to looser groupings...[31]

It is the message and organic unity of the poem, with its combination of embodied sensibilities and sharpened constructions, that make poetry what it is. While attention to formulaic currents can stabilise the meaning of poetry and invest it with certain order and musical cadence, free verse poetry can enlarge the lyrical and semantic scope of poetry, endowing it with polyphonic (harmoniously diverse) capacities that the more monotonous poetry experienced before could not exhibit and flow with to the same extent. What Nāzik describes as the 'spontaneous outburst' in poetry does not need to be rule-bound to restrict its natural flow. And like Gibran and other modernists, Nāzik al-Malāika emphasised the importance of innovation in language in order to express modern changes and address socio-political challenges rationally and creatively through modern discourse. To be modern in poetry meant to bring the ordinary and the extraordinary into poetic expression of often luminous quality, departing from the lush grandeur of the old styles with their unsuitability to the dynamism and political complexity of the new age. The precise word, the sharp and mythic symbols, the majestic metaphors and the musical harmony of the poem as a unit of revelation, embodiment and spiritual ascendance gained currency among a large number of modern poets. What is noticeable here is a linear process of contributions from epoch-marking poets, such as al-Sayyāb and al-Malāika, to poetic reforms that reflect the political and cultural changes in the Arab world and an attempt to adapt to literary and scientific advancements in the world as well. Thus, the poetry of al-Malāika, which addressed natural and political conditions in the Arab world, translated her extended theoretical poetics in poems such as 'The cholera', which she published in 1947 in response to a plague that hit Cairo and resulted in many tragic losses. The image of death permeates the poem:

> *In each place, there is a soul screaming in the darkness*
> *In each place there is a sound of weeping*
> *This is what death had shredded*
> *Death, death and death*
> *O the overwhelming sorrow of the Nile from death...*

The magnitude of the tragedy is densely invoked in a fluid construction that echoes the enormity of its subject. There is a tight structural cohesion to the poem, which locates at its heart death caused by the plague of cholera, creating an organic unity that runs throughout the poem. Despite these innovations, al-Malāika is heir to the Arabic tradition that wields an almost inescapable unconscious influence on Arab poets, because of its ever-present traditional habits of expression, where the language of the past tends to dominate. Interestingly, Yasir Suleiman, who studied her poetry, argues that Nāzik al-Malāika's writing fused secular nationalism with Islamic spirituality in a way that foreshadows the rising tide of Islamism. He writes:

> This 'national spirituality' replaces the earlier secularism of the poet in a way that presages the ascendance of Islam as a primary source of political organisation in the Arab world in the second half of the twentieth century.[32]

More notably, the ascendance of Islamic politics along the lines described by Suleiman can be clearly seen in the poetry of Shawqī, as mentioned in the previous chapter, where politically-manipulated reference to the Islamic past is commonplace. Moreover, al-Malāika's resort to Islamic and traditional images reflects paradoxes and ambiguities, which the poetry of the Iraqi poet Badir Shākir al-Sayyāb projected with an acute lyricism in his famous poem 'Hymn of the rain', *Unshūdat al-Matar*. Besides al-Malāika, the importance of al-Sayyāb in the journey of modern Arabic poetry is widely acknowledged and is revealing of the interplay between poetry and politics in the Arab world. The poet was born in the village of Jaykor, south of Basra in Iraq, and suffered the loss of his mother, Karima Bint Sayyāb, at the young age of ten, commemorating her with deep nostalgic sorrow in several of his poems. In particular, it was the 'Hymn of the rain' which gained al-Sayyāb fame, even though he passed away young and poor and was politically marginalised by the Iraqi Communist Party despite being a member. The poem in question is vivid in its amalgamation of romantic, epic and symbolic dimensions, evoking tradition and modernity in an inventive and acutely memorable way.

Your eyes are two groves of palm trees at the hour of dawn
Or two balconies from which the moon has begun to recede...
I cry out to the gulf: 'O Gulf,
O Giver of pearls, of shells, of death...'...
Not one year passed when there was no hunger in Iraq...
In every tear of the hungry and the naked
And every drop shed of the blood of slaves
Is a smile awaiting new lips
Or a nipple growing pink in the mouth of a newborn babe...[33]

The lines above represent a poem whose depth and simplicity overflows with modernist poetic energy, the essence of which is renewal. This renewal is inclusive of tradition but not bound by it, so it can still craft itself in modernist space, supported by the nation-state and its imperatives of geography and identity, as suggested by Wen-chin Ouyang.[34] Terri Deyoung, who studied the poem thoroughly, offers two main reasons for its importance. These explanations concern the poetic direction of the time, and its political and cultural significance, so she is worth quoting at length:

> To begin with, it is considered the first poem in which he successfully integrates political statement with personal experience. In this view, it combines Sayyāb's nostalgic longing for his idealized homeland, while in hiding in Kuwait from the Iraqi police, with the longing of the people of Iraq for an idealized post-revolutionary future after the fall of the hated Nuri Said regime, which was, for most Iraqis, simply a surrogate for British colonialism...second, it is viewed as Sayyāb's first step toward using symbolism derived from ancient pagan fertility myths as poetic source material. By the late 1950s, these fertility myths of death and rebirth became a convention, both in Sayyāb's poetry and modern Arabic poetry in general, used to portray the vision of an Arab civilization reborn, free to develop its own way, without being subject to arbitrary outside interference.[35]

Throughout the poem runs the idea of a new beginning, as discussed at the outset of the chapter. Rain, the principal motif of the poem, washes away old stains and brings life anew. The symbols, myths and political connotations in the poem speak of the conditions of the Arab world in the 1950s and 60s. The existing Arab social and political structures had been entangled in a traditional web of unpromising interdependencies. Independence from colonial rulers renewed the pride of the Arabs, but soon enough, after a series of setbacks such as the 1967 defeat, it became clear, at least for Arab intellectuals, that the Arab world was still burdened by ideological, patriarchal and political hegemonies, with local rulers and parties disconnected from the real needs of the people and the age in general. Even though several successful political revolutions, swept up in passion and hope, took place to end colonialism, as in Egypt, Algeria and Libya, none of these revolutions brought sufficient social change to reinforce the place of the individual within a strong and rights-minded society and state. Instead, what happened was the proliferation of rhetorical ideologies, subsuming the individual and forcing Arab societies into political directions blighted by dictatorships and religious obscurantism and regression. The opposite development would have been independent, democratic policies and genuine forms of economic Arab cooperation that could with time have yielded a modicum of prosperity and political stability in the Arab world. The absence of a political system with principles of equality, accountability and justice at its heart made poets, who characteristically search for the essence of things, portray the problems as they were and invoke radical solutions. In particular, Adonis assigned 'to the poet a role in society that can be described as futuristic, prophetic and revolutionary'.[36] And the poem of al-Sayyāb, while not obtrusively political, invites natural images, as did that of al-Shābbī before, both crying out for comprehensive renewal in a region whose outstanding literary and cultural past dictated its present. In short, the poem, as Ouyang writes, 'imagines a political community with roots in the immemorial past and at the same time grounds al-Sayyāb's modernist poem in the tradition of Babylonian Ishtar–Tammuz myth and the pre-Islamic *qasīda* [...] More importantly, the individual who imagines his community draws the shape of both text and space as he narrates the nation.'[37]

In another poem called 'The blind prostitute', of 524 lines in length, al-Sayyāb sheds light on major Arab problems with the image of darkness. Abu Hāqqa describes its themes as follows:

> The lines of the poem give examples of the victims of Arab society: the victims of ignorance, injustice, dubious legislation and desires, and the manipulation guiding all that organises the life of the people and underpins their relationships. Those are the victims of blind fate engulfed with severe darkness as if people live in the caves, tombs and wolves' lairs...darkness is not only striking Iraq but the entire Arab world.[38]

A few lines from the poem will suffice to demonstrate:

The night descends one more time, and the city absorbs it
And those passing to the depth...like a sad song
Blossoming like the daffodils brightening up the road
Like the eyes of Medusa,[39] *every heart has been numbed with hatred*
As if they were omens beckoning the people of Babylon with fire...
They said, 'We will escape', and they fled from one tomb to another...
The haggard guard passes, and the prostitutes are tired
Sleep wavers in their eyes as if they are caged birds
Their lips and hands look orphaned, weeping...
Money is the devil of the city...
Life harsher than death, and triumph like extinction.
Tiredness oozing from the blood, and the poison of serpents in the blood...
All men of her village, are not they good people?
They were hungry—like her and her father—miserably destitute.[40]

These lines echo the theme of dark destruction which characterises the most famous poem of the American–English poet T. S. Eliot, *The Waste Land*, by which al-Sayyāb and many other Arab poets were deeply influenced. Eliot's famous line 'April is the cruellest month'[41] signifies the distortion of nature that is its destruction by man. The month that initiates the innocent spring and new beginnings was made cruel by wars and their devastating consequences in Europe during the 1920s.

In al-Sayyāb, the vision of darkness with which society is inflicted tellingly describes the formation of the individual and society in the Arab world. The poem is not exactly one of organised political discourse, but it is infused with socio-political meanings in its demonstration of exploitation in one of the arenas in which exploitation is visceral, ringed with primal degradation and humiliation. The paternalistic and dictatorial ways structures of the Arab world bristle with barriers that impede women from equality and access to jobs which could give them social independence and political security. Instead, some are reduced to prostitution, victims of the oppression of oppressed men. Oppression appears cyclical once there is a system in place to encourage it. As the Palestinian sociologist Hisham Sharabi put it, in relation to the Arab world:

> Thus, between ruler and ruled, between father and child, there exist only vertical relationships: in both settings the paternal will is the absolute will, mediated in both the society and the family by a forced consensus based on ritual and coercion.[42]

In short, the reference to prostitutes with the word 'blind' suggests that the entire society is suffering from blindness, blindness to the weak and oppressed in its midst in particular. While social norms seem a substitute for the absence of the corrupt state in safeguarding individuals and providing them with social networks of protection, these social norms are limited as they do not tolerate genuine freedom and plurality within society. They give rise to individuals who do not realise their personhood in relation to themselves and others. Those who are forced by socio-economic pressures to deviate from societal norms, such as prostitutes become pariahs. Al-Sayyāb, therefore, uses poetry to shine his light on the multiple levels of oppression from which so many people were suffering. Exploitation and oppression are also at work in the relationship between the city and the village, the two principal spaces of social organisation.[43] The city becomes a theatre for greed, governmental oppression, bureaucratic ineffectiveness and inequality; while the village loses its young people who go to seek a better life in the city because of the state's negligence.[44] And so, severe as his evocation of darkness is, al-Sayyāb is steeped in a deep understanding of socio-political deformations in the Arab world. These forms of social oppression, political mismanagement and rhetorical triumphalism, masking the incompetence of the Arab state, in turn propel defeats and discords. The results of these can be seen in several Arab countries throughout the twentieth century, such as Lebanon, Yemen, Sudan and Algeria, and most notably in the social and political devastation of Syria and Iraq in the twenty-first century.

The call of commitment

In the face of social degradation and political defeats, several Arab intellectuals and poets responded with calls for new directions for literature in general and poetry in particular. Of course, these directions were not wholly new. As has been shown above, Arab poets have always engaged with the socio-political currents of their time in a variety of ways. In fact, there is hardly an Arab poet, from the modern period at least, whether he be neo-classist, romantic, symbolist or existentialist, whose writing has not been inflected with the complexities of her or his society. Yet in the 1950s and 60s several poets took to the canonical notion of commitment in literature, believing that poets or people of letters should and do mirror the concerns of their society and times, and in the process combine eternal human truths with worldly relevance. 'Literature is for the sake of life', not for its own sake, as the theory once ran. Just as with developments in any other sphere of human knowledge, however, there is often a tendency to systematise scholarly and literary practice with over-theoretical characterisations. Yet the idea of commitment spread among poets and writers in the Arab world under the influence of the French philosopher Jean-Paul Sartre's definitive contribution to the issue. At the centre of Sartre's thinking in this regard was that the writer must be freed of societal and political shackles of any kind, while still paying attention to the injustices in society and the world at large. Freedom and justice guide the vocation of the writer. When Sartre wrote his thoughts on the issue in the 1930s, he referenced the many evident injustices in the world to illustrate his point:

> The writer's duty is to take sides against all injustices, wherever they may come from...from this point of view we must denounce British politics in Palestine and American politics in Greece as well as the Soviet deportations.[45]

In the Arab world, several writers debated the notion of commitment, with some stressing its merits and others elaborating on its meanings or rejecting it altogether in favour of an absolute realm of freedom. Among those are two eminent Egyptian writers, Taha Hussein and Tawfīq al-Ḥakīm, whose views on the matter demonstrate different sides of the debate.[46] Hussein took the view that the attitude of commitment in literature implies and applies pressure to the freedom of the writer. He wrote:

> I do not like to ingratiate myself to the people, to subject them to what they should not be subject to...so let there be no separation between the man of letters and his freedom... and between the readers and their freedoms...we do not need to make aims from everything, and to make an end from everything; but we make of literature an end of itself...let the man of letters produce as his disposition inclines him to and as life which he lives dictates for him to produce, then take his produce and make whatever you wish of it...the primary function of literature (and scholarship and knowledge) is that it summons/raises people towards it; it does not bring itself down to them.[47]

The emphasis on freedom is part of Hussein's vision that it is essential to the expansion of consciousness and to the psychological health of society in general, which literature through its revelatory power can inspire and spread. Without social and political freedom, people live in a state of servility and subservience; their true ambitions for their potential get forced into compromises of unfulfilling and unhealthy nature. There is no doubt that Hussein intends to enlighten the Arab world on the importance of freedom and its merits, having experienced harsh social and psychological constraints as a young talented boy in Egypt that he details in his extraordinary memoir of 1959, *al-Ayyām* (The Series of Days). His message is consonant with an important poetic theme in modern Arabic poetry. Tawfīq al-Ḥakīm, however, while laying emphasis on freedom, also suggests the importance of attention to current reality and its demands:

> We are approaching revolutions tomorrow by the peoples, underpinned by fundamental turnarounds in principles and the developments of ideas, for which it is not easy to predict their consequences or to infer the results. Let events run their course, and let things change and evolve in accordance with the way(s) of existence. And let us change with things and develop, for we are only some of these things. All that we wish and hope for is that thinking should not drown one day in the revolution of the waves, so that it disappears from life and its benefits fade with it. Thinking must always exist, and be of service to all groups in their present time, upholding the higher values necessary to their development as a guarantor of their future.[48]

The theme of commitment became particularly relevant in light of the predominant nationalist and socialist discourses in the Arab world in the 1950s and 60s. The political weight of the moment, then with President Jamal Abd al-Nassir at its heart, was impregnated with promise and seemed inescapable for Arab poets and intellectuals in general. His rhetoric of Arab socialism, unity and dignity rang with enthusiasm throughout the Arab world. Almost like a creative act of high merit, Nassir appeared as a new beginning, a beginning from which could be derived hope for liberation from subservience to the West, coupled with potential for economic prosperity. The Iraqi poet 'Abd al-Wahhāb al-Bayātī (1926–1999), who in his poetry often shifted between socialism, existentialism and pan-Arabism, was one of the pre-eminent socialist realist poets who expressed the promise of the Nasserite revolution in his 1965 collection, *The Book of Revolution and Poverty*, highlighting how the revolution would sweep away the stains of recent defeats and restore the renewal with which the 'Arab essence' and civilisation were historically equipped.[49] Yet by the time Abd al-Nassir became the figure that he was in the 1960s, eminent Arab poets had already developed a consciousness of a critical bent, suspicious of political authorities in general. In a poem written in the wake of the re-election of Nassir in 1965, the important Egyptian poet 'Abd al-Mu'ṭī Hijāzī (b.1935) addressed Nassir as follows:

I fear that my love to you is born of fear
Passing through from bygone centuries,
O commander in chief, lower your sharp sword as you march forward
Poetry refuses to pass under its high shadows...[50]

This is an illuminating opening to the poem, which became popular after being published in *al-Ahrām* newspaper in Egypt. The poet is conscious of the social basis of the Arab world and the patriarchal tendencies inculcated within it, which limit the inclination for constructive criticism of authoritative figures. Many political leaders are addressed as fathers; many people perceived Nassir as a father figure. One of Nassir's formative experiences was taking part in the Arab Salvation Army as an Egyptian army officer, intervening to salvage Palestine from the Zionist conquest in 1948, before becoming a key figure in the Egyptian revolution of 1952. That revolution of Free Egyptian Officers effectively ended the British presence in Egypt as well as deposing the last monarch of Egypt, King Farouq (r.1936–1951). Nassir quickly became the face of the revolution and in 1954 became President of Egypt. It was hoped that the revolution would be not only politically transformative, but also have serious socio-economic implications. As mentioned above, 'Abd al-Wahhāb al-Bayātī saw in the purportedly socialist and pan-Arabist Nasserite revolution a sign of recovery for the afflicted Arab world from defeats, particularly the loss of historic Palestine in 1948. He dedicates the first poem in the *Book of Poverty and Revolution* to 'Abd al-Nassir, *the human*', as he refers to him: *al-insān*. He writes at the end of the poem:

O the poets of the new bounteous revolution
Let your poems to him be without veils
This revolutionary giant is a mere human
He erodes the rock of history,
and lights a candle in the darkness for humankind.[51]

It is the credentials of Nassir as an internationalist revolutionary that the poet emphasises here. He highlights Nassir's promising affiliation to the poor people of the world—he presents him as one of them, a mere mortal, not as somebody above questioning. Nassir's actions were seen as a testing ground for the future of the Arab world. Concerns about the rights of the individual and his place within society, equality among people, the rights of women and freedom in general were raised. It seems, however, that the heavy political weight of the moment reduced the scope of the people's vision. Nassir was idolised for his political discourses and actions, which attracted a lot of sentimental attention in the 1950s and 1960s. This meant that the ever-relevant issue of societal changes along libertarian lines, so necessary for political development in the Arab world, was inadequately addressed. The political discourse of pan-Arabism as put forward and stressed by Nassir became the reference point for many Arabs, including the intelligentsia. Thus the political momentum of revolution was manipulated and derailed from developing into a fully-fledged social revolution towards durable political progress, in which society at various organisational and grassroots levels could take part. The political vision as articulated and enacted by Nassir became the bedrock of Arab inspirations rather than societal and political actions that could have made him one of the people, not a figure above them, as he was made to feel and behaved accordingly. Even though some of his actions appeared courageous and won Arab plaudits as they attempted to stress Arab independence and dignity in the face of Western hegemony, Nassir is therefore one of those post-independence leaders responsible for the institutionalisation of dictatorship in the Arab world, as the poet in question, Hijāzī, suggests.[52]

As Nassir took bold nationalist steps, most notably through the nationalisation of the Suez Canal in 1956, which provoked tripartite retaliation from France, Israel and Britain, his political capital rose. And when Nassir unified with Syria in 1958 and created the short-lived United Arab Republic (1958–1961) as a first phase towards broader Arab cooperation and unity, the Arab world recognised a leader who not only gave eloquent speeches, but also took concrete political steps that responded to the spirit of Arab independence. Yet the insightful poet Hijāzī and others saw troubling signs all along in Nassir's rule. These signs included jailing and torturing of political opponents; continuing reliance on paternalistic, traditional and unsophisticated political structures; and the socio-political and economic deprivation from which many continued to suffer in the Arab world. The adulation that Nassir receives from the poet is therefore tinged with suspicion. There is a long-standing Arab tradition of panegyrics dedicated to Arab rulers, most famously exemplified in the poetry of the tenth-century Abbasid poet al-Mutanabbī (915–965) which overflowed with praise for the then leader, Abū Firās al-Hamadānī (932–968), bestowing on him an almost sacred legitimacy to rule.[53] In Ḥijāzī's case, the custom of heaping praise on an Arab leader to substantiate his legitimacy and gain his favour is portrayed as formative in shaping the people's unconscious. The poet is concerned that the respect he feels for Nassir, at a time when Nassir was widely popular, is not real but instead only the past forcing its habits onto his imagination regardless of present circumstances. Yet while the poet demonstrates his affection for the leader, he asks him not to be dictatorial, not to use his military power against the people, and to lower his sword so that he could recite poetry modestly as one of the people and not above them; in effect, he should let the system of law and order be the arbiter of justice and freedom, and not act as one person without human shortcomings. He elevates the language of poetry as an honourable medium of expression above that of the sword as an instrument of power, which symbolises fear, tension and domination.

The defeat in the 1967 war (*al-naksa*, the setback), when Israel launched a sudden attack on Egypt, Syria and Jordan and occupied the rest of Palestine, came to confirm the intuition of the poet that social and political tyranny was an issue needing to be radically addressed in Arab societies. Populist political rhetoric is no substitute for mismanaged realities, which is what the defeat nakedly exposed. There had been extreme frustrated optimism invested in Nassir before 1967, to which he responded with his resignation; but he came back and stayed until his death in 1970. The defeat brought psychological grief to Arab intellectuals and poets. Introducing herself and her poetry in her edited anthology of *Modern Arabic Poetry*, the great Palestinian poet, literary critic and anthologist Salma Jayyusi wrote, 'the June 1967 war made her suspend publication of her second *diwan*, and since then she has published little of the poetry she has written.'[54]

Following 1967, however, Arab poets confirmed their presence at the heart of the cultural and political scene in the Arab world by responding to the crisis. Most poets reacted to the defeat with a heavy critique of the Arab world. New poetic sensibilities and attitudes emerged into the cultural scene and gave way to a period of rich Arab poetic outcomes. Thus, the second half of the twentieth century, as much as the first half, produced poets of startling quality and depth. Modern poetry in the second half of the twentieth century in particular best exemplified and confirmed modernity's relevance to the Arab world. The kaleidoscopic range of experimentation in form and content displayed visionary depth, musical variation and breadth and aesthetic heights for Arabic poetry of this period, all speaking of a culture that lived on to define and redefine its identity through its unique and historic pulse, namely its language.[55] In addition to the previously mentioned Iraqi poets, al-Sayyāb, al-Bayātī, al-Malāika and others, the poetic pioneers of this period include the Syrian poets Nizār Qabbānī (1923–1998), Adonis (b.1935), Yūsuf al-Khāl (1917–1987), Mohammad al-Māghūt (1934–2006); the Lebanese poets Saʿīd ʿAql (b.1912), Unsī al-Ḥāj (b.1937) and Khalīl Ḥāwī (1922–1982); the Egyptian poets Salāḥ ʿAbd al-Ṣabūr (1931–1981) and Amal Donqol (1940–1983); and many Palestinian poets, the most prominent of whom was Mahmoud Darwish (1942–2008).[56]

The prevailing emotion that characterised Arabic poetry in the context of 1967 was one of anger and rebellion; not only against what had happened, but also against the Arab world itself. Mainly, the anger was directed against the social and political elites of the Arab world who jeopardised and manipulated its resources (most clearly oil) and neglected rationalist developments in sectors such as education and health, as well as investment in social and political reforms. In particular the Syrian poet Nizār Qabbānī expressed the despair of the Arab world in biting criticism. Qabbānī is known for his suggestive and sensual poetry, in which he celebrates and invokes the physical aspects of love with an uninhibited sense of freedom.[57] Considering the trenchant outpouring of disappointment expressed in poetry after the defeat, Nizār Qabbānī spoke for Arab poets in general and their predicament then when he wrote this explanation of the sources of what came to be known as *al-Adab al-huzayrānī* (The June literature), in reference to the month in which the defeat took place:

> *From under our psychological ruins, it emerged,*
> *From our stuffed throats with salt and disappointment, it emerged,*
> *From our smashed bones and our shattered dreams, it emerged*
> *And from our lips which thirst paled, it emerged.*[58]

More notably, Qabbānī wrote another famous poem called 'Notes on the margins of the defeat', in which he offered his verdict on the Arab world with more elaboration. Many Arabs memorised and performed the poem at both public and private events in approval of its sentiments, which ring with melancholy and sardonic defeatism:

> O my friends, I mourn to you the ancient language
> The old books...
> And I mourn to you
> Our fragmented language, like old shoes
> And the vocabularies of prostitution, and the satirical poems, and the damnations,
> I mourn to you...I mourn to you
> The end of thought that led to the defeat...
> O my sad homeland, you have turned me in a moment
> From a poet who writes about love and nostalgia
> Into one who writes with a knife...
> It is no surprise that we have lost the war
> Because we enter it
> With all that the Easterner has of talents for speeches
> With overblown statements that have not killed a fly...
> Because we enter with the logic of the drum and the flute...
> The secret of our tragedy is that
> Our screams are bigger than our sounds
> Our sword is higher than our heights...[59]

The sentiments that Qabbānī expresses in the poem are widespread in Arabic poetry of the time. The central point is that Arab leaders and populist discourses say and promise more than they can deliver. The poem relays a sense of pervasive Arab ineptness. Thus the change required must affect language and discourse in being present-bound and future-orientated, rather than staying caged in the ways of the past. Poets responded harshly, criticising Arab society because they thought that the only progress with genuine potential is one that involves the Arab individual, and mainly those from the new generation, as Qabbānī makes clear at the end of his poem. Evidently, the poet has lost hope for his own generation, but not for the children of it:

> Do not read our news
> Do not follow on our footsteps
> Do not accept our ideas...
> O children, O the rain of the spring, O the grains of hope,
> You are the seeds of fertility in our sterile life
> And you are the generation which will defeat the defeat.[60]

In effect, the present generation could attempt to establish an infrastructure of knowledge and practice to transcend the past and its tried and failed ways. In this context, what is entailed is a Foucauldian view that sees the individual as embodied with socio-political norms supported by power relations. And in this case, the power relations of the Arab world are viewed as instituted within stagnant modes of communication and conduct, in ways that are in disharmony with the modern period, with its technological and scientific and cultural advancements, effectively as experienced in the West. In intellectual discourse, this demand for radical change was expressed most cogently by the Syrian philosopher Sadiq Jallāl al-ʿAzm, who wrote against the background of the defeat in 1968 *al-Naqd al-Dhātī Baʿd al-Hazīma* (Self-criticism after the defeat). His book, as summarised by Fouad Ajami, deals with 'the inadequacy of the Arab social and moral order. Azm begins by examining the weakness of the Arab as a soldier, but he ends up by evaluating the Arab as an individual— his quality of thought, his capacity to make decisions and to shape a viable social order', shedding a severe critical perspective on the socio-political formations of the Arab world.[61]

The defeats of 1948 and 1967 thoroughly wounded Arab pride. One of the fronts that kept Arab poets particularly on edge was that of the Arab–Israeli conflict and its pulsating heart, the Palestinian cause. Most notably, the 1973 war between Egypt and Israel gave Arabs a sense of psychological restoration, as the initial phase of the war confirmed Egyptian advancement, once the Egyptian army had crossed the Suez Canal and Israeli troops were forced to retreat. Yet, in the later stages of the October War, the victory did not seem as certain as it had appeared at the beginning; the US intervened to settle the conflict between the warring parties. This resulted in the 1978 Camp David accord, which settled the Israeli–Egyptian dispute but left Palestine and other Arab countries, mainly Syria, Jordan and Palestine, out of the picture. Egypt witnessed isolation from the Arab world for being the first country to recognise Israel, particularly when the Egyptian President Anwar al-Sadat visited occupied Jerusalem in 1978. In addition, the Palestinians had already made political and nationalist progress when they attacked patrolling Israeli troops in the Battle of the Karama in 1968 near the Jordan valley, and inflicted losses on them that made some poets think that the 1967 defeat was merely a tumble, and eventual victory against Zionism inevitable. As the Palestinian poet Tawfīq Ziād (1926–1994) put it:

> Merely a tumble
> That could happen to any gallant knight
> It is one step backwards
> For ten steps forward...
> What then? I do not know.

All I know is that the land and the years are pregnant.
What I know is that right cannot perish,
Or be beaten by usurpers,
And on my land conquerors could not stay.[62]

Therefore, these isolated events confirmed that the Arab people were people of resistance who could not accept the violation of their sovereignty by international powers or the newly created state of Israel. The values of justice and of loyalty to the land and its memory were resonant in Palestinian poetry of the time, which often exhibited tragedy and hope in the same breath. Moreover, it became starkly clear by the 1960s and 70s that the map of global powers had changed, as the US and Russia competed for world dominance while the old colonial powers, France and Britain, retreated to second place. Since the birth and continuity of Israel were underpinned by Western facilitation, and mainly American and German support after the 1967 war, any action the Arab world took vis-à-vis Israel, or vice versa, incurred a Western response. This response would either work in favour of Israel or calm the confrontation altogether, often to the detriment of the Arabs. The fact that the Arab world was tied to Western powers on unequal terms meant that its people's aspirations for independence were severely compromised. This resulted in politics narrowly guided by the self-centred interests of nation-states rather than by pan-Arab ambitions, as championed by 'Abd al-Nassir. Even those who criticised Nassir and his influence recognised that he was a unique leader, whose aims for an independent and powerful Arab nation were praiseworthy. When he passed away in 1970, Nizār Qabbānī evoked an image of a divided world which was not qualified to embrace the vision of 'Abd al-Nassir, hailing him as a historic leader:

O the last of the prophets, we have killed you
We have killed you...
It's not new for us
to assassinate the Prophet's companions and the saints
For how many a prophet we have killed
And how many an Imām...
Our history is a dilemma
And all our days are Karbalā...

You came to us as a beautiful book
But we cannot read...[63]

Qabbānī places Nassir in the line of the prophets and *imāms* who were born at critical moments for the Arab peoples in order to implement radically needed reform, but failed because of their peoples' ignorance. Historical milestones are used, including the incident of Karbalā: in AD 680 the grandson of the Prophet Hussein was killed at the hands of the army of Yazīd, which provoked schisms in the Muslim and Arab world. Many political developments involving Western and Arab forces found expression in the discourses of Arab poets after the passing of Nassir.

By the 1970s, oil had become the key global commodity; the disparity of wealth this created divided the Arabs further. The West became imperially involved in the extraction and monopoly of Arab oil in return for the alleged protection of oil-producing nations against other regional powers, such as Iran. The Arab rhetoric that condemned Israel and vowed to regain Palestine after 1948 therefore subsided in certain corners of the Arab world, giving way to timid condemnations and ineffective engagement. The initial sacredness attached to Palestine wore off for Arabs involved in oil, as many protest poets noted. Meanwhile, the Palestinians continued to suffer discrimination and deprivation in refugee camps. In 1970 King Hussein, ruler of Jordan, forced them out of his country, the central base of Palestinian nationalism and resistance. The refugees established a foothold in Lebanon, which slipped into a devastating civil war in 1975. The Lebanese war forcibly drew in the Palestinians: they became part of the political fabric of a country whose sects were locked into an intractable civil conflict. In addition, the Israelis targeted the Palestinian resistance, namely the Palestine Liberation Organisation (PLO).

All these developments are represented in the poetry of the iconic Palestinian poet Mahmoud Darwish among others. One event that clearly demonstrated the fissures in the body politic of the Arab world occurred in 1978: President Anwar al-Sadat of Egypt, the propagator of the politics of *infitāh* (openness) towards the West and the US in particular, shocked the Arab world with his peace treaty with Israel at Camp David. The treaty shattered the dream of Arab unity which al-Sadat's predecessor, 'Abd al-Nassir, had made the centrepiece of his rhetoric. It guaranteed sovereignty for Egypt in its heartland in return for normalised relations with Israel, but kept the Palestinians out of the political equation in terms of liberation and independence. Thus, the shared fate experienced by Arabs in 1967 was fragmented, with the Palestinians on the marginalised and losing side. The Palestinians thus became increasingly visible on the international scene as the most prominent victims of colonial powers. The Palestinians were subjected to discrimination inside Palestine, and endured massacres at the hands of Israel and its local allies, such as the Tal al-Za'tar in 1976, and Sabra and Shatila in Lebanon in 1982. They became icons of resistance against Israel due to its incessant aggression against them and their continued nationalist aspirations. Arab poets from Palestine, Syria, Iraq, Egypt and elsewhere responded to this conflict with anger, bordering at times on open vulgarity.

Two of poets whose poetry received a wide Arab hearing and approval were the Iraqi-born and Syrian-national Muzaffar al-Nawwāb (b.1932) and the Egyptian poet Amal Donqol (1940–1983). Their poetry fits what Salma Jayyusi calls platform poetry: poetry that describes the political state of the nation and mobilises its people in the face of national calamities and threats; that reminds citizens of their patriotic responsibilities and rails against tyrannical practices.[64] Through the following poem, al-Nawwāb responded to the massacre of 1976 in Tal al-Za'tar, committed by Syrian and Maronite forces with American and Israeli support against the Palestinians in Lebanon. The poem, characteristically, bares its emotional expressions in full nakedness:

Do the dead care how their graves are decorated?
Does the ewe care about the shape of the slaughtering knife?
What consummate dissonance!
A breast on the ground,
Lying next to two small hands
The size of grape leaves
A child grows up among the burnt corpses
O betraying Arabs...

What are the merchants of al-Sham cooking on hell's fire?
The plague is imminent
When a troubled star full of holes appears
It emits a deadly light
That illuminates the eye sockets of a skull
The wind flickers and plays inside it
At Tal al-Za'atar...

The capital of the poor has fallen, just a little while ago
And in response?
Impotent castanets are clicking and jangling all the way to the White House
The testicles of the Arab leaders trembled with pride...

Naft Ibn Kaaba announced...that a meeting would be called...

Have you heard, O Arabs of Silence?
Have you heard, accursed Arabs?
The hatred has reached the wombs!
Have you heard, accursed Arabs?
Palestine is being erased from the womb!
The adherents of the American religion in Mecca
And the market are at their peak!....[65]

This poem, 'Bridge of old wonders', was both performed live and widely distributed on cassette; it depicts the political Arab condition at local as well as regional levels. It refers to the massacre in the refugee camp of Tal al-Za'tar that killed an estimated 15,000 Palestinians. The siege of the camp lasted for almost three months. The many pleas for help from the besieged fell on deaf ears. People faced death either from hunger and thirst or from shelling by the Syrian and Maronite troops attacking the camp, in which many Palestinian fighters and Sunni Lebanese forces were also sheltering. Syria intervened to put an end to the Lebanese civil war with the approval of the Arab League but immediately showed that it had political interests of its own that clashed with those of the Palestinians and their allies in Lebanon. Thus the Lebanese civil war, which was supposed to be put down by Syria in 1976, lasted until 1989. There was no neutral party in Lebanon that could protect the most vulnerable, namely those Palestinians who had arrived in Lebanon after fleeing another massacre by Jordanian forces in September 1970. The fate of the Palestinians was a tragedy perpetuated by almost farcical levels of political corruption. Israel and America, both involved in Lebanon, approved the Syrian intervention and merely watched as the situation evolved.

Al-Nawwab's poem includes the invented character of Naft Ibn Kaaba, literally 'Oil, son of the Kaaba', a personification of typical Gulf rulers; he calls for meetings with Western powers and begs the White House to reinforce their political alliances, although the US provides arms to Israel, their arch-enemy in the region. What the poet is keen to portray is betrayal of Arabs by other Arab powers despite possessing oil as an effective economic weapon; they could have used this leverage to pressure America into meeting Arab demands, but instead succumbed to further submission. The poem registers a consistent pattern in the political behaviour of Arab leaders in the Gulf who, with the discovery of oil, entrenched themselves in the capitalist economic order as led by the United States and ignored their economic treasure's potential to serve Arab causes such as Palestine. Similarly, when Beirut fell to Israeli invasion in 1978 and 1982 (on both occasions many Palestinians and Lebanese were killed), it was the continuity of the market and its profits that seemed to matter most to the ruler of Saudi Arabia and other oil producing countries, and not the plight of their fellow Arabs. This ineptitude on the part of oil-producing countries, with their concrete means of political bargaining, was incorporated into the poetry of a number of important Arab poets, including Nizār Qabbānī[66] and Mahmoud Darwish. Poets refer to the merchants of Damascus, historically the elite backbone of the Syrian regime, who cower in silence whilst massacres are committed, without revolting or even protesting. They depict severe corruption in the body politic of the Arab world; railing against the political systems of the Arab world for their cruelty and cowardice in serving their own tormenters.

After Egypt signed the Camp David accord with Israel, Arab disapproval manifested itself in the suspension of Egypt's membership of the Arab league, whose headquarters were removed from Cairo to Tunisia. The accord was and remained unpopular in Egypt and the Arab world in general. It did not even end Israeli occupation of Egypt since Sinai remained under incomplete Egyptian sovereignty, but it did open up the country to Israeli political and economic influence. This infuriated Arab poets and intellectuals, who had thought until that point that they were united against the Israeli occupation of Arab territory and in unconditional solidarity with the Palestinians. Amal Donqol's poem, *lā tusālih*, 'Do not make peace', is a living testament to the energy of the protest against Israel, which was reinforced throughout the 1960s and 1970s by Egyptian poets and singers such as Shiekh Imām (1918–1985) and Ahmad Fu'ād Najm (1929–2013). Donqol's poem was widely distributed and engraved on walls in Egypt and elsewhere, particularly its refrain 'do not make peace (or reconcile)'. The refrain continued to speak to Arab audiences facing similar conditions in the Arab world:

Do not make peace
Even if they offer you gold,
Would you see if I took your eyes out
And in their place, put two gems
Would you see?...
Could the blood turn to water in your eyes?
Do you forget my clothes besplattered with blood
And wear over my blood clothes decorated with sugarcane?
It is a war!
It could burden the heart
But the shame of the Arab trails behind you
Do not make peace
And do not seek to escape...

How can you look at the hands of those who shake yours,
And not see blood
In each hand?...

Do not make peace
No matter how much is said of the words of peace
How could the lungs inhale the poisoned breeze?...

Someone who wears the complete garment will be borne
To light up an overwhelming fire
To call for revenge
To give rebirth to righteousness
From the shoulders of the impossible...

Do not make peace
Peace is an accord between two equals
(In the honour of the heart)
It does not demean
From the one who stole the land from between my eyes
And silence releases his sarcastic laughter...

Do not make peace
Do not make peace[67]

In 1967 Israel expanded its conquest and occupied more Arab land, including the rest of historic Palestine, Jerusalem, Gaza and the West Bank, as well as Egyptian territory, the Syrian Golan Heights and the Jordan Valley. The United Nations issued resolutions, most notably 242, calling for the withdrawal of Israel to the borders of 1967. Yet Israel remained intransigently unresponsive to international resolutions, and did not accept any attempt at an overall peace based on its withdrawal to the 1967 borders, although this could have led to a cessation of the Israeli–Palestinian conflict. There are no partial or interim agreements that could palliate the violent and demeaning results of the Israeli occupation on the people of the region, and particularly the Palestinians. Thus any official Arab attempts at peace with Israel look unconvincing and unpromising. The latest major peace agreement, the Oslo accord, signed between Israel and the Palestinians in 1993 at the White House, as predicted by Said, ended with the second Palestinian Intifada in 2000.[68] Israel continued to deprive the Palestinians of their political and human rights through demolitions, settlement expansion, assassinations and other forms of collective punishment. This made the dream of justice and peace look unachievable, with Israel in its current colonialist form, and it is for this reason that many Arab poets and intellectuals called for resistance rather than premature accommodation and coexistence with Israel. Hence the sad refrain 'do not make peace'.

The cornerstone of peace is justice. In the absence of justice, life reeks of distortion and hypocrisy. Although no way of living is completely independent of history and politics' shaping influence, there is nonetheless an independent life free from colonialism which the Arab world has striven towards since the beginning of the modern era and has never in fact realised.

Nevertheless, moored in a tradition invested with stories of pride, coexistence and peace, Arab poets never gave up on the pursuit of an independence in which Arabs will again be able chart the courses of their own lives. The poets, as guardians of beauty, truth, wisdom and dreams, exemplified this in their search for justice and prosperity for their societies. The Arabic dictum quoted in the previous chapter, 'justice is the very basis of authority', is therefore operative here as well. Donqol opens 'Do not make peace' with the idea that there are contexts in which the diplomacy of compromise fails to achieve genuine peace where restorative justice might succeed. Human life requires authenticity; in the face of shattered authenticity, born of fundamental and continuous injustices, peace remains a dream that cannot be prematurely or immaturely imposed. Donqol shows through the constant image of blood that sacrifices and victims will only intensify the conflict but overall he asserts that the Arabs have not reached the position of equality necessary to make peace with Israel. The poem also criticises Arab rulers who are too quick to please both Israel and the superpowers of the day, and who are unaware of the way in which peace agreements like that of Camp David in fact keep their countries weak both in the region and abroad. The poet is in fact criticising an overall Arab ineptness, noting fundamental flaws.

Yet, if there was despair, there was also trenchant defiance. Israel continued to suppress the Palestinians in an attempt to eradicate their vociferous national existence in Lebanon and Palestine. The Palestinian question remained one of the yardsticks by which commitment in Arabic poetry was measured. In particular, it was Beirut in the 1970s and 1980s that served as a centre for vocalising Palestinian resistance and nationalism, which poetry expressed and personified acutely. Interestingly, this period also witnessed successful modernist experiments of a metaphysical and surrealist nature, which benefited the stirring political poetry of competent poets such as Mahmoud Darwish. The Israeli attacks galvanised many Arab poets to record, condemn and invoke Palestinian heroism and its vibrant culture. In the modern period, literary culture, and particularly poetry, became the soulful face and the spiritual heart of Palestinian identity. Several Palestinian poets, such as Fadwa Touqān (1917–2003), Muʿīn Bseiso (1926–1984), Tawfīq Ziād (1929–1994), Samīh al-Qāsim (b.1939), Murīd al-Barghoutī (b.1944), Ahmad Dahbūr (b. 1946), alongside Arab poets such as the Jordanian Amjad Nasser (b.1955), and even the Pakistani poet Faiz Ahmad Faiz (1911–1984), all reacted to the war on the Palestinians in Beirut, asserting values of resistance and steadfastness. Palestinian poets active within Palestine, such as Tawfīq Ziād, Samīh al-Qāsim and Fadwa Touqān, served as rousing voices for the Palestinian Intifada that erupted in 1987. Nationalist Palestinian poems became evocative events participating in a tide of rising support. They were performed with enthusiasm both inside and outside Palestine, with the collaboration of rising Arab musicians such as the iconic Lebanese singers Fayruz (b.1935) and Marcel Khalife (b.1950). Two of the aforementioned poems that exemplify poetry's ability to fuel an atmosphere of resistance were written by Tawfiq Ziād and Samīḥ al-Qāsim and can still be heard today: *Unādīkum*, 'I call to you', and *Taqaddamū*, 'Come forth'.

> *I call to you*
> *I clasp your hands*
> *And kiss the earth beneath your feet*
> *And I say to you: I sacrifice myself for you*
> *And dedicate the light of my eyes to you*
> *And the warmth of the heart, I give you...*
> *The tragedy is that I live*
> *My share of tragedy is that of yours*
> *I call to you*
> *I clasp your hands*
> *I have not spared myself for my homeland or underestimated the power of my hands*
> *I have stood in the face of my oppressors*
> *Orphaned, naked and barefooted...*
> *I have carried my blood on my palm*
> *And have not lowered my flag*
> *And I have protected the green grass above the tombs of my ancestors*
> *I call to you, I call to you...*[69]

Samīḥ al-Qāsim's poem is another example from the poetry of resistance that registers the pulse of the people's struggle:

> *Come forth*
> *Come forth*
> *Every sky above you is hell*
> *Every earth underneath you is hell*
> *Come forth*
>
> *The child and the old man die among us*
> *But neither gives up*
> *And the mother falls down on her dead sons*
> *And does not give up*
> *Come forth*
> *Come forth*
> *With your armoured vehicles*
> *With the skewers of your hatred*

And threaten
And disperse
And make orphans
And demolish
You won't break our depths
You won't defeat our longings
We are destined to be valiant
Come forth, come forth...[70]

The Palestinian cause has since its beginning weighed heavily on the conscience of Arab poets and intellectuals. Though Palestine has been used by various political movements and leaders with narrow interests of their own, its central importance as a country under an alien Zionist occupation bent on continuous colonisation and humiliation made it the crowning focus of Arab nationalism. To this end, poets fuelled their poems with passionate energy, with images of attachment to the land and defiance against its occupiers. Palestinian poets, whether in Palestine or exile, vividly depicted the Palestinian predicament through various poetic techniques and styles, including myths and symbolism, emphasising rebirth and resurrection from the ashes of defeat. Poetry written by Palestinians inside Palestine came to be known as 'Palestinian resistance poetry', and the poems above affirm their resistance and steadfastness. In the same vein, poetry written by Palestinian exiles overflowed with longings for return, inflected with tragic images often including the figure of Jesus on the cross. Overall, Palestinian poetry asserts affinity to the land, with a sense of continuous existential historicity.

In the first poem above, the blood of the martyr still speaks after his death, inspiring further sacrifice. In the second, it is defiance and determination that run throughout the poem. Selfless heroism bred by collective patriotism makes the poet reiterate with confidence that whatever power the enemy uses against the Palestinians, the latter will ultimately triumph, because their sacrifices stem from their faith in their cause and their ability to defend it with limitless capacity for sacrifice. Thus the two poems echo the poetry that we saw in the context of the Algerian struggle, where there was an incessant and bold emphasis on sacrifice and steadfastness in the face of an enemy that robbed the people of their land, while attempting to make them submit to its power. With such poetry, the occupied find their voice by invoking their historical memory, fertilised with images of the land and their habits of life. The poetry in question is not only mobilising but has also a collective therapeutic value: it reproduces history in its pristine sense, before the land was occupied and its people were forced to leave. In fact, much of Palestinian poetry is centred on the re-creation of the homeland through language, immortalising it as it was as experienced by those who lived there before it was taken from them. Poetic language, through its use of metaphors, reproduces historical reality in the form of physical and psychological landscapes which manage to enchant people on account of their historical, political and spiritual values.

Palestinian and Arabic poetry in general after the 1950s had to grapple with contradictory dimensions. Most modernist Arab poets bemoaned the disorganisation of the Arab world, which brought defeats and setbacks. While poets referred to the Palestinian experience, therefore, they also shed light on the state of the Arab world in general, tending to see Palestine as a symptom of that state of disunity, archaic traditionalism, political corruption, patriarchy and disregard for political and human rights. Yet, no matter how much Arab poets expressed anger at the state of the Arab world, there seemed to be total unanimity among them in condemning Zionism, the Israeli occupation and US support for both. It could therefore be said that Arab self-criticism stems ultimately from anxious concern and indeed love for the Arab world.

At this juncture, two thematic directions can be discerned. Some poetry calls for new beginnings in the Arab world, for abandoning the traditional and striving towards a new political system supported by a robust institutional ethos, democratic transparency and sound governance. Other poetry advocates a return to the distant past, specifically the epoch of Arab cultural florescence. The latter includes Islamic references and inclinations, although in general it was the poetry of commitment, as described above, that tended to have political effects, since it was recited and sometimes sung by ordinary people. Realising the political capital of poetry, several Arab rulers or governing elites, such as those in Saudi Arabia and Iraq during the dictatorial regime of Saddam Hussein, attempted to co-opt poets by hosting lavish poetry festivals, such as the annual al-Jandāriyya Festival for Culture and Heritage, and the al-Marbad for Poetry. These attracted famous poets, even though they have specific objectives, such as the Saudi festival which aimed to reinforce traditional cultural values and promote poetry with an Islamic outlook rather than modernist poetry with ideals of freedom and human expansiveness at its heart. The phenomenon resembled the court poets in the medieval ages, when the rulers attracted poets through favours and guarantees of fame.[71]

Modernist poetry, however, with its sophisticated references permeated with philosophical currents and innovative linguistic constructs, is mainly read by highly educated audiences or taught at universities. It is not as politi-

cally effective as populist and crowd-pulling poetry, with its rhythmic immediacy and accessible content, except in the hands of arguably the greatest Arab
poet in the modern era, Mahmoud Darwish. Very few poets of the avant-
garde could break through the walls of populist discourses in which the Arab
world abounds. Yet the role of modernist poets, as most prominently demonstrated by Adonis, was still phenomenal. It has penetrated the poetry of all
classes of poets, consciously or not. To this end, a few notes on the poetry of
Adonis, on his liberated vision and its associations, are due.

The scope of modernity

The eminent literary critic Salma Jayyusi defines the modern in the context of
Arabic poetry as follows:

> The term 'modern' must at once refer both to sensibility and to technique, to vision
> and to style, and no matter how modernist a poet's methods or writing are, it is
> always the way he looks at the world that will help decide how really 'modern' he is.
> Because of the immediate cultural background of the Arab world now, and the little
> time poets have had to undergo an authentic transformation towards a modern
> outlook on man and his universe, the insistence on sensibility and attitude when
> sizing up modernity in any experiment is of paramount importance.[72]

The question that Jayyusi's enlightened definition gives rise to is as follows:
what are the sources of sensibility and attitude which are used here as the
prime measurements of modernity in poetry? Can these sources be seen in
isolation from the defining socio-political conditions that inflect, but do not
necessarily define, them? The latter question is one that the *sui generis* poetic
creation of Adonis can shed light on, operating as it does within a tantalising
world of image-based and linguistic constructions of intrinsically related considerations. While Adonis tends towards denial of fixed roots in his poetry,
opening with its splendid natural spaces for contemplation and aesthetic
astonishment, he ultimately reads into the Arabic tradition whatever serves
his poetic vision. His proselytising about unbound freedom in and through
poetry can partly be seen through a political lens, but only partly, because his
poetics leaves the political undefined, divested of its ideological burdens
through expansive widening and subversion of the known in pursuit of a sublime aesthetic manifestation of something more. The creative logic of energy
in his poetry is unencumbered by the material weight of the visible moment,
establishing another order as palpably vast as language and its chemistry can
allow. Yet an instructive statement such as the following from Adonis, paired

with his poetry below, shows how he is wilfully moored in a tradition of liberal and metaphysical qualities; and that his philosophical and aesthetic rest-
lessness is not immune to historical affiliations and the meaning-invested
world which politics affects in one way or another:

> In the Arab–Islamic epistemological tradition, thought is an answer, and as poetry
> offers no answers it is therefore defined as being entirely separate from thought. But
> while the poet does not provide an answer, this is not to say that he does not think:
> as poetry is a questioning, it leaves the horizon open to inquiry and further knowl-
> edge; it offers no certainties.[73]

That poetry offers no certainties is indeed one of Adonis' central thoughts.
Adonis' argument facilitates several critical aesthetic readings, which can
scarcely be attempted here for reasons of space. If poetry and its material
energy in language are of this world, then poetry echoes its endless facets,
including certainty and doubt. Questions might be raised about the type of
certainties involved in poetry, but that it can manifest certainties in the form
of truths seems obvious. Yet Adonis chooses to emphasise the questioning
dimension in the poetic tradition of the Arab world and rejects the idea of
certainties. Adonis has links with other poets of his school of thought, such as
Yūsuf al-Khāl, with whom he started one of the most important modern
poetry journals besides *al-Adāb*, namely *Sh'ir* in 1957; the journal bore witness
to the limitation of political ideology as superimposed by dictators and ideological movements that lacked sensitivity to other people's ways of life. At one
point in his early life, Adonis was part of the movement of the Syrian Socialist
Nationalist Party (SSNP), led by the charismatic Lebanese leader Antun
Saadeh (1904–1949). Saadeh had a grand political vision that entailed unity
between Syria, Iraq, Lebanon and Palestine. He was cruelly executed in
Lebanon for alleged separatist tendencies. Adonis later regretted that he was
part of the movement, but maintained respect towards its intellectual leader,
who is portrayed in Hesham Sharabi's 1978 book, *Embers and Ashes:
Memoires of an Arab Intellectual*, as a sound man committed to humane values.[74] The key point to draw from these aspects of Adonis' biography is that
Arab life was saturated with ideologies hampered by narrow certainties and
reliant on uninspiring readings of the textual heritage of the Arab world, as
well as a more positive encounter with European modernist poetic trends
from French and European poets such as Mallarmé, Verlaine, Lorca and
T. S. Eliot; all these influenced the search for vibrant new beginnings in
Arabic poetry. It is against this backdrop that Adonis' poetry inclines towards
and accentuates questioning. Experiencing political spaces stifled by certain-

ties that constrain alternative and radical intellectual questioning make the elevation of questioning by free and thoughtful poets such as Adonis an imperative. Yet this questioning is not innocent of political ideals, since it exists within a poetic vision that gives priority to poetry and the motion of its chemistry over accommodating existing ideologies. Such poetry aims for change at the level of sensibility and attitude, which will inevitably spread to affect other spheres of human activities. On a grand scale, Adonis is a poet who 'wants the poet to dethrone God and replace him, viewing history as an endless series of beginnings'.[75] In this respect, Adonis has more politics, albeit philosophical politics, in his poetry than he admits. His views need to be seen within the historical as well as the present context of the Arab world with its abundance of dysfunctional ideologies, such as socialism and a narrow nationalism in whose name several Arab dictators have governed, as in Iraq under Saddam Hussein (r.1979–2003), Syria under Hafez al-Assad (r.1971–2000) and his son Bashar al-Assad (b.1965), and Libya under Mu'ammar al-Qaddafi (r.1969–2011). These ideologies exist alongside many patriarchal social, religious and political trends that cajole people at various levels of society into submitting to oppressive authorities. At its heart, Adonis' poetry offers an ambition for a world liberated from such authorities and enlivened by human agents, rather than reduced to socially and politically manipulated lives. It offers a world in which freedom, conscience and consciousness, with all their complexities, are active, and not relegated to the margins of life:

From dialogue

Neither God nor the devil do I choose
Each is a wall
Each closes my eyes for me—
Can I exchange one wall for another
And my confusion is the confusion of an enlightened one
The confusion of one who knows all things...

The language of sin

I burn my heritage; I proclaim my land is virgin,
And there are no graves in my youth
I walk over God and the devil
My way is more distant than the ways
Of God and the devil—

I pass through my book
Through the procession of the dazzling storm
Through the procession of the green storm

I shout, there is no heaven, there is no falling after me
And I erase the language of sin...[76]

These two poems, from Adonis' famous book *Mihyār the Damascene*, are deconstructionist and rebellious to an extreme and their spirit is echoed throughout the book. The human voice is powerful. The speaker partakes in the creation and expansion of her or his own world beyond the binding imperatives of the identity that birth and soceity require. Agency is asserted through repetition of 'I'. The forces condemned in these poems are God and the devil, both of which are sources of submission and temptation that trample upon the human agent's willpower and conscience, before constraining both to their own dictates. Adonis rejects them because they are unseen authorities which do not correspond to the complexity of a real human being whose actions are not only good and evil as set in stone at particular times in history, but extend beyond both. In the words of the French existentialist writer Albert Camus, Adonis fits the description of 'the metaphysical rebel' who is:

> certainly not an atheist, as one might think him, but inevitably he is a blasphemer... human rebellion ends in metaphysical revolution. It progresses from appearances to facts, from dilettantism to revolutionary commitment. When the throne of God is overthrown, the rebel realizes that it is now his own responsibility to create the justice, order, and unity that he sought in vain within his own condition and, in this way, to justify the fall of God. Then begins the desperate effort to create, at the price of sin if necessary, the dominion of man.[77]

In the same vein, Adonis reiterates the limitless creative reservoir of his own humanity, in his case creative through language. In essence, the poem rings with the rhetorical mantra of the Enlightenment, 'man is the centre of the universe', and echoes the philosopher Nietzsche's view regarding the death of God. Adonis' vision in the poems is clearly revolutionary; it tears away at the solid beliefs of many in the Arab world, shattering stable meanings and values in favour of expansiveness in identity, whereby the human agent is the centre of meaning and action. In this sense, Adonis' sensibility is a brainchild of Enlightenment. It is worth quoting at length a passage from the philosopher Roger Scruton, whose summary of the configurations of European Enlightenment helps to illuminate Adonis' poem:

> In the first flush of scientific confidence, the thinkers of the Enlightenment tried to carry over into every human intellectual endeavour the search for first principles which, in Newton's physics, had been attended with such success. This search brought with it a sceptical attitude towards authority, rejecting everything that had

no secure foundation in experience. In history, morals, metaphysics and literature the Enlightenment attitude briefly prevailed, giving rise to the phenomenal ambitions of the French encyclopaedists, and to their materialist, almost clockwork, vision of the universe. It produced the political theories which motivated the French and American revolutions, and the systematic explorations in chemistry and biology that were to find fruition in nineteenth-century evolutionism. It also brought about the technical achievements which precipitated modern industrialism, and while thus preparing the way for the miseries of revolution and factory labour, it infected the minds of the educated classes with a serenity of outlook, and a trust in human capacities, that weathered the assaults of Hume's scepticism, of Vice's anti-rationalism, of the growing introversion and doom-laden mysticism of the romantics. This was the Augustan age of English poetry, the age of Johnson and Goldsmith, of Voltaire, Diderot and Rousseau, of Lessing and Winckelmann. From the point of view of the historian it is perhaps the richest and most exciting of all intellectual eras, not because of the content, but because of the influence, of the ideas that were current in it.[78]

Discourses of enlightenment touched the Arab world as well, but in a different way to their effects on Europe. As Said writes, 'the grand narratives of emancipation and enlightenment mobilised people in the colonial world to rise up and throw off imperial subjection; in the process, many Europeans and Americans were also stirred by these stories and their protagonists, and they too fought for new narratives of equality and human community.'[79] Adonis' enlightenment echoes similar objectives for the Arab world, in the sense of creating a wellspring of active ideas that will with time become sensibilities and actions. His poetry exudes the energy of a rebel bent on changing the 'traditional socio-political make-up' of the Arab world, particularly as constituted within narrow religious and sexual norms, towards the building of an equal and free human community. Once the human agent is equipped with visions about and for their own humanity, then she or he can turn them into opportunities for socio-political consciousness and spiritual empowerment, towards realising what the Moroccan poet Mohammad Benis (b.1948) calls 'the existential experience in life',[80] which necessitates open exploration. The pioneering journal *Sh'ir* therefore adopted the prose poem to rebel against poetry with fixed forms. In the words of the significant Lebanese prose poet Unsī al-Ḥāj, 'it represents the most expansive form that the modern poet has reached in terms of technique and content'.[81] Yet Adonis suggests that modernity in poetry differs from that in science. Whereas science follows a linear logic that should be adopted regardless of origin, in the case of art, and poetry in particular, the poet should tap into the modernist strands in the Arabic tradition primarily, and then be open to modernist expansion.[82] Adonis is not fascinated by the West to the extent that he could forget its shortcomings. In his poem 'Grave for New York', he articulates and condemns the darkness of capitalism, competitive individualism and political hegemony with intense revulsion:

New York—Wall Street—125th Street—Fifth Avenue
A Medusan spectre ascends between the shoulders. A market with slaves of every race.
Humanity living like plants in glass gardens. Unseen, invisible wretches submerge
like dust in the web of space spiralling victims:
The sun is a funeral
The day a black drum...
And I confess: New York, in my country the curtain and the bed, and the chair
and the head are yours. And everything is for sale: the day and the night, the Black
Stone of Mecca and the waters of the Tigris. I announce: in spite of this you pant,
racing in Palestine, in Hanoi, in the North and the South, in the East and the West,
against people whose only history is fire.
And I say: ever since John the Baptist, every one of us carries his severed head in a
tray and awaits a second birth.[83]

In his several works of criticism in particular, Adonis suggests that the Arab world possesses the means of its enlightenment within its own rich tradition, but that this has been negatively manipulated by several orthodox extremes, impeding its creative openness and adaptability.[84] The many tragedies of American policy in the Middle East, as documented by conscience-driven writers such as Noam Chomsky, are depicted by Adonis as untreatable wounds that sully relations between nations.[85] Such tragedies have been most manifest in Iraq, particularly with the infamous 2003 American invasion. The important Iraqi poet Saadi Yousif depicted in evocative verse the suffering of the Iraqis, who were subjected to extreme humiliation by American troops. One particularly harrowing poem is 'The wretched of heaven'; echoing Frantz Fanon's title, *The Wretched of the Earth*, the poem depicts the suffering of the Iraqis with searing poignancy:

We will go to God naked,
our shroud is our blood;
our camphor, the teeth of dogs,
turned wolves.[86]

Yousif's lines reflect the devastating effects of the sordid relations between expansionist capitalism and colonialism, as seen in the invasion of Iraq. In Adonis' 'Grave for New York', therefore, the heart of American capitalism is soulless, confining its own people and subjecting the world to its drive for profit. As a visionary producing poetry that affirms people's capacities for justice and productive work, Adonis highlights the theme of longing for a second birth for the Arab world, one that will be inspired by the prosperous ages of cultural vibrancy as well as coexistence in places such as Andalucía in Spain before 1492.

Adonis' vision is for the future. He sees the possibility for sound Arab thought 'when the Arab thinker starts to think of what he did not think of, that historical suppression, and the spheres of superiority: religiously, intellectually, physically, socially and politically'.[87] This holistic approach does not seem feasible in the context of the Arab world's condition, a context of widespread submission of the individual within a community controlled by grasping elites. Responsible individualism within a just society can result in a healthier social and political community but the challenge of fundamental change in the Arab world is considerable. Adonis admits 'I repeat that I personally do not dare to practise this kind of thought, and I do not find one Arab who possesses such courage. So what is the point of what we write here about heritage, originality and modernity? The answer is that what I write is only interrogative, it is an attempt on the doorsteps, which turns sometimes into small knocks on the shut door.'[88] Clearly influenced by Adonis, the Moroccan poet Mohammad Bennis expresses what 'the small knocks on the shut door' sound like in his poems 'The second coming' and 'Belonging to a new family':

1.

A prophecy shakes us out of our graves
Away from bullets
Away from old loyalties
Forward forward!
In you I see
Those that authority has slain
put on leaf and flower, and fly
to create out of those killed senselessly
the banners of the end
and the beginning.

2.

My father recommended safety
Fearing to contradict law and order
He memorised the legal code, advised me:
If you're wise, stay out of politics

How can we sit on chairs, strapped down by advice
Recommending safe submission?

How return?
Without taking action
Words lie dead on library shelves
Canned in manuscripts, newspapers, books.[89]

The multiple sources of authority in the Arab world and the submissive affiliations they tend to create reinforce a culture of stagnation in which the spectres of the past dominate to the point of negating the demands of a more dynamic present. Hence the poet cries out for new beginnings rooted in freedom, social responsibility and legal order. Parallel to this, the Egyptian poet Salāḥ ʿAbd al-Sabūr, in his poem 'People in my country', draws a picture of what nuanced as well as evocative ordinariness looks like in Egypt, and indeed elsewhere in the Arab world:

People in my country are ferocious like falcons
Their singing is like a winter tremor in the top of trees
Their laughing sizzles like fire in the wood
Their footsteps want to sink in the earth
They kill, steal, drink and belch
But they are men
And are good-hearted when they have a handful of coins
And they are believers in Destiny.[90]

The poem shows a facet to the Arab world in which the lack of social and protective political order is compensated for by exceptional individuals: they have sharpened senses, they provide for themselves, and they engage in social activities to help them maintain a kind of ease and continuity in ordinary life.

Conclusion

Much of the poetry of modernity expresses existential contradictions and possibilities, suffused with hope and exhortations for new beginnings. Yet there is also much in modernist poetry that invokes simple ordinary moments with their blessings and curses. Examples include poems by the Egyptian poet Salāḥ ʿAbd al-Sabūr, and the Iraqi poet Saʿdi Yusuf (b.1943) among others.[91] It is not possible to cover all aspects and implications of modernist Arabic poetry, given the vast range of poetics that emerged in the second half of the twentieth century. Nevertheless, the modern Arab world faced enormous internal and external challenges over this period, one of the most visible being the establishment of Israel on Palestinian land. These challenges affected modern Arabic poetry in an existential sense: almost every, if not all, Arab poets felt the heat of political conditions in a way that could not but find place in their poetry. Jayyusi expressed the political and aesthetic faces of modernist Arabic poetry as follows:

> A deep commitment to aesthetics found itself, therefore, embracing an equally deep commitment to politics and life, with the two merging together into one unified experiment and experiencing, as a consequence, the pulls and strains of contradictory directions. There is no poet of importance (or otherwise, in fact), who has not been involved with the political situation in the Arab world in one way or another.[92]

This chapter has looked at a range of poetic sensibilities shaped by the particular conditions of the poets and their own visions. Almost all are aware of shared Arab literary and intellectual heritage in a way that colours their poetry with passion for a united Arab world liberated from external domination. Some, such as Gibran and Adonis, wrap their poetics within sublime constructions, veering towards revelation and linguistic ingenuity. Others choose to more directly craft their poetry to the political configurations of the current moment. Despite these differences, both types overlap more than they care to admit.

One startling poet whose early vocation reflects these contradictions is the Palestinian poet Mahmoud Darwish. Darwish provides a genuine embodiment of the collective sounds of the Arab poet, with eyes on the past, the present and the future. His poetry is vividly alive, permeated with radiant musical richness fed initially by the experience of his own people, the Palestinians. It is also grounded in his sensitive understanding of various human conditions, combining historical observations with personal introspective experiences. In the following chapter, which I devote entirely to the study of Darwish's poetry in relation to the themes of nationalism, humanism and violence, I explore samples of his textual output with reference to the relevant theoretical insights of Frantz Fanon and the Austrian writer Sigmund Freud.

PART TWO

THE POETRY OF MAHMOUD DARWISH

HUMANISM, NATIONALISM AND VIOLENCE

'If you want a red rose,' said the tree, 'you must build it out of music by moonlight, and stain it with your own heart's blood. You must sing to me with your breast against a thorn. All night long you must sing to me, and the thorn must pierce your heart, and your life-blood must flow into my veins, and become mine.'

Oscar Wilde, 'The Nightingale and the Rose'[1]

Modernity in Arabic literature is multifaceted and there is a constant debate as to whether it is rooted in the literary Arabic tradition or whether it is imported.[2] In particular, this debate concerns the genesis of the Arabic novel, but it is also relevant to modern Arabic poetry, since the free form in which Arabic poetry appeared from the 1940s onwards was quite unprecedented. Whatever the debate has attempted to prove, it seems reasonable to assume that modern Arabic literature in general (with poetry being no exception), regardless of the important outward influences it has absorbed, has authentic origins and retrospective echoes of its own. This authenticity is situated within the historic genius of the Arabic language, as demonstrated by its extensive literary and cultural creations, resonating with both local and universal relevance.

Of course the literary Arabic tradition was interrupted by other forces. These include the effects of colonisation, modernisation, and post-colonial conditions and thought.[3] There are several Arab poets mentioned in the previ-

you cannot separate the seed from its climate.

ous chapters in whose work the influence of tradition is evident, even though they adopted and developed literary forms which were truly innovative and characteristic of the modern period.[4] In doing this, they were in dialogue with Western literary and philosophical traditions, particularly in relation to modernity and its implication for the human subject.[5] In the modern period, no poet or writer of substantive worth could have written without acknowledging modernist philosophical and literary trends.[6] It is therefore the merger of sensibilities from various traditions that determines literary Arabic modernity.

Against this background, the significance of the Palestinian poet Mahmoud Darwish (1942–2008) is of particular interest, because of the Palestinian–Arab context from which his unique and sustained poetic voice derives, as well as the developments through which his work has progressed. In poetry, figures such as Adonis, Yūsuf al-Khāl, and Unsī al-Ḥāj represented modernity as a transcendence over politics in the pursuit of unravelling the fragmented and unconscious self, in whom resides the chemistry and the metaphysics of existence in both psychological and philosophical senses. For Darwish, however, this largely introspective sense of modernity clashed with the collective fate of his people, who had fallen victim to an occupation that continued to deprive them of their essential sense of security, most often expressed in the modern period through identification with a nation-state. Being born and growing up in the midst of such a tragedy, Darwish became its pre-eminent poetic voice. In this context, poetry is not merely an answer to individual calls but is also endowed with collective resonance and significance. Yet the genius of Darwish stems from his unique ability to make the collective personal and the personal collective in an intimate way, lending his poetics local and universal as well as modern and traditional dimensions. Darwish is particularly special, because the modern—as the sum of subjective impulses—and the traditional—as the sum of collective echoes and aspirations—coexist within his poetry, and neither is excluded to the detriment of the other. It is the human subject as a crystallisation of instincts, conditions, will and vision that translates into poetry of inclusion and plurality, with a cadence and lyricism that enlivens its philosophical content and its intrinsic humanity. It is poetry as an abode of beauty, and beauty as an antidote to oppression and narrowness, beauty as resistance, that informs our understanding of Darwish's poetry. He writes:

> The absorption of poetry into the power of our intuitive life is an act of resistance, so why do we accuse poetry of apostasy if it unveils inside us sensual aesthetics and freedom of imagination, and resists ugliness with beauty? Beauty is freedom, and freedom is beauty. Thus, poetry that defends life becomes a form from the forms of invaluable resistance.[7]

146

But to act upon this hybrid understanding of poetry as explained above, Darwish underwent a poetic journey of sorts. This journey is populated with ideas about nationalism, resistance and humanism as reflected upon by post-colonial and international writers who have been at the forefront of libera-tionist and modernist thought. In this spirit, this chapter presents a theoretical and empirical reading of Darwish's poetry and its treatment of the themes of humanism, nationalism and violence within the context of the Israeli–Palestinian conflict. In particular, the chapter analyses his poetry and prose in conjunction with the views of the Austrian thinker Sigmund Freud (1856–1939) and the Martinican psychiatrist Frantz Fanon (1925–1961), as voices of modernity, emancipation and humanity. These three leading thinkers have enhanced our collective understanding of the human condition in conflict-ridden contexts. I emphasise the importance of Freud and Fanon here because modern Arab poets such as Adonis and Darwish interacted with such think-ers, embodied their universal thoughts and aspirations, and echoed them in their poetry. Freud engaged critically with Jewish nationalism in its formative years in the 1920s and 30s, whereas Fanon was directly involved with the Algerian struggle against French colonialism in the 1950s. Darwish was a poetic chronicler of the Palestinian question in all its dimensions, particularly since the 1960s.[8] All of them articulated aspirations for universal justice and freedom, while taking part in their peoples' struggles and dilemmas. By emphasising the complementary roles of all members of society in the struggle against the colonisers in his portrayal of the Palestinian struggle, Darwish appears closer to Fanon's anti-colonial nationalism. Nevertheless, while emphasising the historical conditions that gave rise to Palestinian nationalism, Darwish grew to be critical of it in a tone that is reminiscent of Freud's criti-cism of nationalism and of collective identities in general.

Palestine and Darwish

Darwish was born on 13 March 1942. Until the age of thirty, he was the vic-tim of constant political ruptures. His predicament, consisting of displace-ment from his home, imprisonment, exile and war, was in many ways emblematic of the overall Palestinian experience, especially that of his genera-tion. The Palestinian people were suddenly uprooted from a territory which once made possible stable childhoods, grounded in historical continuity, to which political concerns were relatively secondary. Darwish vividly evoked this background of sudden displacement in 1969, in his first interview with an Israeli Jewish journalist, Joseph Algazy, for the Israeli newspaper *Zo haderech*, which belonged to the Communist Party of which Darwish was a member. For the political and psychological richness it affords, it is worth quoting at some length:

> I remember myself when I was six years old. I used to live in a beautiful, peaceful village, called Birweh. It was located on a green hill, above the valley of Acre. I was the son of a family of modest means, living on agriculture. When I was seven years old, the games of childhood stopped...and I remember how this happened...I remember this exactly: one summer night, when the villagers used to sleep on the roofs of their houses, my mother suddenly woke me from sleep. I found myself with hundreds of the inhabitants of the village running to the forest. Bullets were flying above our heads, and I did not understand what was happening. After a night of desolation and escape, I arrived with one of my relatives, who were dispersed in all directions, in a strange village where there were other children. I asked naively, where am I? And I heard for the first time the name Lebanon... It seems to me that that night put a violent end to my childhood; my childhood void of hardships came to a sudden end. I now felt that I belonged to a world of the old, the mature. Ever since those days when I came to live in Lebanon, I have not forgotten, and I will never ever forget, my recognition of the word 'homeland'. For the first time, and with no mental preparation, I found myself standing in a long queue to get food that the UNRWA distributes to refugees. The first meal consisted of yellow cheese. And there I heard countless new words, which were to open a window onto a new world: homeland, war, news, refugees, army, borders, and through these words I began to study, understand and recognise a new world with a new situation...it deprived me of my childhood.[9]

This account is similar to many other Palestinian stories of displacement and personal and collective struggle.[10] The final declarative statement, 'it deprived me of my childhood', condemns Zionism as a colonial movement that cut away everything in its path in order to fulfil its ambition of founding the State of Israel in 1948, at the expense and to the detriment of 'the other', the Palestinians. This trauma was redoubled when Israel occupied the rest of Palestine and still more Arab territory in 1967. Darwish expressed satisfaction, or felt 'psychologically comfortable', in the words of the Egyptian critic Rajā' al-Naqqāsh, about the fact that he was in an Israeli prison soon after the defeat, or *Naksa*.[11] He did not see it from the outside but from the dungeon of an Israeli cell, from an abyss that could not go deeper. This was the relative transcendence of the shattering event of 1967, which perplexed many Arabs and frustrated their poets' hearts and intellectuals' minds, as explained in the previous chapter.[12]

The violence inherent in these experiences of occupation and displacement makes Darwish's poetry vividly insightful with regards to his reflections on and treatment of violence and its victims. Since the beginning of the Palestinian struggle in the 1960s, Darwish was an early chronicler, registering the pain and the aspirations of the Palestinians to return to their homeland. Darwish's experience of the Palestinian predicament is immediate, as he was imprisoned several times by Israel, the last of which was in 1969, when he was incarcerated for twenty days. Yet he was also exposed to a variety of Israeli Jews, some of whom he admired and respected, highlighting their good influence on him. One example was his teacher of literature, Shoshana. In his words,

> Shoshana taught me to understand revolution as a literary work; and she taught me the study of Bialik [a well-known Jewish poet], focusing on the poetic energy, rather than his passionate political enthusiasm. She did not try to fill us with the poison of an official school curriculum which encourages the denial of our heritage. Shoshana saved me from the hatred with which the military ruler filled me. She broke down divisions that the military ruler created.[13]

After viewing this context, in which humanism and nationalism are inextricably bound, it is instructive to turn to relevant theoretical opinions that give more perspective on Darwish.

Violence as a challenge to humanism

One particularly overlooked view of nationalism is that of Sigmund Freud. He viewed nationalism, which is often treated as a natural outgrowth of the nation-state system, underpinned by symbolism and discourse,[14] with suspicion and dread. He rejected it in favour of universalism and individual freedom that could transcend national boundaries, and he appreciated reason as a harbinger of truth and collective sanity. Equally, Freud was against the interference of external political pressures on internal desires; he saw them as a hindrance to freedom and creativity. His rejection of resistance was categorical for, in the words of Jacqueline Rose, he saw in it a 'psychic reality that blocked the passage of the psyche into freedom'.[15] Freud grounded his reasoning in an archetypal dislike of nationalism, religion and any other collectivised identity rooted in ritualistic and exclusive bonding rather than societal and legal premises that are open to the world and embrace its diversity, empowered by a rational basis for preservation, protection and prosperity. He extended his rejection of nationalism to Jewish nationalism, viewing it as misguided. In a letter Freud wrote in 1930 to the leader of the Jewish Agency, Dr Chaim

Koffler, who had previously sought his help in criticising the British policy of limiting Jewish immigration to Palestine, Freud made his views on Jewish nationalism clear:

> I concede with sorrow that the baseless fanaticism of our people is in part to be blamed for the awakening of Arab distrust. I can raise no sympathy at all for the misdirected piety which transforms a piece of an Herodian wall into a national relic, thus offending the feelings of the native people. Now judge for yourself whether I, with such a critical point of view, am the right person to come forward as a solace to a people deluded by an unjustified hope.[16]

Freud saw absolute freedom in pure states of existence and creativity, unencumbered by nationalist or traditional commitments. Such idealistic inclinations regarding humanity in general did not, understandably, stop him from identifying with his people, the Jews, in any context of anti-Semitism. He writes 'since you have abandoned all these common characteristics of your countrymen, what is there left to you that is Jewish?...a great deal and probably its very essence.'[17] Freud enfolded his pacifist attitudes within complex contradictions that may seem irreconcilable but as a champion of humanism, he is interesting and relevant to the instance of Darwish and his poetry. For, like Freud, Darwish was steeped in humanist understanding and ideals, that were to be tested during the Israeli–Palestinian conflict. Darwish made many impassioned pleas and appeals bemoaning the stupidity of violence and its potentially endless entrapment. Unlike Freud, however, Darwish embraced resistance in general along with the popularised term 'the poetry of resistance', whose meaning he gradually explored and extended. The dialectical dilemma in Darwish's case is acute when one considers his individual persona and experience as against his collective context and sense of attachment and responsibility, which accompanied him to the end of his life.

Frantz Fanon is another illuminating figure on the themes of nationalism, violence and identity. He is particularly relevant for his views that opposed Freud's. Freud focused on the inner world of the individual in relation to the external environment, exhorting disassociation between the two. He writes in *Civilization and its Discontents* that 'ultimately, all suffering is merely feeling; it exists only in so far as we feel it, and we feel it only because our constitution is regulated in certain ways'.[18] Fanon, like Freud, is not short on human and worldly ideals, but his analysis penetrates realities rather than speaking above them, necessary though that might be for the healthy civilisation to which Freud admirably aspired. As an intellectual activist and psychiatrist during the Algerian revolution against French colonialism Fanon notes 'terror, counter terror, violence and counter violence: that is what observers bitterly record when they describe the circle of hate, which is so tenacious and so evident in Algeria.[19] Fanon is no advocate of violence, but he sees no alternative to resorting to it in situations of extreme colonial injustice. He writes of the condition of black people in *Black Skin, White Masks*: 'I do not carry innocence to the point of believing that appeals to reason or to respect for human dignity can alter reality. For the Negro who works on a sugar plantation in Le Robert, there is only one solution: to fight.'[20]

In this sense, taking Darwish's focus on the Palestinian experience, and viewing it from the parallel prism of those great thinkers, his poetry is grounded in humanist aspirations and nationalist principles that are in constant dialogue and interaction with one another. Fanon warns of blind nationalism in stark terms: 'if nationalism is not made explicit, if it is not enriched and deepened by a very rapid transformation into a consciousness of social and political needs, in other words into humanism, it leads up a blind alley'.[21] Humanism and poetry are not necessarily natural bedfellows, as Darwish discovered when allying himself with the tradition of humanism while at the same time belonging to the secular tradition of Palestinian nationalism. Poetry may embody ideological narrowness when immersed in sentiments of exclusion and violence that divest it of the humanist values of inclusion and deference to the other. Indeed, since the beginning of Darwish's poetic career, and despite his intense and passionate outpourings of emotion for his colonised homeland, he often related his poetry to a wider human and universal experience, from which the nationalist subject of his poetry, Palestine, was paradoxically precluded. His poetry can be seen as an attempt to compensate for a homeland that he knew to be his yet was beyond his reach, because of its occupied status. Yet before expanding on this notion and how it bears on the themes of violence and humanism in his poetry, let us bring Said into the discussion.

Edward Said, the Palestinian–American intellectual, creates a revealing synthesis of Freud and Fanon in his book *Freud and the Non-European*, along the lines mentioned above. He says that Freud's views on culture and nationalism are informed by psychological experimentation and introspection; and that these are geared towards universalising tendencies rather than actual cultural configurations stemming from real and varied life experiences, which would widen the methodological and epistemological scope of human understanding. Said's view of these thinkers' divergent approach to culture can be summed up in his words:

however much or little one agrees with Fanon...there is no doubt that the whole idea of cultural difference itself—especially today—is far from the inert thing taken for granted by Freud. The notion that there were other cultures besides that of Europe about which one needed to think is really not the animating principle for his work that it was in Fanon's...[22]

Said's view of culture concurs with Fanon's in considering culture and its enactments as filled with socio-political content. Art is therefore an expression of this content. In relation to art, however, the question of culture is complex, given its tendency to transcend immediate politics; poetry universalises the particular, whereas politics particularises the universal in order to articulate and deal with it practically. In this spirit, Said also wrote about Darwish's poetry, to which he devoted an article in 1994:

> Poetry for Darwish provides not simply an access of unusual insight or a distant realm of fashioned order, but a harassing amalgam of poetry and collective memory, each pressing on the other. And the paradox deepens almost unbearably as the privacy of a dream is encroached on and even reproduced by a sinister, threatening reality...this strained and deliberately unresolved quality in Darwish's poetry makes it an instance of what Adorno called late style, in which the conventional and ethereal, the historical and the transcendently aesthetic combine to provide an astonishingly concrete sense of going beyond what anyone has ever lived through in reality.[23]

Said's view of culture and the location of the individual within it is grounded in conditions which even poetry, that 'distant realm of fashioned order', cannot entirely escape.

Nevertheless, Darwish, as a universal and national poet writing on a cause that has seen much violence, demonstrated proportionality and introduced twists to his poetry. In this, his poetry embodies Fanon's vision of nationalism as well as Freudian universalism. '[T]he harassing amalgam of poetry and collective poetry', as Said describes it, is achieved through balances that absorb the nationalist Palestinian subject while embodying and aspiring to a vision of poetry with universal echoes. Such aspiration in poetry exceeds and indeed resists the oppressive colonial political context and embraces freedom as an ideal of which poetry is an exalting emblem.

Darwish: Raw beginnings and subtle ends

At the end of his famous poem *Sajjil Anā 'Arabī*, which was first published in 1964 and is widely recited in the Arab world until this day, Darwish issues a threat veiled within a reasoned argument:

I do not hate people
Nor do I intrude
But if I become hungry
I eat my usurper's flesh
Beware...
Beware...
Of my hunger
And my anger![24]

There is nothing to be said about a human being who wants to eat the flesh of his enemy, except that all other possibilities must have been exhausted. Darwish's early writings abound with base images of nature attempting to reverse the condition of injustice that has been inflicted on the Palestinians. Fanon insightfully illuminates this image of violence in cases of anti-colonial struggles: 'For the native, life can only spring up again out of the rotting corpse of the settler.'[25] Nonetheless, it is worth bearing in mind Darwish's humanist touch when creating images of violence within his nationalist involvement. 'I do not hate people' is a declarative line summarising a sentiment that runs through Darwish's early poetry. 'People' here is an inclusive word that suggests peace with humanity at large at its most basic and primordial level. The declaration is raw: it takes one back to early states of nature, essentially to endemic anger fuelling violence, the inevitability of which Fanon documented and reflected on in his writing about the Algerians and their resistance to the French colonisers of their country. It is clear that Fanon's theoretical and empirical understanding of nationalism in contexts of colonialism fits Darwish's early poetry in particular. There is a sense of inevitability to Darwish's engagement in the Palestinian revolution, an inevitability evoked by natural images in their base form. In one stanza of another poem, entitled 'Diaries of a Palestinian wound', which Darwish dedicated to the prominent Palestinian poet Fadwā Touqān (1917–2003), he writes:[26]

This earth which absorbs the flesh of martyrs
Promises summer grains and planets
So worship it!
We are salt and water in its heart
And in its lap...a wound that fights!

Martyrs are praised, given promise by the earth within whose folds they reside. There is inbuilt violence, hope and promise in this short stanza. Martyrs are valued for their fighting, which is rooted in their love (and worship) of the earth, which absorbs their blood and produces grains and planets out of it.

Violence at the individual level is here, as Fanon describes it, 'a cleansing force. It frees the native of his inferiority complex and from his despair and inaction.'[27] The idea that nature, which somehow encompasses intimate secrets beyond the colonisers' grasp,[28] revolts against the oppressor is prevalent in Darwish's poetry, but nature does so with the aid of human agency, fighters and martyrs. Another approach that Darwish adopts is the evocation of religious–mythic figures, such as Jesus and Job, inviting or paralleling their suffering, prophecies and symbols to record the Palestinian experience:[29]

For I am burning on the Cross of my worship
So I will become a saint...
With the uniform of a fighter[30]

Or

Today, Job screamed to the expanse of the sky
Do not make from my case a lesson twice[31]

The cross of life, creation, lineage, society.

The fighter is redeemed and gains sainthood by his fighting; he does not shy away from the cross but worships it even until he is past burning. At the heart of this image is the resurrection that follows an ultimate sacrifice. The fighter embodies Darwish's Jesus here, the Jesus who redeems humanity through his crucifixion, as recounted in the Christian tradition. In the second lines, the Biblical figure of Job, who endures relentless suffering as God tests his loyalty to him and his resolve and patience in the face of adversity, cries out to humanity not to take a lesson from his experience, not to repeat it, for it is severe and painful beyond words. Thus, in his early writings, Darwish resorts to deep levels of expression and emotional intensity to chronicle the Palestinian experience of dispossession, exile and the inherent violence in all these experiences. Yet alongside this Darwish registers humanist sentiments, unconstrained and unqualified; as an example, he seals the aforementioned poem *Jawāz safar*, 'Passport', with a slogan-like declaration, 'all the hearts of people are my nationality'.[32]

The seeds of humanism in Darwish appear early on, in 1968, in his poem 'A soldier dreams of white tulips'. Here, in a dialogue between himself and an Israeli soldier, the latter reveals to Darwish his thoughts and emotions, recorded in the poem with resigned neutrality and sympathy:

Do you feel sad? I asked.
Cutting me off, he said, Mahmoud, my friend,
Sadness is a white bird that does not come near a battlefield.
Soldiers commit a sin when they feel sad.
I was there like a machine spitting hellfire and death,

Turning space into a black bird.
He told me about his first love, and later, about distant streets...[33]

The poet delves into describing the quotidian dreams, thoughts and practices that are part of a soldier's life. The evocation and elevation of everyday
experiences later became a hallmark of Darwish's poetry. The choice of title,
'A soldier dreams of white tulips', suggests ordinariness and beauty amidst the
chaos of violence and war. The poem in its totality hints at the porous nature
of national boundaries, and perhaps the inherent shackling inadequacy of
nationalism, a Freudian theme that will become clearer with further analysis.
This poem therefore irked many nationalists when it was published, who
accused Darwish of *tatbī'*, normalising and accommodating the occupation,[34]
rather than continuing the trend of resistance which Darwish was depicted as
championing by the Palestinian writer Ghassan Kanafani (1936–1973). In
this sense, Fanon's words resonate with Darwish's predicament at this stage,
the 1960s and early 70s, and indeed later:

Illuminated by violence, the consciousness of the people rebels against any pacifica-
tion...The action which has thrown them into a hand-to-hand struggle confers
upon the masses a voracious taste for the concrete. The attempt at mystification
becomes, in the long run, practically impossible.[35]

This is an appropriate point at which to turn to the poetry Darwish wrote
in the 1970s and 80s, for these were epic decades for Palestine's struggles and
dilemmas, and for Israel's violence and destruction. Here, Darwish reaches
peaks of expressive emotion, intellect and portrayal that deepen and nuance
his poetry; but perhaps most importantly, he preserves a vivid record of the
ultimate abyss to which the Palestinian fighters and people were driven in
Lebanon. Resistance in his poetry is made more concrete by the violence that
characterises this period. The poet does not hesitate to be a freedom fighter
when the very survival of his people is at stake.

Another bloody turn, and loss bemoaned

Darwish went to Lebanon in 1972. Conscious of his presence and creativity,
the Palestine Liberation Organisation (PLO), recently forced out of Jordan
by King Hussein in what was known as Black September in 1970, clamoured
to incorporate Darwish in its intellectual circles. Once entrenched in exile,
Darwish met living martyrs, people who were soon to be assassinated or fall
in the battles and fierce confrontations that characterised this era of civil war
in Lebanon. There were two massive Israeli incursions, the second of which in

1982, led by the Israeli defence minister Ariel Sharon, was mercilessly aimed at eradicating or driving out the PLO from Lebanon. In this context, Darwish called upon the martyr, who embodies the earth, to intercede and facilitate their return home. Biblical tradition is very much present here, if inverted and subtly parodied. Darwish establishes an organic hierarchy, at the top of which stand the martyrs who mediate between the land and the people, followed by the refugees, and the other strata of the Palestinian community. What follows are lines from the poem itself, dedicated to the assassinated Palestinian leader Abū Alī Iyād (1931–1971) and tellingly entitled 'Returning to Jafa':

> *Do not say, our Father in heaven*
> *Say, our brother who carried the land for us*
> *And returned...*[36]

Darwish imbues the martyrs with supernatural powers and divine attributes, made possible by nationalist sentiment. If nationalism as prose is steeped in exaggerated heroism and mythical elevation, nationalism as poetry turns the dead in their graves into gods. By praising victims, nationalism, as known from existing literature, endows them with traits that render their death a triumph.[37] Freud would effectively say that it animates their existence with delusions—delusion being a byword for immaturity and infantilism in Freud's view.[38] Darwish, however, does not use or imply the concept of delusion; nor does he portray any aspect of the nationalist struggle in a delusive light. He resembles Freud in one sense; in accruing delusional aspects to nationalism in general. Yet he is closer to Fanon in another; in understanding that the nationalism of nationalist struggles against occupation stems from the severe depravity and denial of the occupied that triggers violence. Fanon is aware of the depth of longing for freedom and rectification of injustice that underpin violence and unceasing struggle: 'the native's violence unifies the people'.[39] Apparent in these few lines is the plight of the Palestinian refugees, their unaccommodated existence in many parts of the Arab world, exposed to hardships and obstacles that provoke longing for return to their homeland. Darwish makes possible this return by using the proxy of the martyr, who carries the longing of the refugees with him as he returns to the land that he has embodied for so long.

We saw at the outset of this chapter how Darwish's childhood was ruptured, and how he was forced into exile at an early age. His unceasing return to the past, to this state of deprivation, echoes significant Freudian themes. Darwish highlights with particular poignancy that 'no individual can be satisfied with his own personal answer to a question that was collective from the beginning, since the tragedy of the big displacement'.[40] Darwish deploys notable (Freudian) psychological terms to describe the condition to which he was reduced. Freud originally conceived of displacement as standing for the mobility of mental life,[41] but in Darwish's sense displacement comes across as the shattering of a core that should be reclaimed, even if metaphorically. In this view, the mind is rooted in primary habits, experiences and scenes, and yet rootless in its capacity for adaptation and fluid imagination as befits its context, as the case at hand demands.

Lebanon, where Darwish experienced unqualified violence, created a need for what might be called poetic adaptation. It is beyond the scope of this chapter to delve into the Lebanese civil war (1975–1990), which was exacerbated by the violence and destruction of Israeli incursions. As the veteran Middle Eastern correspondent Robert Fisk describes in his book *Pity the Nation: Lebanon at War*,[42] the fierce struggle for power in Lebanon, entailing a wide range of local, regional and international players within the confines of a limited space, resulted in gruesome spectacles that tainted all those involved. Darwish resorted to the epic and ethereal to document this experience and describe its emotional and psychological undercurrents. The language he used makes an epic narrative of the conditions in question by intensifying the imagery and the metaphorical associations. It depicts the epic as part of a dramatic reality in which violence is entrenched and far-reaching. And in the context at hand, the Palestinians were existentially threatened. Two books in particular register this stage, namely *In Praise of the High Shadows* and *Memory for Forgetfulness*. Here, instead of the martyrs being saints or residing in another world of happiness, their body parts become weapons to be used in the battle for survival in Lebanon. There are strong echoes of what Fanon describes as 'absolute violence' here:[43]

> You have no brothers my brother, you have no friends,
> O my friend, no fortresses
> You have neither water nor medicine, nor the sky nor blood nor a boat
> You have neither the frontline nor the backline.
> Besiege your siege...for there is no choice
> Your shoulder has fallen, pick it up
> And hit your enemy...there is no choice
> And I have fallen next to you, pick me up
> And throw me at your enemy...for you are now free and free and free
> Your fallen or wounded victims are a magazine inside you
> Throw it...hit your enemy...there is no choice...

Our body parts are our names
Invest your siege with madness
And with madness
And with madness
Your loved ones have gone. Gone.
You either have to be
Or you will not be...[44]

Absolute sense of language used to represent absolute violence, engulfing all and evoking madness as an antidote to madness. Darwish creates a sense of madness through his repetition of the word 'madness', reinforcing its material reality as a kind of confrontation. Linguistic repetition and parallelism of the type exhibited here is integral to poetic composition, according to Roman Jacobson.[45] Yet they are also part and parcel of anti-colonial struggles. As Fanon put it: 'this, then is the correspondence, term by term, between the two trains of reasoning'.[46] Darwish describes the state of the Palestinians in the face of the 1982 Israeli incursion, calling on them to rise, fight, 'for there is no choice'. He then concludes with a reference to the timeless Shakespearean adage, 'To be or not to be'. The wounded or the martyrs, who in earlier poems rest after they had sacrificed themselves for the homeland, are used as fuel for what has been left of the Palestinian revolution in Lebanon. Their body parts become activated weapons for other fighters who resist against Israel's intentional war of annihilation. This is nationalism and violence at their zenith, which Jean-Paul Sartre in his introduction to Fanon's landmark book, *The Wretched of the Earth*, highlights with bitterness at his fellow country-people (the French aristocracy in particular) who cannot see the violent seeds they had planted during their colonisation of Algeria: 'for violence, like Achilles' lance, can heal the wounds that it has inflicted. Today we are bound hand and foot, humiliated and sick with fear; we cannot fall lower.'[47] If a French philosopher could describe the state of his people in such terms, considering their immoral colonialism and its effects on the psychological health of the colonised nation, what could the colonised be expected to say, given the devastating violence inflicted on them? Darwish seems to take this last statement by Sartre, 'we cannot fall lower', to its furthest conclusion, resorting to madness[48] as the last frontier for the colonised in the face of the coloniser who had sunk so low in his repression and oppression of the colonised. Fanon recognised this organic chain of violence, depicted vividly in Darwish's lines above:

> But it so happens that for the colonised people this violence, because it constitutes their only work, invests their characters with positive and creative qualities. The prac-

tice of violence binds them together as a whole, since each individual forms a violent link in the great chain, a part of the great organism of violence which has surged upwards in reaction to the settler's violence in the beginning. The groups recognise each other and the future nation is already indivisible. The armed struggle mobilizes the people, that is to say, it throws them in one way and in one direction.[49]

Yet Darwish does not stop at this violence and the panorama of devastation it creates in his poem. He hints at the Freudian idea of delusion that inheres in any nationalism. Thus Darwish seals his great poem by pointing out the lack of symmetry between the nationalist's ultimate goal and what is lost along the way to its realisation:

How grand the idea
How small the state![50]

In a thoughtful paradox, Darwish registers here the broader idea that transcends the actual size of the nation-state and becomes the expansive, homeless idea of humanity, which is palpably denied to the Palestinians, given the conditions of injustice in which they are mired. The idea that obsesses the fighter is larger than the cause she or he is fighting to obtain. Here Darwish is at home with both Freud and Fanon: the former as an adversary of nationalism, and the latter as its surgical analyst and champion in the context of anti-colonial struggles. This is so even if, at the literal level, Freud's account of nationalism and nation-state ideology seems to be more influential. What Darwish does here, as an intellectual, and increasingly as a poet–philosopher,[51] is to dispel the myth of the nation-state. Exhibiting a lexical euphoria, he shatters its origins and stable meanings, in order to bring the Palestinian struggle, anguish and longing for the homeland to the fore. As Freud seems to shatter the origins of the Jewish faith by suggesting that Moses was an Egyptian before being claimed by the Jewish people, Darwish introduces tremors in the Palestinian pursuit of their nation-state. Darwish has no Moses to play with but there is nevertheless a dogged Palestinian pursuit of a nation-state (another modern Moses), which he suddenly questions. Humanism which is concerned with the spiritual wellbeing of the human being recognises no holy idols; it knocks them down lest they forget higher ideals amidst an all-out violence that no state or collectivised identity could secure.

Freud does not mean to deny a collective identity to the Jewish people so much as link it with wider worlds, to wrestle Jewish nationalism away from being trenchantly linked to a territory, putting the idea of justice and truthful humanity before any other nationalist considerations. Rose explicates this with characteristic eloquence:

Freud therefore turns Moses into an Egyptian, lets the stranger into the tribe. He castigates the ruthlessness of monotheism, breaks apart the unity both of the people and their faith. He places murders at the origins of the group. But this is, finally, no simple iconoclasm. The integrity, the narcissistic unity and at-oneness of the group, *returns*...But he has done so at a time and in the framework of an analysis which suggests that identity, while it may indeed be necessary for the survival of subjects and peoples, is no less a danger to both.'[52]

Increasingly, Darwish dissolves the 'I' and invites the 'other', looking at the future from its brightest spot rather than the darkness of the present or the past for that matter:

'I or he'
That's how war starts. But
It ends with an embarrassing meeting:
'I and he'[53]

A journey to the heights

Darwish has always been a champion of the Palestinian struggle for collective freedom and political sovereignty within a recognised and inclusive nation-state. Considering the historical premises of the Palestinian cause, he endows and expands on the humane attributes inherent in the conditions that gave rise to the aspirations of the Palestinians' national movement. He continues to concretise as well as humanise the Palestinian struggle with more inclusive awareness of profound psychological configurations. But Darwish suggests that nationalism should not be an end in itself. As with Freud, the dialectic between local identity and the human universal acquires acuteness in the poetry and philosophy of Darwish. In his mourning of the Palestinian leader, Yasir Arafat (1928–2004), he writes, 'and we will not be what we want to be unless we know how to halt the process of exodus from our history and from human history, and how to return to both of them, with all that we have of energy, experience and talent.'[54] What Darwish never denies is the essential beingness and humanity of the 'other', as fervent nationalist discourses often do: 'an identity does not negate an identity. What perplexes the identity and agitates it is when it is conditioned by the negation of the identity of the other.'[55] Darwish directs his statements here at the Israelis. In this sense, Darwish echoes what Freud called for many decades ago: 'This is a plea for a model of nationhood that would not just accept the other in its midst, nor just see itself as other, but would grant to that selfsame other, against which national and political identities define themselves, a founding, generic status at the origins of the group. Freud knows that this is a form of sacrilege as well as a huge risk, and not just to himself...'[56] At the heart of the Palestinian situation is the double Israeli denial of the other, the Palestinians in their political and human rights. Hence, independence and liberation are key words in Darwish's diction. Here Darwish captures Fanon's idea regarding the centrality of humanism for nationalism:

> *He said to me on the way to his jail:*
> *When I am freed, I know*
> *That the praise of the homeland*
> *Is like its disparagement*
> *A profession like all professions*[57]

Thus, nationalism should not be an end in itself. By 2002 and 2003, years which witnessed another escalation in Israel's violence against the Palestinians, as well as reactive Palestinian violence, characteristically Darwish's voice takes on the sharpness the situation in question compels. This sharpness includes revisionism. For unlike early writings, when martyrs are redeemers and intercessors for the living, martyrs become victims and initiators of their actions. The literary critic Angelica Neuwirth suggests that Darwish in his new collection, *Hālat hisār*, deconstructs the image of the martyr; thus 'martyrdom is no longer a social rite with redemptive power, but an exclusively individual act motivated by personal pride and defiance of despair'.[58] Sound as this suggestion is, it is possible to add that Darwish revises his earlier poetry; hence he engages in revisionism rather than deconstruction's limited attempt at reordering what has been constructed. On the one hand, martyrs die for their particular homelands and are celebrated by their people; on the other, they are universal victims of irresistible circumstances. Darwish laments martyrs as well as shedding light on the broader existential and power parameters within which their demise occurs:

> *Our losses: from two to eight martyrs*
> *Every day,*
> *And ten wounded*
> *And ten houses demolished*
> *And fifty olive trees uprooted*
> *In addition to the structural damage which will be inflicted on*
> *The poem, the play and the unfinished painting.*

Life in its widest sense constitutes the material ingredients of art. Once the organic unity of life is disturbed by violent conflicts, art shares in the loss suffered by other elements, even though in its abstractness or projection through other lenses art seems to transcend time-bound reality. Everything seems reversed when there is violence; it is hard to extract normality from what is totally and inherently abnormal, hence:

The martyr warns me: Don't believe their ululations
Believe my father when he looks at my photograph weeping
How did you reverse our roles, my son, and walk ahead of me?
I should have been the first, I should have been the first![59]

The actual object of hailing, the martyr, acquires a mature humane voice that chimes with universal chords of suffering. Ultimately martyrdom is a premature death that naturally induces its due lamentations and sorrows. What then of nationalism and the liberationist role it has in the context at hand? Nationalism and nationhood shroud all forms of sacrifice within cloaks of heroism but reach their limits when they fragment and become objects of their own destruction. For the Palestinians, it was the task of the intellectuals, as Fanon would have wished, to guide, to imbue nationalism with humanist inflections, so that it does not become an object in and of itself; so that it is always looking at another horizon, parallel or beyond the nation-state; so that the humanity of the struggle is not superseded or made secondary. As Fanon puts it, 'The living expression of the nation is the moving consciousness of the whole of the people; it is the coherent, enlightened action of men and women. The collective building up of a destiny is the assumption of responsibility on the historical scale. Otherwise there is anarchy, repression and the resurgence of tribal parties and federalism.'[60]

Fraternal frictions

In the first decade of the twenty-first century, the Palestinians entered another stage in their struggle for freedom from Israeli occupation and their struggle for power among themselves. In January 2006, Hamas, the Islamist Palestinian faction founded in 1987, triumphed in the parliamentary elections over the long-standing Palestinian nationalist faction, Fatah. Gaza was crippled by an Israeli siege; Hamas was hindered taking the reins of power from the Palestinian authority and Fatah, its dominant faction. The struggle for power between the Palestinian authority and Hamas marked a new chapter in the history of the Palestinian national movement. So far, and despite all the splits and infighting between the different Palestinian factions, Fatah has succeeded in monopolising and centralising the use of violence, a condition that the German sociologist, Max Weber, considers essential to the creation, viability and continuity of a nation-state.[61] Yet in keeping with Fanon's insight, cited

162

above, increasingly Palestinian politics has become infected 'with the resurgence of tribal parties', a condition which led to a civil war between Fatah and Hamas in the Gaza Strip and ended in the latter controlling Gaza and the former the West Bank.

Darwish was a tireless chronicler of the Palestinian struggle. With the Palestinian infighting in the picture, his position at this stage takes another turn. It cannot be said to cancel what he stood for before but it engages in further revisionism and becomes more Freudian in its universality and appeal. The split between the Palestinian territories, of course imposed by the Israeli occupation, has been reinforced by Palestinian infighting and animosity. Two different ideologies, with different power agendas, clashed violently, each accusing the other of being less nationalistic and less trustworthy in the context of the national cause of the Palestinians. Thus the poem that Darwish published after the 2007 Hamas–Fatah power struggle demonstrated a deeper criticism of the self-idealisation and violence often indulged in by unbridled nationalism. Freud's insights, as explained by Rose, are of notable relevance here: 'Nationhood is, or can be, a religious passion. Freud may have wanted to believe that religious beliefs would go away; but instead he seems to be issuing a rather different warning—against the power of national identities, as everything in more recent times confirms, to endow themselves with the aura of the sacred.'[62] Probing a similar point in his poem, Darwish writes:

'From now on, you are another!'
'Was it necessary for us to fall from a very high height, and see our blood on our hands...to realise that we are not angels...as we thought?'

Later he declares:

'What is our need for Narcissus so long as we are Palestinians?'

And he ends the poem with:

'I do not feel ashamed of my identity, for it is still under construction. But I feel ashamed of some of what has appeared at the beginning of Ibn Khaldūn's prolegomena.'[63]

In another prose-poem, produced in the same year (2007), entitled 'From now on, you are you!', he writes:

Al-Karmilu Salām. wal-bundiqiyatu nashāz.
Al-Karmel is peace, and the rifle is an abnormality.[64]

Palestinian nationalism, namely the struggle for an independent nation-state, has been made concretely legitimate by the conditions that gave rise to it but Darwish does not let this uncomfortable reality go by without serious questioning. Palestinian blood has been for so long described as a 'red line', *khattun ahmar*, among the Palestinians themselves, but now they themselves have spilled it with intensity and hatred. 'We are not angels...as we thought?' Darwish writes: in effect, if we are not careful with our nationalism, it will consume us, indeed, it has done so. He echoes Freud in linking nationalism with narcissism when he uses the same mythical figure: Narcissus is the one whose own image fascinated and saturated himself, so that he ceased to see beyond himself. This mirrors the self-obsession of the nation-state; hence 'as we thought'. Darwish also evokes the thoughts of the great fourteenth-century Arab philosopher Ibn Khaldūn, who in his prolegomena diagnosed how *al-'Asabiyya*, strong bonds of belonging and solidarity, create and also destroy tribes, nations and groups. The *(al)-'Asabiyya* of Ibn Khaldūn, as the Moroccan philosopher Mohammad Abid al-Jābry explains, is 'a knot that is social, psychological, conscious and unconscious as well; it binds the individuals of the group; it is based on kinship; it binds them continuously, increasing and it tightens when there is an external danger that threatens these individuals, as individuals and as a group'.[65] The definition and description befits the Palestinian case, but it is the breach of solidarity among the Palestinians that Darwish is ashamed of. *Al-'Asabiyya*, which in the first Khaldunian sense means solidarity on the basis of which groups, tribes and nations are constructed, turns into extremism when infighting becomes the order of the day, and is thus a mirror for the Palestinian condition *par excellence*.

In the second poem quoted above, Darwish expands his revisionism by describing the 'rifle', once a powerful symbol of the Palestinian revolution, as an exception, unlikable, an abnormality, *nashāz*. He had said farewell to peace in its most idyllic sense, as it exists in nature, *al-Karmil*, decades ago when he left Palestine in 1970. Now in one of his last poems, aptly entitled *lā urīdu li-hadhi al-qasīda an tantahi*, 'I do not want this poem to end', Darwish collapses all boundaries of nationalism and nation-state, and endows poetry with the unqualified freedom that the Palestinians, whose aspirations he aired for four decades, are yet to attain:

> I don't want this poem ever to end
> I don't want a clear target for it
> I don't want it to be the map of an exile or a country
> I don't want this poem to end
> with a happy ending, or with death
> I want it to be as it desires to be:
> Someone else's poem, my opponent's poem, my equal's
> poem...

I want it to be the prayer of my brother and my enemy.
As if the one addressed in it is me the absent speaker.
As if the echo is my body, as if I am
You, or others, as if I am my other.[66]

This is an outcry and affirmation of freedom in its most idyllic state. There is not a hint of negativity or exclusivity in this poem towards any constructed human reality. Negativity is inherent to any liberationist nationalism, and any individual commitment to it, as Edward Said wrote of the Palestinian condition: 'The situation for us [Palestinians], since 1948, has been heavily political, in the sense that our self-expression as a people has been blocked. So since every poet in a way answers to the political and historical needs of the time in some way [...] there is an implicit relationship to the political...even in the most non-political of all forms, a relation of negativity.'[67]

Having collapsed all boundaries and exhibited such a generosity of spirit, Darwish embraces his own death, sensing in death a hint of return, a freedom from history and all its derivatives, an idea which analysts of Freud's work considered his most radical: 'the aim of all life is death', wrote Freud. 'The wish to minimize tension', wrote Cohen about Freud's idea, 'derives from a wish to extinguish it, to return to the stasis of inorganic matter from whence we came and to which we'll return: "all organic drives are conservative, are acquired historically and tend towards the restoration of an earlier state of things".'[68] Although the congruency with Freud becomes manifest later, Darwish had played with the idea of freedom in death in his 1982 *diwān*. There, he evokes the Palestinian condition in Lebanon, evoking how the Lebanese poet Khalīl Hāwi (1919–1982) had chosen his freedom by choosing suicide in the face of the Israeli invasion:

And Khalīl Hāwi does not want death despite himself,
He listens on his own wavelength
Death and freedom
He does not want death despite himself,
So let him open his poem and go...[69]

The few lines from Darwish's long poem, *Hālat hīsār*, at the end of this chapter will further show the Freudian–Darwishian harmony, in the first's prose and philosophy, and in the second's poetry and sense.

Conclusion

No theory should overwhelm the very materials it serves to illustrate. Freud, Fanon and Darwish wrote and theorised within not entirely similar historical periods, and with, to some extent, different peoples and contexts in mind. The idea that human conditions afford striking similarities as well as differences, as Ibn Khaldūn recognised centuries ago,[70] can guide an analysis of how Freud's thoughts on belonging, nationalism and nation-state, Fanon's on anti-colonial struggles, liberation and nation-state building, and Darwish's on longing, resistance and human conditions in general, overlap. At the beginning of the Palestinian national movement, Darwish is in step with Fanon's ideas about nationalism. Fanon's cardinal thought, that a struggle for liberation requires cohesion and unity that touches all the strata of the colonised society, finds reflection in Darwish's poetry at many levels. This includes mourning the martyrs, hailing the heroes and their leaders, and in effect making the land, and nature in general, a grand backdrop for the celebration and the exhibition of the deeds of the nationalist. Fanon warns poets and intellectuals who betray the calling of their people. Similarly, Darwish evokes the complementary roles played by the fighter, the martyr, the poet, the mother and nature.

But nationalism, whichever garb it wears, proves insufficient to the imagination of a free poet, who is committed to universal solidarity and what basic psychological human dispositions and aspirations teach. Freud becomes relevant in the late period of Darwish's poetry for his insights on nationalism and the nation-state. The image of Narcissus, the obsessive sacredness that nationalism assumes, the break-up of solidarity for personal and partisan interests, and the extremism that taints the nationalist all loom large in Darwish's poetry and open nationalism up to further questioning. Yet though such poetry is presumed to be free of ideological and causal shackles, it cannot exceed its historical conditions. As Darwish writes, 'The poet cannot be freed of his historical condition. But poetry provides us with a margin of freedom and a metaphorical compensation for our inability to change reality. It takes us to a higher language from the conditions that keep us from being in harmony with our human existence. And it can help us to understand the self by liberating it from what could hinder its flight in a limitless space.'[71] In Darwish's lines below it is possible to find another nod to Freud's radical suggestion that death (but not the process or the method of it) is a secret wish that all organic objects aim to fulfil. Total liberation in life is not exactly within the realm of absolute possibility, for one is born of father and mother, the seminal figures of attachment to which one returns, as Freud recognises. The poet, like any other thinker, is encased in his time and place. It is only in eternal rest that true freedom is realised:

He says, on the verge of death,
I have no more earth to lose
Free am I, close to my ultimate freedom, I hold my tomorrow in my own hands
In a few moments, I will enter my life
born free of father and mother
I will choose letters of lapis lazuli for my name.[72]

5

THE POETRY OF HAMAS

Throughout the ages, Arabic poetry has exhibited spiritual tendencies of various types, some of which are born of internal artistic energy, others of which are inspired and directed towards the evocation of definite divine entities. But ever since the rise of Islam in the early seventh century, since the Qur'an with its timeless linguistic qualities emerged as the principal holy book of the Muslims, references to God and his attributes in various contexts have become more common than ever. The language of the Qur'an and the message of Islam as a way of life embodying *Dīn* (religion) and *wa-duniyyā* (life itself) became part of the fabric of the social and political discourses of Muslims, during certain periods more intensely than others. With the emergence of Islamism in the modern period, first as a confluence of ideas and later as organised movements with religio-political agendas, poetry by Islamist figures became ever more entangled with the project of Islamisation, which essentially aims to underpin political organisation and practices with the blessing of religious legitimacy.

Following the example of many Arab politicians, particularly those from Islamic backgrounds, Hassan al-Banna (1906–1949), founder of the Muslim Brotherhood in 1928, sprinkled selected verses from the Qur'an and lines of Arabic poetry throughout his political treatises, in which he advocated a central place for Islam in the life of the *umma* (Islamic nation). One central message that his writings reiterate, particularly in *al-Rasā'il* (The letters), is that the Muslim nation must derive its inspiration from its Islamic heritage: governance draws on the spiritual as well as materialist dimensions of life in a way that Western civilisation in its modern materialistic form allegedly does not.

The hierarchy of loyalties to which Muslims are exhorted to adhere starts with God, then His prophet, and trickles down to include trusted Muslim scholars and believing parents. The rules of the modern nation-state, its legal and socio-political underpinnings, should not, according to al-Banna, overrule the Islamic ethos of loyalty to Islam or its spiritual message of monotheism. To this end, al-Banna quotes one of the early Muslims, Salmān al-Fārsī (d. 656), who, when asked about his loyalty, answered:

> *My father is Islam; I have no father except it*
> *Even if others expressed pride in Qays or Tamīm.*[1]

With its message of monotheism and unity, Islam overrode all tribal alliances to Qays or Tamim, no matter how powerful. But Islam did recognise the value of one's birthplace and community through many practices and sayings that amount to acts of faith. These can be interpreted as accepting and in fact encouraging socio-political grouping along nation-state lines, although they maintain that fundamental universalised Islamic teachings should always sanctify the conduct of governance. The mainstream modern Islamist figures and later groups set out to find ways to accommodate Islamic ideals with the modern political imperatives of actual nation-states and their interests.[2] Al-Banna was not a poet himself, but he used poetry as a source of legitimacy for his Islamist political views. Yet the second most important and influential Islamist figure in the history of the Muslim Brotherhood in Egypt, Sayyid Qutb (1906–1966), was in fact a poet among other things. Qutb is often perceived as a fundamentalist Islamist who advocated an exclusive Islamist rule that did not accommodate secular elements of any type. In several of his writings, most prominently *Milestones*, Qutb grounds his convictions in an Islamic way of life by relating it to that of the Prophet and his companions. Qutb condemned all modern systems as underpinned by nationalism, capitalism and socialism. Anything that veers away from Islam and its monotheistic core, its emphasis on loyalty to God and his Prophet's teachings should be abandoned and replaced with the rules of Shari'a, through which all spheres of life can be regulated and covered, be it economy, politics or art.[3] The sense of 'othering' and ideological self-righteousness in Qutb is extreme; we see its ramifications in poems such as that of Mushīr al-Maṣrī of Hamas.

Much of Qutb's poetry emphasises the righteousness of Islam and is ideologically critical of the West, degrading its way of living. Yet Qutb's poetry is varied, including religious, mystical and romantic sentiments. In his poem

'The new universe', he praises love and poetry and their power to renew the spirit of life:

> *Salute this new universe*
> *Sing and fill life with singing*
> *Love is its most creative act*
> *I have composed poems recalling its creativity...*
> *Through it, we live a new world*
> *So how beautiful to sing with sweet poetry.*[4]

It is interesting that Qutb would envisage a new, almost romantic, order in his poems, although he never truly defines it. For it was with the rise of nationalist Islamist movements that Islamist poetry, grounded in the politics of the followers of Islamist movements, acquired the mobilising power that nationalist poetry often assumed in the twentieth century. It is important to note that the poetry of these movements differs from that discussed in the earlier chapters. It is encapsulated within a narrower ideological strain, in which the immediacy of politics and convictions impinge on the poem. If a poem has any existential qualities, they are often accidental rather than part of a broader vision of aesthetics in which the poetic spirit is free to explore its possibilities. The poetry in this and the next chapter belongs to a tight sphere of loyalties, beginning with God and religion and extending only to the political Islamic ideology of the movement the poet adheres to or supports. In this context, ideology is defined as a set of definite and 'fulfilling' beliefs that, on the surface at least, dictate the discourses and actions that bind its followers together and render them affiliates of one group rather than another. In this sense, ideology manipulates reality, whether with language, human action or socioeconomic relations.

Against this background, this chapter will look at samples from the poetry of the Palestinian Islamic resistance movement, Hamas, and will highlight the language, themes and connotations of this poetry. The next chapter highlights the poetry of the Lebanese Shi'a movement, Hizbullah, thus demonstrating two poetic attitudes that stem from different, even if overlapping, ideological and political conditions.

The chapter is intended to shed light on poetry written by two of the most prominent leaders of Hamas who were assassinated by Israel in 2003 and 2004, namely Ibrāhīm al-Maqādmah (1952–2003) and Abd al-'Azīz al-Rantīsī (1947–2004), in addition to the poetry of the living spokesperson of Hamas, Mushīr al-Maṣrī (b. 1976). Both previous leaders, al-Maqādmah and al-Rantīsī, took part in the creation of Hamas and propagated its ideology in all fields, be they political or cultural. They used poetry to present both their experiences in Israeli prisons, and their involvement in the Palestinian struggle. Their poetry expresses sentiments that reveal deep and nuanced cultural, political and philosophical dimensions. The poetry of Hamas can be characterised as one of commitment, suffering, pain, longing, defiance and certainty. It remains poetry of ideology in so far as its language is locked into a definite world of references; the possibilities of its interpretation are limited by what it directly says.

Hamas' poetry in context[5]

The poetry of Hamas is unique in the sense that it highlights aspects of Hamas' engagement in the Palestinian struggle that have not yet been studied. Political and cultural commentaries on Islamic movements abound, but give no attention to one of the dimensions of human creativity that is most telling and illuminating with regard to identity. This chapter examines samples of what it calls 'Hamas' poetry', particularly poetry written by two of the group's most influential leaders, Abd al-'Aziz al-Rantīsī and Ibrahīm al-Maqādmah. Al-Rantīsī became the movement's leader following the assassination of the founder Ahmad Yasīn by Israel in 2004. He himself was assassinated by Israel later that year. Ibrahīm al-Maqādmah was also assassinated by Israel in 2003. Both had similar life experiences, and ultimately shared the same cruel fate, like many other Palestinian intellectuals, including the well-known novelist Ghassan Kanafani (1936–1972). The poetry under consideration is an integral part of the ideological cultural forms in which the Islamist group takes pride, and which they distribute widely.

With the rise of Islamism represented by Hamas and Islamic Jihad in Palestine, the landscape of Palestinian poetry became more nuanced.[6] Hamas, which gained popularity in the Palestinian public sphere, has had a profile of poets whose poetry is organically linked to an Islamist ideology. As it describes itself, Hamas emerged from 'the womb of the Muslim Brotherhood' in 1987. It did not take much for Hamas to become a dominant political force in Palestine, given the fragility of the mainstream secular movement, mainly Fatah during that period, having sustained heavy defeats and engaged in an unpopular peace process. In addition, Hamas' emergence coincided with rising trends of Islamism in the Arab world, which Hamas seized on through its relatively efficient charitable activities. The leaders of Hamas shaped its vision and articulated it in various cultural outlets. Poetry in this context served as a barometer of sentimental release and evocation. Hamas is an Islamic movement, and as such it could not have reconciled itself to the secular poetry that has pervaded the Palestinian cultural landscape preceding its emergence. In addition, as I have said elsewhere, Hamas 'has a short history but a dense and extensive one'.[7] Hamas' poetry came to represent this density, which its rise to power within a complex geopolitical Middle Eastern and Palestinian scene embodied. Hamas' poetry translates deeply held sentiments amongst its members and leaders. To emphasise and publicise the value of its poetry, Hamas has set itself the task of publishing poetry on a regular basis on its website and in other media outlets as well as publishing its leaders' poetry in collections. In this context, poetry serves as a medium for political mobilisation and ideological consolidation.

Al-Rantīsī's poetry comes in a collection called *Hadīth al-nafs*, 'A Conversation with the Self'; while al-Maqādmah's work comes in a collection entitled *Lā tasrqū al-shams*, 'Do not Steal the Sun'. In a memorable phrase, Taha Hussein, the eminent Egyptian intellectual, referred to the speech of the Arabs as consisting of *nathr, wa shi'r, wa Qur'ān*, 'prose, poetry and Qur'an'.[8] Thus, it is possible to find a trace of each of these mediums—prose, poetry and Qur'an—in all Arab speech or writing, and there is an interdependent relationship between these three components. Yet it is important in this respect to view Hamas' ideology as consisting of a discursive body of knowledge and practices that draw on various sources, not all of them religious. While religion inspires and consolidates its ideology, Hamas' ideology has been flexible; responsive to changes and innovations in interpretations in ways that make it a political organisation with religious roots, even if the latter, religion, as Jeroen Gunning writes in the context of Hamas, 'is used to set the parameters within which debate is acceptable'.[9]

Against this background, the poetry under consideration in this chapter documents different aspects of the poets' involvement and perspectives as Hamas leaders. It reflects their experiences in Israeli prisons, their encounters with their families while imprisoned, their responses to news from outside the prison, their imagined memories of Palestine, their admiration of their founding leader, Ahmad Yasīn. It also reflects Hamas' determination to be a major player in the conflict, in the vilification of leaders that Hamas disapproves of, and in specific incidents with Israelis. Their poetry shows firm confidence in the victory that the Divine has promised, as well as an entrenched commitment to the Palestinian struggle. These themes are integrated into their poems while foregrounding an ideal Islamic history, which Hamas reclaims and struggles to re-establish. It should be emphasised, however, that while there is a great deal of similarity within Hamas' poetry, not least in the frames of reference, there is considerable variation in the style and specific circumstances and vision of each leader. This variation is particularly evident between al-Rantīsī and al-Maqādmah's poetry. In the former's writing, the intended message is clearer, and more powerfully articulated; in the latter's, in addition to the use of free verse, the message is subtler, interspersed with imagistic references, personally seasoned. Al-Maqādmah's particular personality is present in his poems; whereas in al-Rantīsī's poetry, the degree of his commitment and his identification with a specific ideology is more intense and marked. His personality is submerged into a collective ideology he espouses and calls for, evoking its virtues at every turn of his poetry.

Since Hamas' electoral ascendance to power in 2006, there has been an abundance of poetry written by Hamas members and activists. In this context, Hamas' poetry and literature in general provides an interesting point of contrast to the hitherto prevailing secular poetry and literature in Palestine.[10] More often than not, ideologies are made of manipulated language, in which loose references are brought to account for concrete reality wider than these references suggest. Hamas has exploited the failures of the Oslo peace process and those who played a part in it in a way that puts Hamas forward as the sole torchbearer of Palestinian nationalism. As is exemplified in the poetry of its leaders and activists, it has supported the view that only a movement endowed with Islamist ideology could save Palestine from an otherwise imminent doom. Islam, in this context, is the ultimate and the archetypal point of reference, whether at joyous, sad, nostalgic, defiant or pitiful moments. It is noteworthy that Islam here gains a specific political understanding that Hamas enacts and adjusts to befit its ideological–political goals. In this respect, it is instructive to take note of Loren Lybarger's point: 'the objective of the Islamists is some form of sharī'a-based state and society within the boundaries of what is now Israel, the West Bank, and the Gaza Strip in their entirety...because ending occupation and achieving a territorially bounded state are its primary objectives, Islamism in the Palestinian setting becomes a type of religious-nationalism.'[11]

In what follows, I will elaborate on the aforementioned themes in the course of the analysis of Hamas leaders' poetry.

'Abd al-'Azīz al-Rantīsī, Hadīth an-Nafs

In the first poem in his collection, Abd 'al-Azīz al-Rantīsī calls to his son, referring to him by the 'tender' diminutive Uhaymid. He urges him to sleep well so that he as a father can be less anxious about his son's anxiety over his imprisonment by the Israelis:

O Ahmad, sleep, do not shatter my soul
Sleep where the doves rest...
My little one, these chains are a test from Allah
He has destined them as a test to people;
O, my son, do not weep
notwithstanding the shackles, I would mount the clouds...
if they separate me from my loved ones,
or shred my heart with the heads of their arrows;
if they disturb my sleep, and the sleep of my Ahmad, I would not bow to them
and I would not lay my sword down...
this is the path of those who know and fear Allah
this is the path of the immortals
the path of the great...at the frontiers, draw a smile on your lips
and be patient, my son, darkness will fade tomorrow.

At the beginning, the poet states a tragic dilemma, but while fleshing it out with some details hope and promise, often the promise of the Divine, intervene to cut short further despair and announce the inevitability of victory that God has promised to the faithful. Al-Rantīsī's poetry is written in classical Arabic language, referenced within an Islamist reading of Islamic history. It is also rhymed metric poetry, which is similar to the neo-classical poetry discussed in the first two chapters. Each complete line ends on the same letter. In this poem, the letter 'm' is used; thus we have *al-manām*, sleep; *al-hamām*, doves; *al-Ibtisām*, smile; *al-anām*, people, etc., establishing a rhythmic melody, based on what is called mono-rhyme and two-hemistich verse. This is a clear indication of respect and commitment to the old Arabic tradition of poetry writing.

The second poem of al-Rantīsī brims with ideological references, concerned with a broad position representing a worldview that he bemoans is diminishing: namely, the absence of Islamism from the public sphere. As often, the position is articulated as a problem, one that calls for sadness, but gradually optimism comes through and hope emerges to diffuse the overwhelming sadness over the absence of Islamic governance. The poem under consideration is entitled 'The prisoner said':

I called to my neighbour: what is the news?
the prisoner replied without a respite
you who are awake, let the world cry out, peace has waned
with the absence of Mohammad's doctrine [system of governance, hukm],
the rise of the banner of the infidels
hatred has become policy, and oppression has reached unbearable limits...

Al-Rantīsī enumerates serious hardships and tribulations encountered by the Palestinians in the first Intifada, and especially by Palestinian children at the hand of Israeli soldiers:

They have beaten him hard with their stick
their bones have been broken
their hands were tied,
shackled, despite their young age...
At the end of the poem, the light of the moon signals hope:
her face [probably his wife] *has brightened, foreshadowing victory*
she disappeared with her brightness and purity
and I returned to look at the moon.

Religious ideologies have firm points of reference. They are sustained by hope and promise and this is clearly manifest in al-Rantīsī's poetry, which interacts with all levels of the Palestinian struggle, whilst situating them within an Islamist conceptualisation of life. Here a comparative point can be made with secular poetry, which more often than not thrives on mysteries rather than certainties, of which religious poetry is less rife, in the sense that the point of reference are firmer and inter-communally known.[12]

In another poem, al-Rantīsī starts with himself, where he is and what he is facing. In it, he is the centre of attention, which he creates for himself, asserting his ideological and communal identity:

I am the prisoner in the Naqab
I am the valiant, O Arabs
I have prayed, worshipped God
I have defeated the oppressors; I have known rage...
embrace the religion, and the revealed message,
endowed with fortitude and robustness for all times.

Islam is meant to endow those who follow it with inner strength in order to face hardships with the certainty that they will ultimately triumph; that they are tested momentarily, and therefore should not despair. But it seems that the highest point in human sentiment is reserved for existential feelings unencumbered by ideologies. No religion seems to have sanctioned existential sentiments as such, but they have streamlined them into specific ideologies, which interpret and season them with ideological, ready-made explanations. Al-Rantīsī paints in the following poem a vivid image of his tears, rushing down his face at the thought of his son, Ahmad, and his wife:

love has engulfed my soul, as I remembered Aḥmad today
the eyes generously poured down tears
tears run down effortlessly over my face.

At the end of the poem, and after this sad and nostalgic note, al-Rantīsī offers a message of love and yearning to his wife, testifying that she is the secret of his steadfastness and resilience:

All love be to my wife
I bear witness, she is the secret of my resilience and boldness when I waver.

As often, this poem ends on an optimistic note, registering here that he has been emboldened by his wife's support. Al-Rantīsī credits his resilience to his wife.

Women have often been portrayed in Hamas' discourse as lending support to men, who are supposed to lead the struggle physically. The implicit point in such discourse is that the emotional reservoir of women has an unrivalled value. Throughout al-Rantīsī's poetry, women give unconditional love, and they embolden their husbands' views, support their fighting sons, and protect the honour of society from obtrusive liberal interventions, which could render people loose and unanswerable to norms of chastity and social conduct as constituted within Hamas' ideology. The broader implications of Hamas' discourse in so far as women are concerned is that, while men lead, women are called upon to boost the morale and safeguard the resilience of men. This idea was articulated in an interview with one of Hamas' most senior female leaders, when she referred to the way in which women are mobilised in Gaza to support Hamas' activities. Using the masculine form of the language, MP Jamila al-Shanti articulated the position of Hamas women: 'we are proud of the degree of loyalty shown by Muslim sister(s); each is willing to respond to any call made to her; she awaits any caller (*munādī*) to call to her for the sake of the Islamic project'.[13]

Another dimension revealed by the study of such highly charged ideological poetry is its latent element: what leaders of Hamas could not say in plain language could be said in poetry. Poetry here is an intimate communing with the uncensored self, in which imagination, in this case, is answerable to the poet's convictions.[14] Hamas is a territorial movement, in the sense that it restricts its socio-political and military activities to the Palestinian territories. Officially, Hamas has shied away from lending overt support to Islamists with immediate international ambitions, or those who have been vilified to an uncomfortable degree as regressive in their social and political conduct, behaviour based on Islamic grounds. In the following poem, however, al-Rantīsī draws inspiration from the fight of the Afghans against the Russian occupation of Afghanistan, seeing them as a promising Islamist-orientated example of resistance, which the Palestinians should emulate to achieve victory over the Israeli occupation. Al-Rantīsī was vocal in stating his views and more often than not in speaking his mind, a description that could not be extended to all Hamas leaders:

> *Despite the fresh wounds of Gaza, and the bullets that hit me from the Jews*
> *despite my ruined house, I salute our Afghani people*
> *In the East, in Kabul, they are establishing a state,*
> *Raising the banner of the caliphate despite the aggressors...*
> *O, our brothers, Hamas raises the same banner on the soil of our homeland*
> *the soul of your martyr will meet our martyr in heaven...*
> *a thousand salutes to you, Hikmatyar*
> *O leader of the soldiers at the frontlines*

In this poem, al-Rantīsī salutes the Afghan people for their fight against the Russians, a fight that has inspired Hamas' against the Israelis. On a macro-ideological level, Hamas resembles the Afghan resistance: the Afghans stood their ground in fighting against the Soviets and now so do Hamas against Israel—or at least, this is how Hamas wants to be seen. In his writing, the founder of the Muslim Brotherhood, Hassan al-Banna, emphasises the founding of a Caliphate as the long-term noble goal of any Islamist movement.[15] It is here that there is a visible discrepancy between the official nation-statist discourse that Hamas puts forward and the cultural and political discourse of the Caliphate system that it aspires towards.

Other poems by al-Rantīsī tackle different themes, such as the importance of education, which is given a heavy Islamic inflection as a great source of strength and hope for the resurrection of the declining Islamic *umma*. The poem under consideration highlights a Qur'anic verse concerned with education: 'Those truly fear Allah, among His servants, who have knowledge'.[16] Echoing this verse, he writes:

> *God reveres all people of knowledge*
> *and who fears God is feared by all parties*

Another poem praises the founding father of Hamas, Ahmad Yasīn. The poem asserts Yasīn's ideology and the Islamic path that he has charted for Hamas and that has been followed by many faithful followers, making Hamas the hope of the *umma*, the 'nation of Islam'. Further praise goes to the most military face of Hamas, namely Yahya Ayyāsh (1966–1996), who took an active part in suicide bombing missions in the first half of the 1990s:

> *O Yahya, today the umma would wake up*
> *erupting out of its slumber*
> *Muslims would fight to restore our past*

and our soldiers would enchant:
we are destined to the promise of God with victory for al-Qasām [the military wing
of Hamas]
you have planted the waists of men with bombs
you have written for us great lessons with your pure blood

Ayyāsh here is depicted as the archetypal fighter of Hamas, whose method
of fighting conveys selfless devotion to a cause. There is an organic relation of
solidarity between Hamas leaders, its fighters and its popular base. The leaders represent the led, and the led obey and interact with their leaders.
Mutually, they praise each other's sacrifices and highlight each other's courage. In this respect, Hamas differs from the Palestinian Fatah, which has
splintered and appears less cohesive in its discourse, representing divisions
which run throughout its cadres at all levels. Jeroen Gunning's statement
gains some aptness: 'Hamas appears to be largely capable of ensuring compliance through a combination of the political legitimacy derived from its
representative authority structures and the authority derived from being
"representatives of God".'[17]

In addition, in other poems in the same collection, *hadīth al-Nafs*,
al-Rantīsī reveals his frustrations and renders the sad moments of his life in
vivid and tender language in a way that makes some of his poems universal.
Palestine in these early poems is depicted as a binding cause for whose sake
sacrifices are inevitable. In the following lines, where we see the self speaking
inwardly to himself, the language is less ideological, and very personal:

What about you living in sadness
you desire luxury but you stumble over insurmountable hardships
what could you do if you ended up without the homeland
you want to live your youth.

In these lines, al-Rantīsī shows an existential paradox, wherein Palestinian
lives have been disrupted and deprived of normality. On the one hand, there
is the desire to live in peace and to see fulfilment of one's needs and desires,
and on the other, there are human forces that have rendered impossible the
fulfilment of these needs and desires. Confronted by this dilemma, al-Rantīsī
chooses to resist injustice. He is inspired by Islam although a grand Islamic
ambition outside a specific context is not his main motive for involvement in
the Palestinian struggle, as a reading of some of his other poems might suggest.
Al-Rantīsī's poem is moving; it offers insights into Palestinian history and his
own life, representing a dilemma at the collective and the individual level. But
it could also offer insights to a movement at its embryonic stage and the

doubts and scepticism its leaders were likely to have experienced as to their effectiveness and the likelihood of success and popularity:

Better to die than to live as a coward...
here you are rotting in a prison with no price
tomorrow you die, and you will be buried
O, pity on me, to whom you would leave your sons
and the wife you will leave behind to the wolves...
I fear that you would be exiled tomorrow
you would leave your house derelict; complain over the ruins
you search for a trusted friend
to cry for you or share the suffering with you...
I forewarn you, my son,
not to bow to an idol, not to return the sword to the sheath
go in life as you like; I would not be satisfied with such a life without struggle.

This is a moving poem, clouded by paradoxes and occasional mysteries, such as when he fears that his wife would be left to the wolves if he dies. The wolves here are depicted as representing the ultimate danger; he is understandably racked with worry over the state of his wife and his sons if he were not with them. Here, the poet depicts himself as 'the man, guardian, of the house' who should ensure the safety and security of his family. But finally, al-Rantīsī calls to his son not to give up: what is at stake deserves our sacrifices; it should not be accommodated as normal, as such an accommodation would be tantamount to surrendering to forces that deny us a life in dignity and peace.

At this juncture, it is worth providing a general summary of al-Rantīsī's poems. Al-Rantīsī deploys powerful language to present his convictions; all of them are concerned with the cause of Palestine. They all have an Islamic inflection of some kind. They refer, as we saw above, to an Islamic past that should be reclaimed; and bemoan the decline of Islamic values, as a result of un-Islamic rulers in the Arab world. His poems celebrate the steadfastness of the Palestinians, and Hamas and its leaders in particular, and pay tribute to God's protection and the support of those who follow his instructions. His poems are written in classical Arabic, and they follow the traditional Arabic Qaṣīdah 'ode' rules. There are, however, some poems by al-Rantīsī that show a communion with the self, wherein he highlights paradoxes and dilemmas in the context of his involvement in the Palestinian struggle. There is an internal conversation in these poems, taking place in light of the political conditions in which he is implicated. As such they are more personal poems.

Ibrahīm al-Maqādmah, lā tasrqū al-shams

The poetry of another influential Hamas leader, namely Ibrahīm al-Maqādmah, is written in a free-verse form. Most of his poems are meditative and inward looking, providing latent reflection on his own involvement in the Palestinian struggle, and the different travails that define it at the personal and collective levels. They also reveal the ideological background that defines his vision of the struggle and sustains him through it as well. While in Israeli prison, al-Maqādmah highlights in a moving poem his encounter with his wife and his child through the prison bars:

> *The prison bars separate us*
> *through them, I listen to her resounding voice*
> *she cries deeply, O, my father*
> *it stirs my heart with the most melodious music*
> *she leaps like a sparrow forced into a cage*
> *she rises every time yearning surges in her to Fatima*
> *she embraces my heart, tied to the prison bars*
> *tearfully, she brings news of the children*
> *she shows pride in her brothers growing older*
> *of her uncles, enveloping her with care, never faltering in supporting her*
> *O Fatima, the blossoming spring of the heart.*

There is an intense and tender listing of feelings that the poet has observed in his visitors, his wife and his daughter; it offers a mutual yearning for the father to be with his family and his family to be with him. The bars through which they meet part them from each other, setting in motion sentiments of longing. But they use the time allowed to them to communicate by exchanging news, particularly the visitors' news, as life outside prison is more dynamic and prone to changes than life inside prison. A few lines after the excerpt translated above, al-Maqādmah highlights that this suffering and the pain of his incarceration in prison are not for nothing:

> 'Be patient,' he calls to his daughter, 'the pain decreases [is worth it] if you fight for a noble goal'

His longing for his daughter reaches a peak, before reassuringly declaring at the end of the poem that we are set to triumph:

> *Her soul touches my soul...*
> *My God, I have come to you obedient and humbled*
> *and I will not compromise* [or give up], *preserve the essence of my heart...*
> *my little daughter, be certain, be confident of righteousness and victory,*
> *no matter how bleak the moment is.*

Most of al-Maqādmah's poems echo a sense of longing for his family as well as a sense of defiance. In fact, it is characteristic of Hamas' poetry that it is poetry of defiance *par excellence*. This type of defiance comes across as divinely inspired, and as such it cannot be broken or undermined. We saw this in the first poem by al-Rantīsī above, and we see it here. Despite the personal despair, loss and disturbance they experience as a result of their direct involvement in the Palestinian struggle, they remain defiant and hold on to their positions. Sheer defiance characterises the leaders of Hamas, most of whom had undergone extreme suffering of some sort. They remained manifestly defiant through the hardest of times: whether in Marj al-zuhūr, where Israel deported Hamas leaders and kept them stranded in a no-man's-land between Israel and Lebanon in 1992, or in Israeli prisons, or later when they were threatened by Israeli bombing.

In the following poem, al-Maqādmah enumerates a list of harsh measures to which he was subjected in Israeli prisons, but he issues a declaration of defiance, calling the punishments useless as far as the Israeli objectives are concerned, in their attempt to break his will or his hold on his principles and his fight for his beliefs:

> *The night approaches and they knock on the locked door*
> *my pulsing heart: bring your chains, bring your machine guns, your bombs*
> *try all the methods of torture, do not be ashamed*
> *deport my family to wherever you want...*
> *all the methods of torture are in vain...*
> *pour the coldest of water on me in the coldest of weathers...*
> *threaten as you like*
> *torture as you like*
> *I prepare for tomorrow; for the bright future.*

Defiance in this poem is evident, alongside the certainty of a bright future. Certainty of victory in Hamas' discourse is a cornerstone concept. It is a movement that derives its ideology from divine sources, '*Harakah rabbāniyya*', as Hamas describes itself. Longing is a common sentiment in Arabic poetry in the twentieth century, and Palestinian poetry in particular. As Jayyusi writes, 'it is perhaps possible to say that Palestinian poetry is the poetry of longing par excellence, of an external dream of return and rebirth'.[18]

In al-Rantīsī's poetry and also in Ibrahīm al-Maqādmah's, the bright future which awaits the Islamic movement entails the liberation of all of Palestine from Israel and the Israeli occupation. It entails an Islamic state of sorts, wherein the Qur'an and the discourse of the Prophet serve as the underpinnings of the law and the regulations of that state. In Hamas' discourse in general, there is a kernel of pragmatism, in the sense of accepting a two-state solution with Israel, and accommodating the coexistence of secular forces and factions within an Islamic society. But perhaps that accommodation is more functionalist, for pragmatic reasons. So long as the Islamic state is not in a powerful position, and not in command of virtual authority that would allow it to impose its will on others, it has to accommodate them. This position is clarified and explained from a religious point of view by a prominent Hamas leader, namely Mushīr al-Masrī, in his book *Participation in Political Life in the Context of Contemporary Regimes*. Within the grand scheme of Hamas' ideology, an independent Palestinian state is only a stepping stone towards the realisation of a larger Islamic polity that would encapsulate territories larger than Palestine, and ultimately would culminate in an Islamic Caliphate. Thus, both poets bemoan the collapse of a grand Islamic system of governance, a Caliphate. As such, they vow to carry on the struggle until that state is established; Ibrāhīm al-Maqādmah writes in his poem 'Do not steal the sun':

> For the sake of Islam, we struggle
> We stand by Islam, and we do not fear the slaves [meaning those who submit to a rule other than the rule of Islam]

And it is in this context that their struggle is characterised by defiance and certainty that the goal will be achieved. Though Hamas' wishes and visions have grand overtones in terms of Islamic governance and authority, its leaders remain committed to Palestinian independence and sovereignty first and foremost.

But as the Hamas leaders struggle to attain their goal, they convey entrenched suffering, longing and hope. Al-Maqādmah highlights his encounter with his family while in prison in another poem, an encounter that made him reflect introspectively on human sentiments and their formation:

> Two minutes or three
> do not dream of other than these minutes
> how sweet the intense emotions are...
> how strange the intense pain is
> how saturated with meaning the longing is

Other poems establish a soliloquy, whereby the poet compensates for his separation from his fellow prisoner friend by highlighting that he has not forgotten him, that they are connected, and that their souls migrate like birds:

> How strange your soul Shraytah is, traversing in my being
> my soul travels between your prison and mine

Hamas' poetry, as typified through al-Maqādmah's verse, shows us leaders selflessly devoted to a cause they believe in. This selfless devotion anticipates extreme dangers, including death:

With death, we make the dawn of tomorrow
through our wounds, and the troves of martyrs,
the flower of al-haqq [righteousness] *would blossom*

But there are times when the pain of the poet being separate from his family, is too great:

We perish like a plant in the desert
I died like a plant in the desert
shall I cry over you [his son]? Tears would burn me
shall I forget you? The air would forget me
I take refuge in the Divine, the God of the universe to console me

When it comes to his family, his sons, his longing for them is deep:

you are there
you attract my shattered heart
you burn it, shred what is left of it into pieces, the moon burns

As his son cries in front of him, he calls to him to halt his tears:

Preserve your tears
they burn me, my vision

In this poem, invested with pain, the poet recollects the memory of his child's death and that he could not attend his funeral and lay him to rest:

O, the mother of Ahmad [his wife]: *this is a wedding for Ahmad*
the dream gets bigger, as Ahmad gets older
the more he hurls stones at the soldiers
whenever he is wounded
when he screams in the faces of the soldiers:
the army of Muhammad will return, will return.

What we see in this poem again is a sense of extreme pain and hardship diffused by the promise of the Divine. After the evocation of fire as a sign of despair and pain, the poet evokes the sea, as a sign or symbol of healing; the scene of the sea stretches the imagination and calls for contemplation:

O sea, in youth and old age I adored you
I adored your water and your sand
I have not feared you, was not awed by you
I exchange love with you
can lovers betray?
Do they need to be haunted by a ghost of revenge?

This comes as a moment of liberation, in which beautiful 'ideology-free' lines of poetry flow unimpeded by ideological shackles that might have suggested an explicit declaration of love in romantic and existential terms. The poet declares his love for the sea, lets his words slide down a slope of emotions, culminating in the final painful thought. His separation from his wife and his family, his longing to be with them and the pain that he experiences all stoke his passion for revenge on those who caused him this emotional deprivation. But he is asking about revenge rather than declaring that he will avenge both his son's death and his enforced separation from his family.

Other poems by al-Maqādmah highlight the same issues that al-Rantīsī tackles, reflecting a collective concern and shared perspectives. The space given to Yahya Ayyāsh in the poetry of Hamas is greater than any military leader in the history of Hamas. The elevation of Ayyāsh constitutes part of 'a tradition of adulation in Arabic poetry for the hero'. As Jayyusi writes, 'the adulation of the hero, so prevalent in the old poetry, remains alive today whether the hero is a valiant freedom fighter and seeker of justice who continually faces death or the poet himself who speaks as a teacher, leader and prophet, as one who bears a great and sacred responsibility on his shoulders and who suffers and is roused to anger because of other people's wickedness or sloth'.[19] None has received as much reverence and adoration as the *muhandis*, 'the Engineer', Ayyāsh, who moved between the West Bank (the village of Rafāt near Nablus) to Gaza to organise and direct attacks and supervise them with deadly effect on the Israelis. Ayyāsh advanced the position of Hamas at a time when the Palestinians felt that he addressed their vulnerability by standing up to Israel with its powerful military machinery and its destructive forces. But ultimately the suicide missions he masterminded tainted the morality of the Palestinian cause with their indiscriminate and callous nature in the eyes of many Palestinians, as well as in the eyes of many in the world. To this end, Ayyāsh represents a case of callousness and mindlessness, which the occupying Israeli forces initiated and fostered by their aggressive and deadly attacks over many years against the Palestinians. Ayyāsh is central to the cruel formula of violent action and reaction ('a principle of reciprocity', as Khaled Hroub calls it, as perceived by Hamas).[20] Ayyāsh's supervision of many suicide missions inside Israel proved deadly to Israelis, but made him a hero among some Palestinians, chiefly Hamas affiliates, who saw in his selfless devotion to the struggle and his ability to 'strike back' an answer to their helplessness and defencelessness in the face of such a powerful machinery of arms and armaments. Al-Maqādmah celebrates Ayyāsh's life, highlighting his heroism and his unique militant mark. Powerfully and nostalgically, al-Maqādmah addresses Ayyāsh:

Your bombs have been launched, clearing the clouds away from the sun
Ayyāsh, you are the light in a world in which fog prevails
Ayyāsh, you are the tiger who takes on the roaming dogs
Spread your light, this people no longer endures torment
finish off our misery [bomb it], *open ways to our sweet wishes*
Ayyāsh, do not leave and leave our dream to ravenous wolves.

This is another powerful poem; one that lays on the shoulder of one fighter much of the fighting's burden, and equally much hope and confidence. There is pain and agony in this poem over Ayyāsh's demise. The poet sees in Ayyāsh the perfect embodiment of a struggler, an archetypal symbol of hope and heroism.

Much of the world, if not the entire world, is seen through Ayyāsh's eyes in this first stanza of the poem. There is a mutual identification with him and his vision. One's world is what one experiences and makes of it. Al-Maqādmah, just like the Palestinians, is forced into seeing the world through bitter experiences, which collectively have been painful and unyieldingly frustrating. But more often than not, hope is derived from the most painful of conditions. That is what the message of the poem's second stanza best embodies:

Ayyāsh, you are alive, despite the fact that you are covered with earth
we have signs of you in the discourse of the Prophet and the book [the Qur'an]
others are dead in spirit, even if they yield positions and ranks
Ayyāsh, you are the true symbol in the face of hardships
others are fake, when we scrutinise them we discover a mirage
Ayyāsh, do not leave, Goldstein awaits an answer
wombs would not be sterilised after you to produce a thousand fighters...
bombs and bullets are our means and they are the fuel of our discourse
negotiations and compromises have rubbished our rights, and demeaned them...

These lines contain a number of points and messages, ones that have been represented in much of Hamas' discourse and in many of Hamas' poems, including al-Rantīsī's. There is a clear criticism of those who engaged in peace negotiations with Israel, to which Hamas has been vocally opposed. Those, meaning the Palestinian authority leaders, are described as 'fake', inauthentic, and inadequate for the mission of liberation. Secondly, there is the name Goldstein, the extremist who massacred many Palestinians in Hebron whilst they were conducting dawn prayers in 1994.[21] Ayyāsh reacted to such extremism and brutality with suicide bombings, which left many Israelis dead and others injured. But al-Maqādmah does not let up, stating in effect that Hamas would produce more like Ayyāsh, who would strike back and inflict as much damage, all on the way to independence and an Islamic state whose constitution and conduct would be inspired by the Qur'an and the discourse of the Prophet, as indicated at the beginning of the poem.

In total, it can be said that Hamas' poetry is an optimistic poetry; it is confident of victory, and in this sense it is no different to other ideological poetry. Jayyusi has described it aptly: 'the ideological poets, the Marxists and the nationalists, were the more optimistic of the avant-garde poets, reflecting a deep faith in the possibility of human struggle to bring about the final triumph of optimism and faith, of strength and determination'.[22] But whereas the Marxists and the nationalists drew for optimism and determination on historical myths, Greek, Christian and others, universalising and secularising them, the Islamists drew on Islamic figures, battles and other Islamic sources, and imbued them with mythological reverence. Al-Maqādmah refers to Bilāl, the caller to prayer who was appointed by the Prophet, enduring in the process extreme acts of torture from those who opposed the Prophet and his message: *teach me, Bilāl of the good, teach me.*

In the last poem of this collection by al-Maqādmah, the title of the poem represents a condensed version of much that makes up his and his movement's worldview, which sees life as a passage to the afterlife, hence 'A conversation at the gates of heaven'. In this imagined conversation, the poet evokes the theme of the suicide bomber who chooses the afterlife over life:

He walks uprightly
clear in his vision
his steps are measured and his conscience is at rest
he anticipates his fate...
if he misses out on leisure in life, there is ultimate leisure and beauty in heaven...
after Dayr Yasīn, Qibyia, Shatīla, after Qana [massacres committed against the Palestinians by Israel at different points in their modern history]
how much blood has been spilled
there are no more innocents...
after the veto of uncle Sam, there are no innocents any more
there is no innocence in life...
we were thrown out naked
vengeance would not die any one day
the blood of my loved ones will not be water...

This is a very ideologically motivated poem, based on the principle of 'an eye for an eye'. There is desperation, certainty and defiance. The grievances of the Islamist movements in Palestine, and perhaps elsewhere, can be understood in light of the fact that they include people who suffered extreme injustices, who internalised that suffering and as a result are willing to sacrifice their own lives to rectify these injustices. Also, it is a poem that engages with international politics, and especially with American politics in the region. It suggests that they turn a blind eye to Palestinian rights and suffering, and encourage Israel in its path of colonisation of Palestinian land and resources. Such politics creates and normalises violent sentiments of vengeance, when innocence and peace should be the norm.

But perhaps another dimension to this last stanza can be identified through analogy. The great Palestinian poet Mahmoud Darwish has a line that evokes the afterlife, based on the Qur'anic and religious stories that describe it. Darwish's line, *Fawdā 'alā bāb al-qiyyāmah*, 'chaos at the gate of resurrection', is mysterious, less sure of the aftermath of life, no 'conversation' as we see in al-Maqādmah's poem, but 'chaos'. There is a marked difference. Poetry could be impregnated with worldviews, with philosophies. Palestinian poets differ and their poetry can be seen in different lights and from different perspectives; al-Maqādmah and al-Rantīsī's poetry represents more or less unified dimensions within a plural Arab culture of communication, in which differences in poetry could be read as marking different philosophies, different ways of seeing, whilst still drawing on the same sources and accruing to them different meanings and significations.

After 2000

Another Hamas leader who writes poetry and often performs it before crowds is Mushīr al-Masrī. Al-Masrī is a powerful speaker within Hamas, and is one of its rising young leaders. He includes poetry in his speeches which more often than not praise Hamas, its ideological stances and its Islamic values, values which he views Hamas as exemplifying. Unlike al-Rantīsī and al-Maqādmah, who founded Hamas, al-Masrī espoused its ideology at a young age at the Islamic University in Gaza, where he became an active member of Hamas. Over time, he became one of its leading theologians, putting forward in his political writings religious justifications for Hamas and indeed the political conduct and convictions of the wider Muslim Brotherhood movement. In the poem under consideration, al-Masrī uses intense metaphoric language to praise one of the young Hamas suicide bombers, namely Said al-Ḥutarī (1979–2001), who detonated himself in a nightclub in Israel and caused several fatalities and injuries. The poem conveys ideological closure. The only righteous path for Palestinian politics is the one he puts forward and which Hamas represents. Philosophically, the other—the Palestinian authority and its backbone organisation, Fatah, or any other secular force—is totally excluded; all others are negatively portrayed. It represents an extreme version of Islamism, which is usually more associated with al-Qāʾidah than Hamas. Throughout its history, Hamas has shown pragmatism and promulgated a nation-state discourse rather than a universalised Islamist one. Al-Maṣrī addresses the suicide bomber, Said al-Ḥutarī, in the first stanza of the poem as follows:

> O, you who burn me with your pure fire...take your share from my fire
> My exploding rockets had thundered upon you...and my flashes glittered
> Take these shares...take them off the old debt
> I am a deaf rock from the fire at the bottom of the abyss
> I have rocketed the inhabitants of hell with it...with a ballista
> Write down my name: [Said]... And thousands are on the way
> The daylight faded...so I do not sense sunset or sunrise
> My work involves all explosives... my rights have been lost...

Mushīr al-Masrī was born in 1978 in Gaza. His brother, Fāris al-Masrī, was assassinated by Israel during the second Palestinian Intifada. His Masters thesis, referred to above, which has become an important reference for Islamic movements, is entitled *The Participation of Islamic Movements in Political Life in Light of the Current Governing Regimes*. It offers insight into the thinking of the Islamist movements as well as their worldview in general. Relying on major texts from the Islamic tradition as well as modern Islamist writings, and using linguistic and textual definition and analysis, al-Masrī reinforces the view that governance belongs to God. It should be sanctioned through religious commandments and rules; any political programme must be entrusted around the basic premise that religious legitimacy is central. In the book, Masrī suggests that it is permissible for Islamic movements to participate in politics alongside secular movements such as the Palestinian Fatah. But such participation seems tactical and interest-driven. So long as Islamic movements do not possess enough power to unseat their secular opponents and govern in accordance with the imperatives of Islamic rule, they can join others and form coalitions. Yet once they are in a position of power and able to preserve it, then they should not be party to a secular political structure, as secularism is grounded in man-made paradigms whereas governance should be sanctioned by God and grounded in a system that includes appreciation of an afterlife. The poem in question, however, should not be taken as a translation of Hamas' ideology as outlined by Masrī in his aforementioned book. The poem goes beyond that in the utter gloominess of violence and narrowness it projects; but its political context should be accounted for. After 2000, Israel employed colossal violence against Palestinians in general, and the Gaza Strip specifically, afflicting it with a humanitarian crisis. The poem is shot through with the spirit of revenge, referencing the base and inhumane. The poem suggests that moments of violent intensity heighten hatred, normalise it and render the image of the Other as less than human. It confirms the dangerous one-sidedness of human emotions once the Other is totally excluded from the purview of the self; and that violence can assume a logic of its own which, if unchecked, becomes its own reality:

> Tighten my belt which is filled with bitter death
> Add ten bombs to it, for today is the day of revenge
> I will grill with its fire those who have built (the Knesset) from my bones
> With this belt, the sun dawns from the deepest dark
> This is my able horse...I pat its forehead with love
> A hero who rid the earth of jinni before he was weaned
> He speaks hell when he neighs amidst the herd...without a bridle
> I will remain a ghost for Izz ad-din...for he has been moulded from granite
> Like a mountain, standing on the bloodsucker, the illegitimate son.

The glorification of suicide bombing is absolute in this poem. In effect, the poet creates an image of the hell in which al-Masri wants al-Ḥutarī to consign his enemies, whereas the suicide bomber is given heaven with all its imagined comforts, riches and rewards. It is the sentiment of total revenge that governs the logic of the suicide bomber here, and closes any other options for resistance and struggle. The poem as a whole, with its narrowness and violent severity, violates the basic existence of the other, in her or his existential sense. It is indeed lamentable that suicide bombing has become such a prominent method of fighting, aligned with such narrow ideological and vengeful poetry that praises the act in certain parts of the Arab world. In this context, it is illuminating to quote the French philosopher Levinas who is a pioneer in writing about the concept of 'the Other' in philosophy: 'I find myself facing the other. He is neither a cultural signification nor a simple given. He is, primordially, sense...because only through him can a phenomenon such as signification introduce itself, of itself, into being.'[23] It is the loss of the primary human sense towards the other that makes this poem dark.

Meanwhile, as we saw throughout this chapter, Hamas' poetry is varied. Within the spectrum of Palestinian poetry, which reflected several humanist concerns, as was discussed in the context of Darwish's poetry, Hamas' poetry is popular among Hamas' constituency, which is considerable enough; and it fluctuates as the political conditions themselves change. Later poetry related to Hamas came to echo the advanced weaponry and the almost exclusive power that Hamas possesses in Gaza, as well as its resistance to Israel's cruel siege and devastating wars against Gaza.

Conclusion

This chapter has reflected a position taken in a previous publication,[24] where I suggested that there is a culture of communication in each society, born of linguistic and cultural integration. The phrase 'culture of communication' compels us to look at how much of the past is in the present, in terms of the discourses of individuals and communities. It allows us to measure and discuss diversity of opinions and philosophies among people with a shared culture of communication, rather than see cultures in unqualified, narrow and categorical terms. It was seen in this chapter that poetry has endured as a major component of the Arab culture of communication, continuing to be the highest form of expression and evocation, and to be used by various political groups to articulate their ideologies as well as aesthetics; they draw on a rich literary and historical background, some more metaphorically and others more literally.

The poetry of Hamas is notable for its traditional and classical nature, for its immersion in the moment in a way that makes any existential aspects accidental rather than an integral part of its epistemology. It is poetry that grew out of colonial conditions like those that once afflicted Algeria, as was explained in the second chapter. It represents one facet of Palestinian nationalism, with roots in an Islamist ideology. Such ideology is self-sufficient in its political and artistic sense. While it is driven by a desire for liberation from the Israeli occupation, it is also animated by the desire for an inclusive Islamic order. Hamas, and indeed its poetry, do however reflect diversity among its affiliates. It adapts to modernist trends as much as it adapts to political conditions, even if it remains rooted in Islamic principles that guide its relations with other political forces.

It is against this background that Hamas' poetry can be understood. I highlighted several aspects that reflect Hamas' ideology and more generally show the interweaving of the personal and the political in particular political and historical contexts. The Palestinian experience of dispossession, Israeli occupation and continued oppression should be viewed as the overarching mould within which cultural forms of expression of the Palestinian experience should be understood. Though it is true to say that poetry is a milieu for individual expression, whereby the individual is in communion with him or her self, this cannot be totally divorced from the political and historical contexts. Poetry, in this sense, is both individual and collective, and it is because of this inter-weaving that I referred to the above poems as 'the poetry of Hamas', reflecting shared political affiliation, experiences and vision.

The poetry of ʿAbd al-ʿAzīz al-Rantīsī and Ibrahīm al-Maqādmah portray aspects of life with which many Palestinians identify. The prison is one experience with which many Palestinians identify: a place of suffering, injustice as well as recollection, reflection, defiance and hope, giving rise to poetry loaded with ideological and political meanings but also interspersed with existential inflections for people involved in a collective struggle at great personal cost. Their families are at the centre of their concern, but the broader anxiety is Palestine under oppressive occupation. Al-Rantīsī's, al-Maqādmah's and al-Masrī's ideology compel them to see the solution in an Islamic way of life. Islam operates here as a window of hope and assurance that this state of oppressive affairs is momentary and could end in victory for those who are determined to fight to rectify injustices done to them and their homeland.

The next chapter looks at the poetry of the Lebanese Shiʿa movement Hizbullah and traces its origins, meanings and contexts.

6

THE POETRY OF HIZBULLAH

Hizbullah began as an Islamist resistance movement in 1982, founded to address the social and political needs of the deprived Shiʿas who were under-represented in the sectarian Lebanese political system. The poetry of or about Hizbullah is diverse and can be broadly defined as poetry authored by Arab poets, writers, supporters and sympathisers as well as ordinary people who respond deeply to the events in which Hizbullah is a central player, and who are embraced by Hizbullah either formally or informally. Though Hizbullah's poetry interacts with various historical events and serves to mark them, it is fluid and reiterative in its inclusion of several themes and reference points representative of both Hizbullah's ideology and day-to-day political and social dynamics. In this respect, the themes of resistance, connectedness and conti-nuity of past glories, heroism, certainty of victory, defiance and patience are notable as constant poetic preoccupations. These themes were substantiated by Arab poets who embraced Hizbullah and its ideology, suggesting that poetry, as a form of discourse, reflects a pan-Arab solidarity with Hizbullah that is manifested in the repetition of discourses of connection and loyalty to the group through various poetic creations that represent one socio-political faction and reality rather than another.[1]

Poetry as political practice

The argument this chapter puts forward and illustrates is that the role of poetry, particularly political poetry of the type discussed here, is complementary to other forms of Hizbullah's communication practices. In the case of Hizbullah, poetry serves to solidify and constitute ideologies, hail Hizbullah leaders, fighters and affiliates, and enhance their appeal and authenticity.[2] Poetry is generally perceived as a residue of past authenticity, underlining the authority and legitimacy of those who use and embrace it, and this aspect comes across in the writings and speeches of Shi'ite pioneers whose ideas and activities gave rise to the organised political community epitomised in Hizbullah today, including Musa al-Sadr, the founder of the Movement of the Deprived, who disappeared in 1978 in the Libyan desert. Al-Sadr's conception of culture is worth noting here. For him, culture is 'what connects heaven and earth, life and the afterlife, the individual alone and the society with God... Thus culture acquires divinity, holiness and power, and in this, it satisfies all the feelings of human beings.'[3] Such an organic and holistic view of culture, according to Joseph al-Agha, has increasingly become symptomatic of Hizbullah as it operates and competes with other political players within Lebanon, and in its 'treatment of Islam as a cultural and social force', underlining that Hizbullah seeks to be, in effect, 'an existential necessity'.[4] It is in this sense that Hizbullah's poetry and the poetry associated with it are integral to the group's worldview of rootedness within its socio-political conditions. In other words, it serves as an integral part of its political communicative reservoir, partaking in all its political and existential aspects,[5] or as an extension— another level of communication that bestows on its members and the wider Shi'ite community in Lebanon a sense of authenticity and rootedness.

Like other political actors in the Middle East who fitted poets within their circles and within state structures to legitimise and authenticate their political programmes,[6] Hizbullah embraced poets within its ranks to project a comprehensive image of itself. To this end, throughout its history but particularly after the 2006 war with Israel, Hizbullah staged poetry festivals such as the 'Festival of the Poetry of Resistance', *mahrajān al-shi'r al-muqāwwim*, and published many poems. With its popularity increasing, Hizbullah began recording and archiving poetry associated with both itself and its ideology, using high-quality CDs and DVDs and distributing them through its media outlets. Thus, though poetry is often fluid and related to early traditions, it can also be used politically in intentional and calculated ways, and can be incorporated into communication practices and strategies, particularly when it is manipulated to lend legitimacy to political discourses and when the poets in question fit with or embrace a particular political ideology.

It is important to acknowledge the presence of Iran and its particular political ideology within Hizbullah's poetry, which projects the group as located in both Arab and Iranian cultures. It is also worth noting that Hizbullah's loyalties and alliances are varied, reflecting its hybrid identity: Hizbullah is an Arab Lebanese party, rooted in its Arab environment, yet it is also firmly connected to Iran, with its distinct literary and cultural tradition, providing it with an intricate web of links and a rich source of cultural and political outputs in terms of literature and discourse.[7] As such, it is a party empowered by an extensive reach of knowledge, which makes its ideology both structured and diverse in content, which merits interpretation in its own right. The hermeneutic approach adopted by the French philosopher Paul Ricoeur and referred to as 'semiotic, interpretive' by Clifford Geertz helps engage with the poetry of Hizbullah not only as a reflective facet of ideology but also as a system of knowledge and affectation underlined by socio-political conditions encompassing the identity of the individuals and group in question. As Geertz argues, 'the whole point of a semiotic approach to culture is...to aid us in gaining access to the conceptual world in which our subjects live so that we can, in some extended sense of the term, converse with them.'[8] With this in mind, the chapter now turns to an analysis of the poetry itself.

Beginnings in oaths and sacrifice

Every member of Hizbullah is initiated to the party with a pledge, *qasam*, which is poetic in nature and congruent with nationalist and patriotic oaths of allegiance to the party and its ideology, thus forming what Foucault implies to be acts of initiation in discourse.[9] There are two main oaths of allegiance, reflecting different periods of Hizbullah's history and referring to different leaders. The first oath relates to the period of resistance beginning in the 1980s and continuing until the 1990s, and the second represents the period from 2000 onwards, when Hizbullah's cultural and political capital in the Arab world expanded. Broadly speaking, in the first period, Hizbullah poetry is rooted in its Shi'ite milieu and Iranian connections; in the second, it is broadened to include wider Arab audiences. In the latter period, Hizbullah's identity became more fluid, with many well-known Arab poets hailing Hizbullah and celebrating its military achievements. In return, Hizbullah gave those poets platforms at poetry festivals, in publications and through media exposure, thus playing the role of the patron once preserved for the Sultan and later for various Arab leaders, such as Saddam Hussein, who included poets within the hegemonic cultural apparatuses of the state. Arab poets who embrace Hizbullah, however, live in various Arab countries with their own cultures and authorities, and therefore their relation to Hizbullah is affinitive rather than one bound to rulers by structures of power.

The first oath this chapter refers to is as follows:

> In the name of Mecca and Galilee with the mount
> Martyrdom has eternally been our dream
> And our slogan is 'let us begin the noblest of work'
> For Glory, O Amal!

And the second reads:

> In the name of the blood of the stolen Jerusalem
> We have kept dignity, and we will not forget
> Khyber and the grand battle of Badr
> We will remain faithful to the oath, O Nasrallah!

The author of the first oath is unknown, but the oath is still in use as a relic from the past, while the second is more formalised and is used by Hizbullah members and supporters when they pledge allegiance and loyalty to the move-ment on formal occasions, in public rallies and in popular gatherings.[10] Both oaths represent continuity, but also the evolution of the party. The first oath refers to the revered leader Musa al-Sadr when evoking 'O Amal!' Al-Sadr had been a central figure in the revival of the Shi'ite in Lebanon and the formation of Amal before disappearing in 1978.[11] The second oath is sealed with the evocation 'O Nasrallah!', a reference to the current and longest-serving leader Hassan Nasrallah. Both oaths register important points about Hizbullah's identity and its rootedness in a wider realm of convictions that transcend political calculations. Hizbullah has always maintained its Islamist identity, while linking itself to important Arab causes and emotional sites, such as Mecca, the site of Islam, and Palestine. Jerusalem also figures prominently in much of Hizbullah's discourses and actions. Both oaths emphasise Hizbullah's pan-Arab identity, thus dispelling suggestions that it is Shi'ite-centred in its worldview and concerns. It is beyond the scope of this chapter to attempt to distil all the dimensions entailed in the aforementioned oaths. Nevertheless, it is noteworthy that the first highlights the commitments of Hizbullah mem-bers to fight the Israeli occupation of Lebanon, which continued in Lebanon from 1982 until 2000; but the statement 'that martyrdom has eternally been our dream' asserts the Shi'ite identity of Hizbullah in the importance of sac-rifice/martyrdom and the rejection of humiliation, which is what the seminal figure in Shi'ite history, Imam Ali's son Hussein, stood for in the battle of Karbala (AD 680).[12] For Hizbullah, sacrifice and martyrdom are aspects of cardinal importance as a means of liberation from the Israeli occupation. In the second oath, it is the figure of Hassan Nasrallah that dominates. Again, the grand battles of Islam are evoked to reassure the fighters that the victories and glories of old battles will be repeated in the present. The first oath in particular is characteristic of the early period of Hizbullah's history, in which various discourses, including poetry, focused on reassuring and emphasising old beliefs connected to the Shi'ite faith, while reaffirming the centrality of resistance and sacrifice. It was during the 1980s and 1990s that several Lebanese Shi'ite poets and a few others interacted with the ideology of the movement and produced poems that were memorised and repeatedly recited by Hizbullah members and within Shi'ite circles. In this context, one can see these recitals and interactions as active communication practices that helped reinforce Hizbullah's identity and appeal. Resistance as manifest in poetry highlights the collective endeavour and spirit of the community, which is emphasised in the writings of the leaders of Hizbullah, such as those of Naim Qassem.[13] The ideological resonance of the oaths and the cyclical view of history they maintain highlight the importance of poetry as an essential form of communication that serves to authenticate Hizbullah's identity. Furthermore, it is the language of such poetry that constitutes, along with other language forms, the raw materials of ideology and faith, which this chapter aims to explore further.

The seeds of Hizbullah's poetry

Hizbullah's poetry appeared initially in the newspaper al-'Ahd, Hizbullah's main journalistic outlet throughout the 1980s and much of the 1990s. The paper included a cultural supplement that published poems, cultural and historical reflections on the life of the Prophet Mohammad or the first community of the Shi'ites,[14] advertisements for cultural activities, and postulations. In that period, as well as later, political mobilisation went hand in hand with cultural activities that substantiated political objectives and helped give them historical legitimacy. Al-'Ahd regularly published poems and announcements for upcoming poetry evenings, thus reaching out to its intended audiences and calling for them to participate. Such poems addressed resistance, and more often than not included references to particular figures or persons who fell in the course of fighting with the Israeli occupation. The bulk of the poetry published in the early editions of al-'Ahd refers to martyrs and martyrdom as essential ideals and practices, and is grounded in the Shi'ite faith and its emphasis on endurance and sacrifice as constituted in the first community of Shi'ites in Islam, and most significantly represented in the figures of 'Ali and Hussein.[15]

Two incidents in the 1980s that are represented in such poetry are the assassination of the Shi'ite leader Ragheb Harb on 16 February 1984 and the death of Iran's leader Ayatollah Ruhollah Khomeini on 3 June 1989. Their passing is extensively commemorated and portrayed as a turning point in history. Ragheb Harb is described as 'the son of Khomeini',[16] while a poem by Musa Mukhs, who is referred to in the newspaper as a friend of Harb's, commemorates his death as follows:

> *At the forefront*
> *We are used to you, the pioneer of Shari'a, to be at the front*
> *Always in the path of righteousness as a guiding torch...*
> *That's how the heroes with firm positions undertake*
> *The strenuous journey of fear*
> *That's how it was with Moses...and this is what Jesus, the Messiah, said:*
> *The prophets of God are a permanent voice that returns...*
> *That's how the religion of Mohammad was firmly established*
> *As a nation that witnesses the renewal of each period*
> *That's how Hussein said it, heightening the determination of soldiers,*
> *That's how Khomeini shook the moving earth*
> *That's how Ragheb drew the horizons*
> *With the blood of the heart and verses full of good omens...*[17]

The message is one of continuity of a path of sacrifice that was started by prophets and historical figures, such as Moses, Jesus, Mohammad, Hussein and Khomeini, and continued with the martyrdom of Ragheb Harb. The poet Musa Mukhs invokes earlier historical characters whose sacrifices served as examples of courage and determination buttressed by a sense of righteousness. Sacrifice is a key theme in Hizbullah's poetry and is also to be found in the poetry commemorating the death of Khomeini, whose passing was widely lamented in *al-'Ahd*. Khomeini is portrayed as a milestone character whose death imbues the entire world with sadness and regret. In much of the writing devoted to him, prose is mixed with poetry in a way that invokes limitless lamentation over Khomeini's death. In one such poem, which is characteristic of Shi'ite commemoration practices called *latmiyaat'* (lamentations), with a rhapsodic undertone of descent into an overwhelming sorrow and grief, the anonymous poet says:

> *Our salvation, where have you gone?*
> *Our protector, where have you gone?*
> *You left us early...quickly...and left us...*

You left us orphaned...perplexed...why...
Why, O Imam?
With whom have you left us?

Who are we without you? Why us?
And how...how could we be guided in this blackness which you left behind?
Who will heal these endless wounds?
My master...
It was said that the strike that does not break the back strengthens it...
But tell us: what can we do with our broken backs...?

May an eye that did not weep over you go blind
May an eye that did not weep over you go blind
And may a chest that did not lament you get torn apart....[18]

Khomeini had exhorted and encouraged collective grief to mobilise the public and to consolidate the newly emerging Islamic nation-state in Iran.[19] In the paper he is given the status of a prophet with divine and worldly traits. 'Salvation' and 'protection', which his actual presence seems to have bestowed on people, have given way to loss, a loss which not only the Shi'ite community should lament, but also every human being. The lamentation shows a community enthralled by its leaders and doggedly loyal to them as Salvationists, guiding torches of light whose passing breaks a momentum endowed with great promises. However, though the spiritual and political leadership of Iran continue to be dominant figures in Hizbullah's poetry, culture and politics in general, they acquire more nuances with time as pan-Arabism enters into the poetic veins of Hizbullah's world.

In addition to the poetry published in the paper, there were several Shi'ite Lebanese poets whose poetry spread by word of mouth, and became known on that basis. These poets were part of the larger Shi'ite revival movement, which Hizbullah championed, and hence interacted with their environments through poetry that echoed the broader concerns of the Shi'ite community as articulated by Hizbullah in particular. There is no serious conceptual difference between the work of such poets and the poetry published in Hizbullah's outlets, as they both depict similar concerns, affiliations and themes. One such poet is Mohammad al-Qabīsī, who was born in the south of Lebanon in 1945. His words and poems are popularised through memorisation and recital by a large swathe of Lebanese Shi'ites loyal to Hizbullah, but he is not known beyond Lebanon.[20] What follows are translated excerpts from his poetry:

We are faithful to God
For the sake of his love, we desire death

We follow on the steps of the Prophet and his family until the appearance of al-Mahdi
We are the valiant at heart
We sacrifice ourselves for you, O the land of the south,
We are on the path of martyrdom

My homeland is strong and dignity is rooted in it
The voice of the fighter is high
O Jerusalem, we are coming,
O fighter, do not fear the powerful, well-equipped,
And pursue dignity in life
Resist, for the souls of the fathers
Lived in your heart and eyes,
O Jerusalem, we are coming

In the south, a turbaned man had appeared
He has been taken notice of by lions
He (the turbaned man) yearns for heroes with burning desires
And people sleep with his memory peacefully
The mother had wiped away the tear with the handkerchief
Which had trickled down the cheeks of the orphaned
Why do I address a father who does not respond?
Why do I try to console a soul that cannot be consoled?
Why do I look at a south soaked in blood?
With the blood of the crime, spilt by the enslaver,
Melodies had come my way, beckoning children,
They sing, O orphaned, be patient, and recite:
Had Musa al-Sadr passed away with dignity
Or had the fire of oppression been extinguished,
You would have seen all creations killed with one stroke,
From your gigantic reaction when you threatened
But your face is a face of dignity,
It is to be worshipped after your God...
I am seeing persecution as oppression
And by God, the right of people is being stolen...

In al-Qabīsī's poetry, Jerusalem represents an ultimate point of reference, whose liberation is called for as the key to Islamic salvation, but it is also the spiritual and political leadership of Musa al-Sadr that dominates, particularly in the third poem, conveying similar sentiments to other poetry and songs of Hizbullah. To this end, one can argue that poetry grounded in a historical tradition is not like political discourses, which often can and do correspond to the political moment in a parallel way, but are nevertheless more direct. Poetry with reiterative political and cultural messages tends to escape rigid classification, as at heart it depicts, and in this case confirms, the epistemological identity of the movement in question with its emotional and spiritual connotations, as will be further revealed.

Another popular poem turned into a song through the choral singers of *husayiniūn lan narka'* (Hussein's followers who would never bow down), which Hizbullah uses as it lays its fallen members to rest, and which belongs to the above-cited genre of poetry, is:

> *With blood and Hussein, we follow on the steps of al-Khomeini*
> *We have pledged ourselves to you, Hizbullah,*
> *With soul and religion,*
> *We walk and death had returned*
> *For us, as lovers of martyrdom*[21]

Such poems and songs assert Hizbullah's early identity; its primal connection to the seminal figures of Shi'ite history, such as Ali, Hussein and others; martyrdom as a tool of liberation; its claim over a wider Islamic identity referenced by the Islamic republic of Iran and the symbolic heart of which is Jerusalem; bemoaning of injustice and oppression; and finally, fighting as the way forward out of injustice. These samples of poetry belong to the era when Hizbullah was relatively limited in its appeal and reach, and therefore they carry messages of suffering, defiance and reassurance through faith and certainty, rooted in Shi'ite tradition and history.

Political and poetic milestones

Hizbullah's popularity in the Arab world increased in 2000 when Israel withdrew its forces from southern Lebanon, and also as a consequence of the 2006 war with Israel.[22] There were several other events which demonstrated Hizbullah's power but none engendered as much attention and adulation in the Arab world as the withdrawal. When Israel withdrew from Lebanon in 2000, Arab poets of outstanding calibre paid tribute to the liberation of southern Lebanon, praising the resistance and Hizbullah's role in it. Among these were the late Palestinian poet Mahmoud Darwish and the Syrian poet Adonis. While neither produced poems for the occasion, they delivered elegiac speeches impregnated with poetic authority. Adonis was particularly admiring of the resistance, commenting approvingly on its self-perception. To this effect, he wrote:

> When I see what Hizbullah did to 'Israel' and its soldiers in the South, on the borders with Palestine, I feel an inclination towards comparison. Poor people, armed with primitive weapons and in possession of tremendous faith, but they have

held their lives in their hands to decide their own destiny. If we compare what Hizbullah did with the Israeli soldiers, we would find that it has affected Israel more than all the Arab armies combined for four decades. Why? Because if the people took charge of their own destiny, and all of them are involved in decision-making and responsibility, then they cannot be overcome.[23]

Adonis' statement elevates Hizbullah's position by asserting its disciplined and determined outlook, using it as an example of how victories can be made. Mahmoud Darwish, on the other hand, did not refer to Hizbullah specifically, but referred to Lebanon's 'culture of resistance':

We love Lebanon more today, because it has triumphed over the pervasive culture of defeat inculcated within the Arab elites which have turned the concept of personal freedom and sacrifice to materials for daily sarcasm...we applaud beautiful Lebanon, without exaggeration or interpretation, because it has triumphed over its legend, over its playful folkloric weakness; and it has defeated the myth of the invincible Israeli army. The consequences of the withdrawal will not halt the infection of the grand hope which small Lebanon had awakened in a continent thirsty for freedom. And so long as the culture of resistance is part of the fabric of the society, then the withdrawal is possible...and eloquence requires no eloquent.[24]

Both Adonis and Darwish highlight the collective dimension of resistance that led to liberation in southern Lebanon. Both figures, being representative of the highest standards of poetry in the Arab world, in effect enlarged Hizbullah's grand sense of itself as a paragon of resistance.

The poetry connected with the Israeli withdrawal in 2000, however, specifically reiterates Hizbullah's rhetoric, symbols, themes and images, while drawing on the Shi'ite faith. Thus, Lebanese poet Mohammad 'Alī Shams ad-Dīn, in his poem entitled 'The blood of Hussein coined the dawn', writes:

Graves are moving
I see heads raised at the arrows
I see the roots resisting the winds
And I hear the graves grinding anger
I feel the sand traversed in the field
And the waves of the sea thrown over the fire
And I say with tears in my eyes
And I do not know, if I should laugh or weep,
Praise be to the one who gave the Umma of the Arabs its new Jesus
From the blood of Hussein
And coined its dawn[25]

The aesthetics and power of this poem reside in its evocation of nature as having been animated with the liberation of the south, as if it had regained a lost order through acts of resistance and steadfastness. The other notable trope in this poem is the evocation of Jesus Christ through using the figurative phrase 'blood of Hussein' (as in the blood of Christ). Both are considered figures of resistance, of persistence in demands for justice, and of resurrection, all of which ultimately lead to the beginning of a new dawn, or a new beginning. In addition, other poems from this period commemorated particular martyr figures, such as the one written by the revered Shi'ite cleric Mohammad Hussein Fadlallah, whose poem is headed with a dedication 'to the Sheikh of the resistance fighters, the revered martyr Sheikh, Ahmad Yahiya'. The poem celebrates the life of the martyr in the light of the liberation, suggesting that it is through sacrifice that liberation was attained, as in the following excerpt from the poem:

> *Longing had attracted you, and fate had saved you*
> *O descending happily...*
> *Your turban, soaked with blood,*
> *Is a compass for travelling*[26]

Martyrdom is a major cultural trope in Hizbullah poetry and discourse. In this poem it is associated with travelling, in that it leads to another stage in people's lives: liberation. As such, martyrdom is portrayed as an indispensable tool of liberation, which is celebrated through the invocation of the blood of martyrs. In fact, many of the poems from this period are steeped in the celebration of resistance and those that perished on the road to its attainment. It is worth noting that *al-'Ahd* also published specific chants used after the liberation, engaging with several dimensions related to resistance. Most of them assert loyalty to Hizbullah and its leader, Hassan Nasrallah. Here are some examples:

> *Look at you, Hizbullah, you have asserted your presence...*
> *The Jews went...and you left no collaborators behind*

Another chant runs as follows:

> *Bint Jbayl calls out*
> *We have liberated the land of our country*
> *May God preserve Abu Hadi*
> *Bint Jbayl, the glorious...*
> *Bint Jbayl, the southern,*
> *Will remain Lebanese*
> *It has regained freedom*
> *Through the victorious soldiers of Hizbullah*[27]

These two chants glorify Hizbullah's resistance in south Lebanon and register issues and places that were part of the struggle for the south. In particular, the village of Bint Jbayl has come to be known in Lebanon and elsewhere in the Arab world for being at the forefront of the resistance and steadfastness against the Israeli occupation of south Lebanon. Hence the name acquired strong associations that assert the values of dignity, heroism and steadfastness. In addition, 'collaborators' refers to the Israeli-allied South Lebanese Army, as led by General Anton Lahd, which dissolved and whose members largely fled to Israel after the liberation of the south; 'Abū Hādī' is Nasrallah.

The expansion of Hizbullah's poetic repertoire

The other major historical juncture for Hizbullah poetry was the 2006 war with Israel, when poets from outside the Shiʻite community in Lebanon and the Arab world celebrated Hizbullah's role in the war. It is best to start with Omar al-Farra, a popular Syrian poet born in 1949 in the city of Palmyra in central Syria. Al-Farra's poems deal with social phenomena in Syria and elsewhere in the Arab world, but he became particularly known for a poem called 'Hamīda', in which he gives a voice to a Bedouin girl who prefers death to being forced to marry her cousin. The poem starts and ends with the defiant statements, *mā arīdak, mā arīdak, mā arīdak:* 'I don't want you, I don't want you, I don't want you.' The poem is clearly one of protest against and apprehension about a long-standing social phenomenon that the poet is ardently opposed to. As such, al-Farra gained popularity and influence, and for Hizbullah to have his passionate endorsement was a testament to how far its appeal had spread.[28]

In his famous poem entitled 'The Men of God', a clear reference to the fighters of Hizbullah, we find al-Farra on a different front, a pronouncedly political one underlined with ideological overtones. The poem, which he wrote following the 2006 Israeli onslaught on Lebanon, is an elegy to the fighters of Hizbullah and to the south of Lebanon in general. Though it includes themes familiar from other poetry concerning Hizbullah, it is richer in language and imagery. The fact that it was recited to large audiences in Lebanon and made use of in various media outlets adds to its political and emotional value in the wider Arab world:

> *That's how the Arab blood became a knife that kills*
> *And poetry after silence became resounding*
> *That's how we became, and we will not be if we forgot the Jihad of righteousness and faith*
> *And that people despite humiliation and oppression wave the banner of rebellion*
> *They decide to take the land by force, and they take it*

That's what the men of God did in the day of conquest in Lebanon
My heart inclines towards the south; and how beautiful that the love of my heart is a
southerner,
Here our journeys have assembled, somebody said; take your shoes off,
I could beg you to kneel
We are walking on a holy land
If I could, I would cross it on my eyelashes
Here, they were robbed, here they were crucified, here they dwelled, here they were
prostrated,
Here they suffered rockets, here they stood, here they hoped, here they ascended the
wings of God,
Here they fell down, a stream of martyrs,
Before they vanished, they wrote books without titles
You will read in our school about the men of God, in the day of victory in Lebanon
Because the people reject the idea of capitulation
Because their wounds have bled, their pride of belonging had cried out an anthem of
glory for the homelands
Because the land is their compass
The light of righteousness is their guide
Amongst them, believing men who read
That if they have promised, they will fulfil their promises,
As they have wished, their purity had united them,
Most of their speech is silence, and some of their silence is gestures
They erupted like a volcano that sends to perdition everything in its way
In death, they have a philosophy
They do not fear Him if they were ordered
For their country, they raised the banner of victory, and triumphed
Southerners: the sand of the earth knows them; the salt of it knows them,
A scent from the wellsprings of paradise
Southerners, known by the lightning of thunder,
The spells of rain, the magic of flowers,
The stars of the night know them; the sun of the morning knows them,
And the revelation of water to waterfalls
And they have known the birds of love, the sharpness of the sword,
The poetry of the Persians, the Greeks, the Phoenicians and the Romans
They have understanding and knowledge of those who governed and those who
perished,
And they have knowledge of the rules and scales of poetry,
And how man gets liberated
Southerners, God used to know them, was their leader,
And their commander, so with all humility,
They were the men of conquest in Lebanon[29]

It is instructive to highlight some of the images and linguistic constructs used in the poem in order to explore how ideology operates in poetry; how it elevates, delineates, and creates an aura of its own authority that imbues the organisation in question with importance that amounts to sacredness. The poem capitalises on familiar dimensions related to Hizbullah's ideology. It locates its point of departure in the humiliating defeats the Arabs faced, which consequently, and because of the responsibility placed on Hizbullah fighters, turned their blood into 'a knife that kills'. Hizbullah is the knife of the Arabs, an effective knife that emerges out of humiliation and oppression. Since it is a knife sharpened with a divine sense of righteousness, those who carry this knife 'decide to take the land by force, and they take it'; and as they take the land, and liberate it, they become 'the men of God...in the day of conquest in Lebanon'. Hizbullah's name itself is indelibly linked with Islamic symbols and history, and here the poet opens his poem with this connection, as if to emphasise that it was with such attitudes, with such a background, grounded in 'faith and righteousness', that Hizbullah, represented here by 'the men of conquest', triumphed.

The poem marches forward towards evoking the south, and how beloved it is by the poet. So many literary trends direct their compass towards the south; namely, the southern part of the globe as historically or presently dominated by occupation, colonialism and struggles for liberation.[30] So the south is sung for, made an object of longing and promise, but here the south is specific: it is the south of Lebanon. The international south is wed to a local south where the struggle for liberation and freedom rings loud. The south is portrayed as holy; its holiness stems from the many events and travails it has witnessed: 'here they were robbed, here they were crucified...here they fell down, a stream of martyrs'. Even the image of the crucified Jesus, highlighting the severity of suffering of the people in south Lebanon under the Israeli occupation, is evoked to highlight how courageous the fighters were in the face of the enemy, in overcoming this suffering. The poem is packed with images that evoke Hizbullah's ideology and feed into it. The use of the word 'philosophy', for example, 'in death, they have a philosophy', explains to those who condemn Hizbullah, and Islamist movements in general, for their alleged pursuit of mindless and deadly violence that death is accepted as a philosophy when it is rooted in a struggle for rights, a struggle over a land that is intimately connected with the fighters: 'Southerners: the sand of the earth knows them; the salt of it knows them...' Al-Farra widens the space of his portrayal of Hizbullah fighters, suggesting that they are knowledgeable, professional in fighting, and aware of various traditions. And because they are equipped with knowledge, poetry and history, God was with them; He helped them to triumph in southern Lebanon, and they were humble in their victory. In addition, al-Farra adds to Hizbullah's prestige and popularity by including images from the Christian and Arab traditions, such as the cross, which is a typical image in much of the secular Arabic poetry of the twentieth century.

Geertz reflects on how ideologies construct a world imbued with meanings and assurances that ground them and legitimise the endeavours and activities of their upholders. Geertz writes: 'It is... the attempt of ideologies to render otherwise incomprehensible social situations meaningfully, to so construe them as to make it possible to act purposefully within them, that accounts both for the ideologies' highly figurative nature and for the intensity with which, once accepted, they are held.'[31] While highlighting the significant role of ideology in moulding its subjects, it is nevertheless equally important to recognise history as giving rise to particular orientations that can legitimise a diverse set of actions without attaching an ideological guardianship to them. Al-Farra's poem can be read as a historical product of a particular era, in which Hizbullah is seen as a special liberating force for its resistance to Israel. Therefore, ideology in this context is more than unchecked subscription to discourse and actions; it is also a historical product that individuals participate in and even come to embody, thus becoming willing subjects, both active and obedient at the same time.

The 'Lebanonisation' of Hizbullah in poetry

While it is characteristic of Hizbullah's songs and poems produced by members and direct affiliates. mainly from the Shi'ite community in Lebanon, to be full of references to historical figures and the country's past, poets like al-Farra internationalised their struggle and added significant existential elements. Existing literature on Hizbullah attests to stages in the evolution of the movement as it grew from being Shi'ite-centred theologically and politically to becoming more inclusive in terms of its Lebanese and broader Arabic following. Hizbullah's poetry and songs reflect this evolution, while remaining grounded in Shi'ite history and traditions. An example is the following poem, initially written by Rida Shu'ayb and later made into a song after 2006. Performed by the choral group al-Fajr, the poem was adapted by Tarik Sharifa and produced by Hizbullah's Dār al-Manār:

O, Lebanon, the garden of Eden,
My fascinating homeland
There is no place like you
This horizon belongs to you

O Hussein, your soldiers have returned,
O Hussein, we returned with the God's victory and the blood had won
You have come back, and Abbas, the faithful, leads us,
O Imam, we and your companions are in the same orbit
When we are afflicted,
The thirst of Hussein burst in Abbas's veins,
The earth shocked and the world thundered[32]

Interestingly, the first part of the song echoes the thinking of one of the quintessential poets of Lebanon in the twentieth century, Saeed 'Aql (1912–2014). This refers to the popular characterisation of the country, before the 1975–90 civil war, as 'the garden of Eden'; a unique place of flourishing trade, high culture and civilisation. In the introduction to his play *Qadmus*, the avant-garde Lebanese poet Saeed 'Aql refers to Lebanon as 'a powerful and genius message in the world, which qualifies us to the Lebanonisation of the world, *labnanat al-'ālam*.'[33] Hizbullah's celebration of Lebanese nationalism, even though it does evoke the religious references to the Garden of Eden, is part of its bid to project its identity as a Lebanese party with shared nationalist imagery. At the same time, the same song shows another aspect of Hizbullah's identity, the one rooted in the theological and historical convictions of the Islamic Shi'ite tradition. The poem refers to Hussein, one of the principal figures in Shi'ite history, a reference that, as we saw above, is also evident in the early period of Hizbullah poetry. Hussein's travel to Karbala, which he undertook after the people of Kūfa in Iraq invited him to become their ruler after the death of the fifth Islamic ruler Mu'awiyah in AD 680, is portrayed as a return. Return here is embodied and continued through the men of Hizbullah who fight with the spirit of the Imam Hussein within them, thus providing a powerful symbol which invites Imam Hussein to bear witness to the Hizbullah fighters' sense of ingenuity and righteousness as descendants and protectors of the faith: 'O Imām, we and your companions are in the same orbit.'

History remains a powerful connection as far as the Shi'ite tradition is concerned. In the context of ideology, a relationship does not recognise time or space; it can out-distance space and wait out time. Hence Karbala of Iraq, to which Hussein travelled to rule, can be read as the Lebanon of today, and the seventh century as the current moment in the history of Hizbullah. Hussein's brother 'Abbās, who showed strict loyalty to him when he went to Karbala, is continuously evoked, as is his thirst in solidarity with Sakīna—the daughter of Hassan, the other brother of Hussein, who endured extreme thirst during her arrest and was killed prior to Hussein's arrival to Karbala. This endows the song with emotional values and with powerful historical and political echoes. The events and stories of Karbala offer lessons in sobriety, patience and steadfastness in the face of harsh adversities. And since the song evokes return, return often suggests preservation of a pre-existing order. As such, the continuity of history is contingent to ideologies more so than it is to cultures, which are less reverential and accept criticism of the sacred. In addition, the way the song uses these historical figures and allusions to battles without explaining their details suggests that there exists a 'culture of communication'—one that, in this context, is used by Hizbullah and shared by members of the Shi'ite community already familiar with this potent history and its meanings.[34]

Themes in Hizbullah's poetry

Apart from references to Iran and Shi'ite historical figures, Hizbullah's poetry includes other constant tropes: reverence for leaders, most notably Hassan Nasrallah; the commemoration of martyrs; the evocation of significant historical milestones pertaining to the party's history; and references to Palestine and Jerusalem. These themes will be elaborated on in what follows. The Shi'ite roots of Hizbullah transcend the geography of Lebanon and include Iran with its Islamic system of government. Iran is a constant thread in the narrative of Hizbullah, and one of the major references whose force of presence does not lessen with time. Thus references to Iran in Hizbullah's poetry persisted even after its heightened 'Lebanonisation' after 2006. In the following poem and song, released after 2006, the late Iranian leader Khomeini is imagined within the spiritual genealogy of the Shi'ite tradition. The fact that he is evoked as authoritative is particularly important, since the poem references his revival and advancement of *wilayat al-faqih*, in which the ultimate power and authority are invested in religious jurisprudence and guardianship over a spectrum of social and political matters:[35]

> *We trust the wilayat*
> *It's enough for you (Khomeini) that you had Mohammad in you*
> *You are the imam and in the wilayat we trust*
> *Righteousness is his sword and fairness a witness to that*
> *The fires of Khomeini remain as a banner*
> *To the forthcoming Mahdi, witnessed by tomorrow*
> *The reign of Mohammad was entrusted to our Ali*
> *And to your trust, and the forthcoming Khomeini,*
> *Righteousness is his sword*
> *And fairness is a witness to that...*[36]

Though the song above does not necessarily project a structural integrity, being composed more of statements than a tightly interwoven poetic composition would be, it holds an ideological cohesion that conveys meanings and themes constitutive of Hizbullah within its Shi'ite milieu. The lines of the song underpin the Shi'ite faith while ascertaining its continuity and embodiment in present figures and events. In this context, Khomeini is embodied in the Prophet Mohammad, who, according to the Shi'ite tradition, handed the reins of power to Ali on his deathbed in AD 632. Thus, Ali's descendants are the rightful upholders of power, including Mahdī, the Twelfth Imām who went into occultation (*ghayba*) in the tenth century AD. In this poem and song, Khomeini is also depicted as a guiding torch for Hizbullah, as reflected in the line: 'The fires of Khomeini remain as a banner.' Iran, in this respect, is an important backbone for Hizbullah, and the strength of this backbone stems initially from its theological convictions. Hence, as opposed to solely political alliances, religious ones are often perceived to be and communicated as being stronger and more enduring. The song also sheds light on how integral revolutionary Iran is to Hizbullah in terms of its founding principles as enshrined in the *wilayat al-faqih* as well as the figures that spearheaded the Iranian revolution and later the Iranian state and moulded the intellectual and spiritual guidance of it.[37]

However, while it is important to focus on the Iranian dimension to Hizbullah, which is present in all its outlets, it is equally necessary to highlight Hizbullah's Arab identity and image. This identity manifests itself clearly in poetry. In the following song, also released after the 2006 confrontations between Hizbullah and Israel, from which Hizbullah emerged as a pan-Arab hero thanks to its resistance and steadfastness against the Israeli onslaught, Hizbullah's Arab identity is celebrated through the use of familiar Arab nationalist tropes:[38]

> *I am the Arab, I am the Arab*
> *I who do not fear the tyrant*
> *To die proudly is the highest of wishes*
> *I am the Arab*
> *I am the Arab, I am the faith*
> *The son of the Bible, the son of the Qur'an*
> *I am the Arab*
> *I am the human being*
> *I am the countries*
> *I descend from 'Adnān*
> *I am the Arab who refused to be afflicted with tribulations*
> *I am the Arab*

I am the Arab, I was born free
I am the determination, the revolution,
Fire follows my anger
I am the Arab who refused to be afflicted with tribulations[39]

The repeated and assertive declaration 'I am the Arab' leaves no room for doubt as to the ground on which Hizbullah raises its banner, recalling the shared history and language that underlined the pan-Arab nationalism that classic figures such as Sati' al-Husri (1882–1968) and Michel Aflaq (1910–1989) called for at the end of the nineteenth century and well into the twentieth century.[40] The shared history of the Arabs is captured in the line 'I descend from 'Adnān.' In the classical historiography of the Arabs, 'Adnān and Qahtān are the two major (figures) tribes from which all Arabs hail.[41] 'Adnān is the father of the northern tribes of Arabia, extending from the Hijāz of modern day Saudi Arabia all the way to Syria, Lebanon, Palestine and other adjacent areas; he is essentially the father from which it is believed Prophet Mohammad descended. To go as far as 'Adnān is to confirm roots, to demonstrate allegiance and authenticity endowed with pan-Arab resonance and values. As characteristic of nationalist discourses, Hizbullah celebrates pan-Arabism in this song, conjuring up Arab ancestry and alleged Arabic traits but also hinting at being a particular Arab, one who does not accept humiliation and tribulations but fights against the odds to regain and assert her or his rights.

In this, Hizbullah hits back at those who went down the path of peace agreements with Israel and capitulations to Western powers, chiefly the United States, which it views as hostile to Arab values and aspirations: 'I am the Arab who refused to be afflicted with tribulations.' Refusal requires an active agent, one who initiates and makes history rather than being overwhelmed by it. Thus, Hizbullah projects a principled image, in which only those who accept its underpinnings, its narrative, are included. Moreover, Hizbullah paints itself not as partisan or of one religious conviction rather than another, but more as an inclusive body: 'I am the Arab...the son of the Bible, the son of the Qur'an.' The reference to the Bible and the Qur'an embraces the three major monotheistic faiths, Judaism, Christianity and Islam, within its fold and claims them as an integral part of its worldview. It is, however, important to recall the context of the above song here, which coincided with the outburst of popular support for Hizbullah in the Arab world during and after the 2006 Israeli attack on Lebanon. The party, which used to rely on self-promotion and on its allies, namely Iran and Syria, now found itself at the centre of attention and admiration by a large section of Arab citizens, including secularists, nationalists, Marxists and Islamists. Since heroism, admiration and defiance are familiar tropes in what is known as the literature of resistance in Arabic literature,[42] Hizbullah was embraced and adulated by many Arab poets who applauded its steadfastness and paid florid tributes to its leadership, and particularly to Hizbullah's secretary-general, Hassan Nasrallah.

As was mentioned at the outset of this book, Arab poetry is rife with examples of panegyric poetry addressed to rulers and other figures in positions of power. Hizbullah and its leaders are no exception in this respect. Hassan Nasrallah has been the subject of many poems and songs, particularly after 2000 and 2006, the two events that cemented his reputation as a leader with a significant popular powerbase in the Arab world.[43] In the following song, released after 2006 by *firqat al-fajr*, the legitimising force of history is bestowed on Hassan Nasrallah with several images that present him as a leader in his faith, Shi'ism, and of Hizbullah. The poem is full of images of heroism that are characteristic of Islamist poetry in general.[44] It opens with:

The sun is colder than the heat of our pride...
We have given our allegiance to Nasrallah, your grandson,
The Hassan of Hussein found Haidar[45] steadfast
The laments of Zeinab are still in our limbs
Until we drew our sharp swords
The Mahdi here has come with the wound of our Hussein
We will follow him, and will heal the wounds
O Hussein, we have come back with Nasrallah
And the blood has won

History is presented as a linear narrative in which key figures in Shi'ite history, from Hussein through to Zeinab, Mahdi and Nasrallah, have the main roles. It is particularly noteworthy in this narrative that Nasrallah, to whom the fighters vow allegiance, is referred to as the grandson of Hussein, a common mode of reference in the Arabic tradition as emotional bonds of affiliation overcome spatial boundaries.[46] In addition, the poem and song includes an image of return, a theme that dominates Hizbullah's poetry. This is a return to the eternal presence of mystical Shi'ite models, and their rebirth in figures such as Hassan Nasrallah. The historical links are made through images of intense passion: 'The sun is colder than the heat of our pride...' and strong historical affiliation and remembrance: 'the laments of Zeinab are still in our limbs...' The historical journey that remembers and evokes the principal Shi'ite figures, including Zeinab, the daughter of Ali who was captured in the battle of Karbala and humiliated by the army of Yazid, the son of Mu'awiyah, highlights the literal and uninterrupted historical narrative of sacrifice and steadfastness in the face of persecution as exemplified in Karbala.

After the 2006 war, Arab poets joined in the praise of Nasrallah. In the following poem, the young Palestinian–Egyptian poet Tamīm al-Barghoutī (b.1977), who acquired fame through his presence on the programme *Shāʿir al-malyūn'* (The Poet of the Million), pays homage to Hassan Nasrallah:

> *The doves of the towers pray for you*
> *You teach them generosity, you, the son of the prophet,*
> *You hand them ripe grains with your right hand*
> *They carry them and fly south*
> *They do not eat the grains, but scatter them on the mountains,*
> *For some women and men*
> *They ask them about the direction of fighting*
> *And carry your greetings to them*
> *If a journalist asked the doves*
> *They would say that the sky is there, shading you,*
> *And that you have spread out the sky before them*
> *The air of the country prays for you*
> *The flowers of the meadows pray for you*[47]

Nasrallah is evoked in a way that suggests heroism and hope. Tamīm al-Barghoutī's use of references such as 'doves', 'generosity', 'ripe grains', 'shade', 'flowers' and 'meadows' speaks of fertility and openness to a bright future which, according to him, is what Hizbullah represents. Unlike other poems and songs by close affiliates and members of Hizbullah, carefully crafted along ideological lines, this poem is from an outsider to some extent. But al-Barghoutī's poem is not detached from Hizbullah's foundational ideology, since he refers to Nasrallah as 'the son of the Prophet'. Thus, he affiliates himself with Hizbullah in his evocation of nostalgic and nationalist directions, where battles were fought and notable events involving Hizbullah took place, as when he says: 'You hand them ripe grains with your right hand; they carry them and fly south.' The poem is clearly grounded in celebrating heroism and paying homage to its representative for having 'spread out the sky' before the Arabs after their horizons had narrowed, given the many defeats and setbacks Arabs faced at the hands of Israel. Thus, even objects such as 'the air of the country' and 'the flowers of the meadow pray for you'; how could he, the poet, not join them in eulogy to Nasrallah, whom he credits with invigorating the Arabs with hope in ultimately overcoming Israel? Moreover, al-Barghoutī embraces one of Nasrallah's famous statements, made in one of his speeches in July 2008, following the release of prominent Lebanese prisoners from Israeli prisons; the statement that 'identity is resistance'.[48]

Broadly speaking, committed poetry that interacts with reality and deals with socio-political issues and manifestations gives authority to and opens further avenues for those whom it hails. Tamīm al-Barghoutī's eulogy serves to enhance Nasrallah's visibility and authority on several levels. It hails him; it almost makes him a 'brand'. The hailing and branding are not unique to Hizbullah; this is how many politicians and political parties thrust themselves onto the public sphere, objectifying themselves and their convictions to the point of saturation. Here, Nasrallah becomes the embodiment of the very ideas and discourse he puts forward. This is reflected in a famous song by the renowned Lebanese singer Julia Boutros, released after 2006. The lyrics for the song are taken from Nasrallah's letter to Hizbullah's fighters during the 2006 Israeli onslaught on Lebanon. Nasrallah's letter is indicative of the complementary roles played by the various strata of Hizbullah's members, including leaders, fighters, professionals, members of Lebanon's Shi'ite community and Arab supporters. The letter is itself a poetic engagement by a leader aware of the value of poetry in boosting the morale of fighters during hard times, and as a medium of authenticity and truthfulness that speaks to people's humanity.[49] Here are a few lines from the song:[50]

> My beloved, my beloved, my beloved
> I have heard your letter
> In which there is pride and faith
> For you are, as you said, the men of God in the battlefield...
> You are the builders of a civilisation...
> You are our forthcoming victory...
> The land will be liberated through you
> With you, we change the world and build the best tomorrow
> And with you, we march and triumph, we march and triumph...

The letter/song underlines the interactive nature of Hizbullah's communication practices. It starts with the evocative construction 'my beloved' and is followed with the active verb *istama'tu* (I have heard), echoing an emotional bond that resonates with paternal feelings, not so different from what a father would say to his children, *istama'tu*. It acknowledges their description of themselves, 'the men of God in the battlefield'. From this foundation of loyalty and religious convictions, the fighters become 'builders of a civilisation' as well as a means by which the world will be changed. It is an upbeat letter/song rooted in confidence and an unshakable faith in the veracity of the path, the path of resistance that Nasrallah and Hizbullah champion in their discourse.

Poetry, songs and art in general accentuate the discourse of this path, imbuing it with an emotional resonance and virtuous authenticity. The following poem, read as an introduction to one of Nasrallah's speeches in 2010, makes use of Nasrallah's words in poetic constructions steeped in mysticism:

Four
And the impossible travel...our travel...
The glowing timbers...our bracelets
And the horizon is wider...
Four
And the water still inhabits the warmth of our swords
And the names surmount our longings
And the victory which had been accustomed to our heroisms
Has found a homeland for itself here...
And it will not be overcome...
O our people, the most honourable of people...

The verses were recited prior to a speech Nasrallah delivered in the stadium of Ar-Rayah in the southern suburb of Beirut on the anniversary of the 'Divine Victory' on 3 August 2010. They are close to surreal, symbolic poetry, poetry that, though anchored in the reality of Hizbullah, is not entirely Hizbullah. It has a cadence of its own which exceeds the object of which it speaks. There is ingenuity in the images: 'And the impossible travel...our travel...The glowing timbers...our bracelets.' It is, however, only when the poem is read backwards that we see its elevated style in addressing Nasrallah, as it evokes one of his most memorable lines when he emerged following the 2006 war, calling the people of south Lebanon 'the most honourable of people'. The poem is sealed with Nasrallah's phrase, dispelling its previous sense of mysticism and revealing in the process the subject of its evocation by using the very language Nasrallah utilised to highlight the importance of the event and the people at the heart of it. It speaks of the difficult and painful moments for the Lebanese who bore the brunt of Israeli attacks but endured the fighting and shielded the fighters of Hizbullah from this attack. Nasrallah's language is used to reassure, to encapsulate historical moments of significant value, and conclude a poem wrapped in mystic references.

Palestine is another constant element in the political discourse of Hizbullah, projected in various media outlets and highlighted in almost all of Nasrallah's speeches as a usurped land that should be liberated and redeemed from the Zionists (Hizbullah's preferred term for Israel). In the following anecdotal poem, the language amalgamates existential aspects and political messages, intertwined within an anecdote told with panache and style by the poet Omar al-Farra. The poem was read in 2007 at an auditorium in Beirut to a packed audience of Hizbullah supporters, who seemed mesmerised by the performance. The relationship between the audience and the poet in this case is one of intimacy and mutual recognition of the topic of which he speaks and the language of the poem; it is written and recited in colloquial Levantine, rural Arabic, and there are folkloric aspects to it. The love story at its heart further adds to the poem's vividness. The title is *Khuttār* (The uninvited guests, or the guests who come without prior notice). Here are a few lines:

Khuttār [the uninvited guests] *came to us in the evening and we were not prepared for their coming*
As I glimpsed the beloved of my heart with them, my mind went absent,
We wanted time to melt, and the clock to stop,
And forget the nights of sadness and the greedy eyes
With my eyelashes fluttering in order to see you
Looking with delight, when you say goodbye,
My fear is that our separation and your absence will be long,
Those daggers will strike at me for a long time,
One night, I came to you while in desperate need
With the heat of timbers as our witness, and the poetry of love at night,
It is possible that I could die at dawn, if you leave this night,
You who are going to Jerusalem, my love travels with you,
To attend the wedding nights, and grow apple trees,
We missed the sun, while the bosom is full of wounds,
O, my wound, murmur, murmur,
The sound of darkness is shameful
I have befriended estrangement and longing
And the singing nightingale
I did not see a day of companionship, nor is my heart comfortable even for a moment
O you, who are driving the stars,
My aim is the robe of the uninvited guest, just go
Stay with me after your absence, but now go,
'Alilah [I] *awaits the arrival of the beloved,*
Say to my people that the girl is in love
She is looking for the right time, cover her, she is cold,
She hopes for a peaceful sleep, and she hopes for a pomegranate,
O time, time evolves with us, and I am wounded,
I saw hope with patience, a string in the wing of an eagle,
O the exile, the abode of my people, they have forgotten me wounded,
Every time I call out, O beloved, one wave after another,
My eyesight drifts and so does hope, and the wave goes away,
Time has betrayed me, O time has betrayed me, and I said I have grown bored,
Through the eye of a needle, after your separation, I have grown bored,
If I could pour out tears, for I have grown bored of the sea, and no longer tolerate the drips of the clouds
Yesterday, in the day of farewell, I strayed, I saw tears as tears,
I no longer recognise the eclipse of the sun
I did not realise that the sweet had bid farewell, O my heart, the ashes of sadness,

I do not think that he will come back,
We heard the music of the wedding, and their bullets aflame,
Khuttār, unannounced guests, came to us in the morning; they cut the wing of a raven,
And narrated a story about him,
They brought a handful of sand with them, they said to me, your love has gone (died)
yesterday,
While afflicted with the love of the land
Reciting a love poem
Under the shade of a grapevine
Every time, the wound bleeds and I hear a sound of absence (disappearance)
My tongue enchants with happiness
O, mother, the moon is by the door![51]

This poem was not written by an affiliate of Hizbullah, and has, strictly speaking, none of the common prominent figures or even themes of Hizbullah poetry. But it situates its subject within the context of southern Lebanon, and the long-drawn-out battles waged by Hizbullah fighters in the south to regain their land from the Israeli occupation. Besides that, it is a love story with familiar dimensions such as longing, sadness at separation, affection, romanticism and deep hope, suffused with almost universal symbols of love such as 'the moon', 'apple', 'pomegranate', etc. The marriage of these two contexts, love and battles, wounds and death, yields a vivid story, hence the mesmerising effect of al-Farra's recital. The audience reacted ecstatically to his story by applauding the poet, approving the poem's sentiments and meanings. Its existence and reception demonstrate Hizbullah's enhanced status in the Arab world; as further witnessed by the moral support and solidarity Hizbullah received following the 2006 war, reminiscent of the support the Palestinian national movement garnered in 1968 when it too seemed to rattle the power dynamics in the region with its stiff resistance to Israeli occupation.

The poem *Khuttār* tells the story of fighters who went to southern Lebanon to carry out a military operation in the Palestinian territories. This could be read as a veiled reference to the Hizbullah fighters who abducted two Israeli soldiers in 2006 and thus triggered the war. At one point in the poem the fighters seek refuge in a house in southern Lebanon to wait for the moon to disappear so that they can camouflage themselves aided by the darkness of the night and undertake their operation inside Palestine. The poem is narrated by a girl in the house that falls in love with one of the fighters. In his introduction to the poem, al-Farra refers to the girl as 'a symbol of the land'. That the poem anchors its subject in a group of fighters heading south to launch a military operation and along the way, for tactical reasons, going uninvited to a house in the south, suggests an intimate connection between the fighters and the people of the south. In this case, the interaction between the fighters and the people results in perhaps the highest form of human bonding, romantic love; one that the lover, the girl, evokes vividly and longingly: 'Those daggers will strike at me for a long time; one night, I came to you while in desperate need; with the heat of timbers as our witness; and the poetry of love at night; It is possible that I could die at dawn, if you leave this night.'

But since Hizbullah, represented by the fighters, believes that the liberation of Palestine can only happen through resistance and that resistance is its essential identity, and since the girl in love knows that, she cannot stop her warrior lover from continuing his journey. Usually lovers long for their beloved to stay, but she puts the land, as she is the land herself, before her own desires: 'You who are going to Jerusalem, my love travels with you... O you who are driving the stars, I am after the robe of the uninvited guest, just go; remain to me after the absence, but now, go.' But as they embark on their journey, she feels great longing and all that it can give rise to by way of tears, anguish and sleepiness: 'She hopes for a peaceful sleep, and she hopes for a pomegranate.' As her lover seems to disappear for a long time, she despairs and feels the worst: 'No longer the sweet and tender, O my heart, the ashes of sadness, I do not think he will return.' Her intuitions are confirmed when she is told he died during the operation: 'They brought a handful of sand with them, they said to me, your love has gone (died) yesterday.' But she does not wallow in despair at her lover's passing. Instead she sees hope and expresses pride in her lover. Hence the appearance of the moon, the reason why the uninvited guests, the fighters, first sought refuge in her house, becomes a sign of hope for her and happiness. This earth will always shine for her while she defends it armed with hope and optimism: 'My tongue enchants with happiness; O mother, the moon is by the door.'

Al-Farra's poem is packed with meanings and references related to Hizbullah's ideology, practice and presence in Lebanon and the Arab world. He widens the appeal of Hizbullah in the Arab world by including Palestine and using it as the direction in which the fighters of Hizbullah head. Thus, it could be said that at many points in its history Hizbullah has succeeded in expanding its base and extent using cultural and literary agencies and activities politically to prove itself potent: invaluable to the Arab world, and indispensable to the Lebanese state. With the revolutions of the Arab Spring in mind, however, Hizbullah's position and identity, particularly in relation to the Syrian Ba'ath regime that Hizbullah publicly endorses and now fights alongside, is questioned and condemned. Many in the Arab world now view it as barricading itself within its Shi'ite identity in a way that reverses all the pan-Arab and Islamic credentials they once hailed.

The question of whether other poets from the Arab world will flock to sing Hizbullah's praises given its unpopular alliance with the Syrian regime, which has committed serious crimes against its own people, needs to be pursued even if it remains ultimately uncertain. Hizbullah's reputation in the Arab world as a potential deterrent to Israel cannot be underestimated. It remains to be seen, however, whether the double standards it practises when siding with the Arab revolutions but not with the Syrian revolution will override its popular image as a deterrent, since such actions create a resemblance between Hizbullah and the region's oppressive powers and regimes. Already the late Ahmad Fu'ād Najm, one of the famous Egyptian poets who (along with his daughter) played a prominent role in the Egyptian 25 January Revolution, and who wrote a poem dedicated to Hizbullah and praised it after 2006, has asked for clarification from the party. During a live television programme broadcast from Tunisia, he called on Nasrallah to denounce the Syrian regime and distance himself from it: 'Do you like what the Ba'ath regime is doing to the Syrian people...is it useful to support what is happening in any way?'[52]

Conclusion

Hizbullah, like all other political entities, was not founded in a cultural vacuum. From its inception, it enfolded itself within an existing literary and cultural Arabic tradition that dates back centuries. Even its name 'Hizbullah' is derived from the Qur'an: 'surely the *party of God* (Hizbullah) are they that shall be triumphant'. Poetry in the Arabic tradition has often reflected the authenticity of culture and acted as a guardian of its language and an expression of its values and norms.

The poetry of Hizbullah revolves around its identity and taps into the cultural and political Arabic tradition. As this chapter has shown, the poetry highlights the party's beliefs, references, battles, victories and views, whether in relation to itself or the others with whom it interacts; from local agents within the complex sectarian make-up of Lebanon, to Iran, its intimate and co-religionist ally, to Palestine, to the Arab world, and to Israel and America which the party portrays in its discourse as the arch-enemy of the Islamic world. The poetry of Hizbullah becomes particularly important and visible after 2000 and 2006, two significant dates in the history of the party and its appeal. As Lila Abu-Lughod shows in her impressive study of the Bedouin society in Egypt and the role of poetry in expressing openly hidden senti-ments,[53] poetry serves as an invaluable ethnographic material that broadens the scope of analysis, as was also true in the case of Hamas. This applies to Hizbullah in so far as the movement and its political and cultural base are concerned. Though Hizbullah's poetry is predictable and the tropes it covers sound familiar, it still sheds light on the language and sentiments that under-pin Hizbullah's ideology and its relationship with ordinary people. As such, it demonstrates the poetics of an ideology that is rooted in particular socio-political conditions and the emotional reservoirs it creates and inhabits.

PART THREE

7

POETRY AND THE ARAB SPRING

A HISTORICAL PERSPECTIVE

The most fatal disease is for the eye to see
A tyrant doing wrong
Yet having his praises sung
At public gatherings.

Mahmūd Sāmī al-Barūdī (1839–1904)[1]

The only force that is capable of extracting us from the present crisis is this third way, whose history can be traced all the way back to the nineteenth century, which has ignited the 25 January revolution, and which is gaining self-confidence day after day. In contrast to other political forces that bask in past glories or that are mired licking their own wounds, this third way, which does not even have a name, face or shape, is the only force that has a vision. And as politically savvy this third way appears to be, it is its poetry—not its politics—that promises a salvation.

Khaled Fahmy, *The Third Way*[2]

Freedom, 'that terrible word inscribed on the chariot of the storm', is the motivating principle of all revolutions. Without it, justice seems inconceivable to the rebel's mind. There comes a time, however, when justice demands the suspension of freedom. Then terror, on a grand or small scale, makes its appearance to consummate the revolution.

Albert Camus, *The Rebel*[3]

It has been common practice among Arab leaders, scholars and people to punctuate their speeches, sermons and conversations with poetry in a way that lends resonant authenticity to the social or political setting. Referring to the

223

Arabs, the great Arab historian Ibn Khaldūn said for them poetry is 'a witness to their right behaviour and their wrongdoing' and 'a source which they return to'.[4] In the same vein, another significant medieval thinker, 'Abd al-Qāhir al-Jurjānī (d.1078), said that in poetry lay 'truth and wisdom', that it was 'a harvest of the fruits of the intellect', a 'leader and a guide', a 'cultured preacher' and a force for 'immortalizing the legacy of the past'.[5] The poetry in this chapter suggests that poetry can be a guide to the future as well as a perpetual tool of human renewal and maturity. The great thinker Ibn Sīna (980–1037) recognised poetry's collective significance as an enactment of the human will for dignified representation using an apt phrase, al-umma al-shi'riyā, commonly rendered as the 'community of feeling'. This reference to al-umma is different and more profound than the one normally used in the political sense. As R. A. Judy writes:

> I think 'the aesthetic community' is more apt, preferring the traditional Islamic conception of al-umma because it, unlike the contemporary political translation 'nation', does not imply a geopolitics of origin as the basis for inclusion but rather values a shared collective attachment based on a capacity to imagine in accordance with the conventions of linguistic expression. This also marks a tangential improvisation of the political concept of the aesthetic state that opens up a vector for thinking about poetry, or art, in relation to structures of power and governance.[6]

Indeed, the conventions of linguistic expression in the Arab world are the prime mover of its cultural cohesion and its awareness of its identity. These conventions underline the relative unity of slogans that underpinned the sentiments of the Arab revolutions; the shared expressions, statements and poems on which people draw to articulate their concerns and aspirations. This chapter will therefore study samples of poetry that evoke the spirit of the ongoing Arab Spring. It tracks this spirit to the nineteenth century, when an important strand of Arab intellectual thought emerged and called for an end to despotism and authoritarianism. In doing so, this chapter brings the book to a close with examples of meaningful socio-political changes that served the Arab people. Arabic poetry as a bearer of knowledge and values has always encapsulated aspirations for freedom and political emancipation in the Arab world. Different historical contexts gave way to poetry of protest, which culminated in the Arab Spring.

To this end, the chapter starts with notes on an important intellectual whose work ushered a stream of comments and reactions in the Arab world, namely 'Abd al-Raḥmān al-Kawākibī (1849–1902). The importance of al-Kawākibī's thought resides in his acute understanding of despotism as embodied in the then Ottoman Empire, and his prescription of solutions and resistance. His diagnosis of despotism finds reflections in diverse poetic orientations throughout the twentieth century. Discussion of these later poems will form the core of this chapter. They are from different parts of the Arab world, including Tunisia, Iraq, Palestine, Egypt, Libya and Syria. To varying degrees, they represent wider realms of expression and engagement with the issues of the countries in question and the Arab world in general.

The light of the intellect

One of the architects of Arab political philosophy in the nineteenth century was the Syrian educationalist 'Abd al-Rahmān al-Kawākibī. Al-Kawākibī's most significant work was *Tabāi' al-Istibdād wa-Masāri' al-Isti'bād*, 'The Nature of Despotism and the Harm of Enslavement'. He lived through an Arab cultural renaissance and nationalist rejuvenation of considerable political weight. During his lifetime the Ottoman Empire, which had controlled the Arab world for four centuries, was descending into decline. Its rulers, most notably Sultan Abdulhamid II (r.1876–1909), were the target of rage and condemnation from many Arab thinkers for what they considered to be epidemic corruption and despotism. Al-Kawākibī was vocal in this context. His aforementioned book is no less than revolutionary in its call for the overthrow of despotic regimes and the restoration of governance by and for the people. I draw on its significance here because it has been quoted and referred to extensively within the context of the Arab Spring as one of the founding modern Arabic texts against despotism.[7] Modern reference to the text and its message of good governance demonstrates the liveliness of Arab culture and politics in the sense that it is embedded in discourses that wed the past to the present and equip the social memory with collective intellectual references.

Against this background, it is instructive to quote what al-Kawākibī views as the primary cause of revolutions in his anatomical analysis of the traits of despotic rule:

> The masses do not often revolt in rage against the despot except after specific euphoric conditions that spark an immediate reaction, of which are:
>
> 1. After a bloody painful scene, which the despot inflicts on an oppressed who wants to rebel against his method.[8]

The Arab revolution, sparked in Tunisia in December 2010, started against precisely such a background. The actions of Mohamed Bouazizi (1984–2011), the young Tunisian man who set himself ablaze, ignited a spiral of protests, ending with the flight of the dictator Zine El-Abidine Ben Ali after more than twenty years in power. One of al-Kawākibī's seminal thoughts was that people can change their governments and rulers if the latter cease upholding the rights, values and interests of those whom they govern. Among the sources that al-Kawākibī used to advance his revolutionary attitude against the Ottoman Empire and despotism in general were the Arab poets. It is built into his argument against despotism that people can change the course of history by tapping into their collective power against unjust rulers. One of the poets al-Kawākibī quotes to demonstrate his thesis is the great tenth-century Arab poet Abū al-ʿAlā al-Maʿarri (973–1075):

> If a government does not govern us by justice
> Then we are capable of changing it[9]

Governance, justice and ability are intertwined to underpin this simple, yet politically charged line. It gives power to the people to be masters of their fate. But as al-Kawākibī explains, for people to rebel against their unjust rulers and rid themselves of despotism, there must be a reliable educational basis that facilitates and channels mature consciousness into active citizenship. Al-Kawākibī is not a random revolutionary or chaotically minded thinker calling for a revolution without a sense of where it should go, or how it should be translated into effective governance. To this end, being the educationalist that he was, he seals his treatise with the following:

> It must be that the sensibility of the *umma* nation should be made aware of despotism. Then it must be encouraged to look at the political foundation appropriate to it; so that this preoccupies the ideas of all its classes. Here it's a priority that this should remain the preoccupation of the minds for years, indeed for decades, until it is exactly mature, until there is a real longing for the attainment of freedom in the high classes and real hope on the part of the lower classes...on this basis, let the like-minded be farsighted, and let the arrogant be touched and humbled by the grace of God, and let it be known that the matter is difficult; but imagining difficulty does not necessitate trepidation and resignation, but provokes the will of the stronger man.[10]

Al-Kawākibī is mindful that the revolution must take place on a solid intellectual basis if it is to succeed; his sole enemy is ignorance, *al-jahl*, which he writes 'causes every malady' (ibid., p. 187). Al-Kawākibī is important in this context because his rich treatise is one of the solid intellectual signposts in the political history of twentieth-century Arabs. The issues he raised fall at the heart of the current Arab Spring. Meanwhile, al-Kawākibī's time coincided with many Arab poets, such as Ḥāfiẓ Ibrāhīm, Mutrān Khalīl Mutrān, Maʿrūf al-Risāfī and others who condemned the Western colonialism of their coun-tries, while pointing out political and cultural problems in the Arab world. To consider the relevance of al-Kawākibī and other Arab thinkers further, it is instructive to look at the initial slogan that the contemporary Arab revolu-tions raised and retrace it to one of its origins in the landscape of Arab poetry. The slogan 'The people wants the fall of the regime' summarises a history of Arab poetics concerned with change geared towards the betterment of the status quo in accordance with people's will and aspirations.

People power and change

The young Tunisian poet Abū al-Qāsim al-Shābbī (1909–1934) wrote the relatively long poem *irāadat al-hayāh* (The will to life) whose first two verses were quoted and used extensively in the Arab revolutions, by protesters, potential leaders, aspiring poets and writers. His words became a shrine of inspiration and passion for what the people wanted for themselves, their socie-ties and their conditions: to be free and just. Poetically, these lines became symbols of vision and possibility. Beyond the two famous verses, the entire poem is compelling, as are others of his poems that similarly raised political, social, existential and aesthetic issues, as discussed in Chapter 3. Al-Shābbī's poems reveal deeper concerns in Arab societies, concerns that echo in verse what al-Kawākibī put into prose a few years earlier. It suffices to highlight the emphasis that al-Kawākibī lays on people's will to change and live in a society immune from dictatorship and ignorance, ideals which al-Shābbī evokes pow-erfully in his poem:[11]

> *If, one day, a people desires to live, then fate will answer their call.*
> *And their night will then begin to fade, and their chains break and fall.*
> *For he who is not embraced by a passion for life will dissipate into thin air,*
> *At least that is what all creation has told me, and what its hidden spirits declare...*[12]

Life, for al-Shābbī, is not just living; it is constituted within a desire, empowered by will, to fights injustice where it looms large. The voice of romanticism, characteristic of that era, is clear in this poem. It is passion for life that makes life worth its name. For life to be of this sort, dignified and just, there has to be justice as well as a struggle against any form of despotism and enslavement. The poem from which these lines are taken is a compact evoca-tion bringing together life at its musically holistic zenith, celebrating the vir-tue of dignity as enabled through human will. People are wed to their essences, which are rooted in the forms and habits of nature, beautified once they are

able to be free and live with passion in a way that makes them feel and celebrate the dignified grace of their own humanity. Indeed, al-Shābbī's poem,
'The will to life', is an extravaganza of willing passion. Thus, when the poet
asks the earth, 'O mother, do you hate people?' the earth replies:

> *I bless the people of ambition,*
> *And those who enjoy the mounting of danger,*
> *And I curse those who rebel against time*
> *And accept living the life of the stone*
> *For the universe is alive, it loves life,*
> *And despises the dead, no matter how old he grows...*
> *Woe unto that who has not been torn apart*
> *By the curse of the triumphant void!*[13]

The poem singles out the season of spring for beauty, fertility and rejuvenation. The other two seasons explicitly mentioned, the autumn and the winter,
hide the rich bearings of nature and therefore are portrayed as sad and sadden-
ing. It is with spring, whether the spring of age, *rabīʿ al-ʿumr*, or the spring of
nature, that life brims with vitality and openness:

> *The bright in life is that which never dulls*
> *And the heart of spring, accented with scented greenery...*
> *The spring came with its tunes,*
> *Encrusted with dreams and fresh perfume...*

The poet ties the brilliance and magic of spring, *saḥar*, with ambition and
the will to life; and ends the poem with a similar line to that with which he
opened it, but with a new twist:

> *If souls aspire to life*
> *Fate will inevitably respond...*

The poem is an affirmation of life in its deepest and most promising sense,
as represented by spring. It is instructive to see how this poem is revolutionary in its spirit and form: it throws itself into the heart of nature and derives
visions from its perfection, embracing life in both its natural and constructed
composition. It does not stray into people's problems or human systems in
detail, but provokes them to love life, while not prescribing answers for those
that suffer materially. It inspires their will to overcome misery. Here the cor-
relation of this poem with revolution as the product of human will might be
noteworthy.

Revolutionaries in the throes of revolutions do not pay attention to details,
particularly after they have been stuck in an extremely unsatisfying and stulti-

fying situation. The poem here does not digress into impossibilities, but opens endless possibilities.

By the time al-Shābbī wrote these famous lines on 16 September 1933, a year before he died at the age of twenty-five, he had already written several poems similarly directed against dictatorship and other socio-political ills. These also pertain to the Arab Spring, as will be considered below, and particularly in light of their connections to al-Kawākibī's ideas.

The rulers and the ruled

Al-Shābbī's genius in poetry is matched with an awareness of the serious cultural and political problems in the Arab world. He directs his heart-felt concern and critique towards two structures: the political establishment represented by the dictator, and the social structure steeped in ignorance. One of the most relevant works is 'The dictator', a poem which has been widely used in the Arab Spring and particularly in al-Shābbī's birthplace, Tunisia:

> *Oppressive tyrant*
> *Lover of darkness, enemy of life*
> *You have ridiculed the sighs of the weak people*
> *Your palm is soaked with their blood*
> *You deformed the magic of existence*
> *and planted the seeds of sorrow in the fields*
> *Wait. Do not be fooled by the spring*
> *The clearness of the sky or the light of dawn*
> *For on the horizon lies the horror of darkness*
> *The rumble of thunder and the fierce blowing of wind*
> *Beware for below the ash there is fire*
> *And he who grows thorns eats wounds*
> *Look there for I have harvested the heads of mankind*
> *and the flowers of hope*
> *And I watered the heart of the earth with blood*
> *I soaked it with tears until it is drunk*
> *The river of blood will sweep you*
> *And the fiery storm will devour you.*[14]

What this poem shares with the earlier example is an enthusiasm and passion for his subject. Here, the dictator is stripped of all the truths and pleasures of existence. He is a delusional figure, who cannot see the hatred and rage that will one day be unleashed against him. There is a Sufi-like dynamic to this poem, with both the surface and hidden elements of existence in an operative mode. The dictator sees what is manifest but not what is latent, which is the soul of things. This reality became manifestly clear during the Arab revolutions, as the four dictators deposed, namely Ben Ali of Tunisia, Mubarak of Egypt, Qaddafi of Libya and Ali Abdallah Salih of Yemen, all claimed until the very end that their people loved them and considered them father figures. The four leaders often addressed revolutionaries in paternalistic language, referring, as did Mubarak, to 'my sons', *abnā'ī*, or in the words of Qaddafi, known for flippancy and outright humour, 'my people love me'. The delusion of spring that al-Shābbī evokes in this context is palpable.

Thus, while spring in the first poem signifies rejuvenation and beauty for the free and for those passionate about life, in the second poem it is a deceiver. It tricks the dictator into believing that the brightness and lightness of spring is all there is to reality, whereas behind the spring lies darkness which the dictator himself embodies. Here, the poet plays on the malleability of language to anchor it where it serves his insight, so that spring, depending on its upholder and receiver, can either be enveloped within darkness or as it appears, an emblem of vividness and brightness.[15] Furthermore, there is a strong message of justice in the poem, an important ideal evoked by the Arab revolutionaries. Instead of planting good seeds that will reap sound fruits, the dictator sows and brings up thistles amidst flowers that one day will erupt in his face and sweep him away. In short, nature abhors injustice when it attempts to sit comfortably in its midst.

In the third poem of al-Shābbī, 'The outcry', which is also visionary, engaging and passionate, he pinpoints what al-Kawākibī, as highlighted above, referred to as the 'cause of every malady', namely ignorance:

O people, my eyes had been struck with lightning
Ignorance is manifest as the fire of lightning in the sky...

Here, ignorance is responsible for many ills: it causes confusion; it strips people of the will to make decisions, to see and understand what is beneficial to them. The poet cries out in anger at his people for neglecting science and the progress of their ancestors. He uses performative, active verbs to highlight how those ancestors created a civilisation; constructed, preserved, lit and wove glories; and accomplished worthy achievements, as opposed to now:

O people you have become followers...
You have worn ignorance as a garment
Adopted it as a slogan...
O people, how come I see you dwelling in ignorance as an abode?

After highlighting that ignorance is endemic as well as destructive, al-Shābbī writes in the last stanza:

O poetry! You have resounded and made people hear,
But I see my people drunk...
...be patient about what you face
And resound, for it is only time before you are perfected.[16]

In relaying his message about ignorance through poetry, al-Shābbī echoes the sixth-century Arab poet Amru Bin Mu'di al-Zubaydi (525–642). This line of the latter's is proverbial in Arab culture:

You would have made the living hear
But there is no life in those you are calling to

In his poem al-Shābbī does not deny life to his people, the Arabs in general, but he calls them *sakārā* (drunk) with ignorance. It is poetry that releases the message about ignorance, rings the alarm bells, while the poet occupies the position of the seer. Poetry is thus the action itself, whereas the poet is the activating vessel from which issues a variety of philosophical, socio-political and aesthetic values. Poetry can accentuate knowledge and materialise its presence as the poet shows commitment to his craft as well as to the afflictions of his society. As was explained in the third chapter, this theme of commitment, *al-iltizām*, has been prominent in Arabic poetry of the twentieth century. Since it pertains particularly to the poetry of revolution and the Arab Spring in general, I turn to it now.

The persistence of revolution

The epistemological as well as the spiritual value of poetry is well established in the Arabic literary tradition. There has always been a diverse body of poets with a variety of orientations: some more inclined to reflect reality, others encased in visions of a transcendental nature, and still others who have attempted to maintain a balance between their own visions and aesthetic sensitivities and the world and its vagaries. But the established existence of these three major orientations did not prevent clashes and competitions between views and preferences.

It is phenomenal that so many Arab writers in the twentieth century predicted revolutions in their societies and called for a fundamental change in societal and cultural values. The Arabic tradition, whether literary or historical, is impressively rich and diverse, allowing several writers and people of opinion to form reasonably clear ideas about the potential patterns and trajectories that their societies could take. Ideas about justice, prosperity and freedom in their humanistic senses have always been present in one form or another. The poets in particular were agents of such ideas but they differed as to the meaning and content of the revolutions they called for. Yet they nevertheless maintained a consensus against ignorance, authoritarianism and oppression. While Romanticism held the torch of passion at the beginning of the twentieth century and before, Socialism held that of commitment, particularly after the 1950s.[17] One relevant poet here is the Iraqi Abd al-Wahāb al-Bayātī (1926–1998), who in 1965 wrote in his appropriately titled *Diwān Sifr al-Faqr wa-Thawra* (The book of poverty and revolution):

> *O generation of defeat, this revolution*
> *Will erase your shame and shake the rock*
> *It will shed your skin*
> *And plant a rose in your barren lives...*
> *O my generation, it will cast down the idols under your feet*
> *The winds of the proletariat will plough them into the abyss of oblivion.*[18]

The poem opens with an evocation of defeat, a raw experience for Arabs in the twentieth century, particularly in 1967, a mere nineteen years after Israel was established on the land of Palestine in 1948. Two defeats at the hands of Israel within such a short span of time alarmed many Arab intellectuals and poets, some of whom continued to bask in rhetorical vacuity while others engaged in a serious critique of Arab societies and called for a meaningful change that could engender a system of governance based on a solid structure of state order.[19] Such a change would be revolutionary, and since the focus of this chapter is on revolution and the Arab Spring, it is important to highlight the kind of change as well as the agents of it.

Revolution is indeed the resounding theme in al-Bayātī's poetry. It is a burning desire that, as Abū Hāqqa wrote, entailed hope for the following:

> Salvation through the road of a revolution that changes ideas, customs, conditions, systems, souls, and the life of the society, and the means of living, and turns bareness into prosperous gardens, and plants in the minds of the young, who are the generation of the future, and the subject of hope and possibility, new ideas that will be like rain whose water washes the face of the earth and the faces of the people, so as to wipe away its dust and its miserable look, and make of the misery which has rooted itself in the souls of the Arabs bridges and lampposts, and flowers and signposts, with what these words symbolize of construction and composition, enlightenment, prosperity, and the development of the agricultural and industrial sectors, and the contributions to the human civilisation.[20]

What is notable about al-Bayātī's poetry, observable in other works of that era (and even before), is the elaboration of desired outcomes for the revolutions, namely the end of poverty and social equality through a fairer distribution of resources and wealth: in others words socialism, as advocated by Jamal 'Abd al-Nassir. Arab poetry adopts this international template of reasoning and infuses it with Arab values and habits of expression. The poetry goes beyond highlighting and raging against ignorance, and promotes itself to the realm of ideology by suggesting an economic model that will potentially save the Arabs from their woes. As was explained in the second chapter, two iconic Egyptian poets, Ahmad Shawqi (1868–1932) and Ḥāfiẓ Ibrāhīm (1872–1932), had already highlighted the importance of *al-Ishtirākiyya* (socialism) for the Arab world, seeing in it a means to the achievement of long-suppressed desires of equality in their societies. In al-Bayātī's poetry, *al-Ishtirākiyya* is implied through its bearers of change, namely the poor and the lower classes, those who will carry the torch of change in the Arab world. Al-Bayātī carried this theme forward from other Iraqi and Arab poets, such as Badr Shākir al-Sayyāb (1926–1964). In another poem he emphasises the historical and political agency of the workers:

> *O God of the downtrodden poor,*
> *We have not been defeated,*
> *But it is the grand peacocks*
> *Who have been defeated alone*[21]

People are exempted from defeat here, while their leaders are blamed for it *tout court*. The 'grand peacocks' are the leaders who led the Arab nation (*umma*) from one defeat to another. And it is the workers, the proletariat, who will one day triumph over them and hold the reins of governance, responsibility and justice; it is this sector of society that the poet stands with and speaks for. Arabic poetry from the 1950s onwards abounds with references to defeats, revolutions and change. It should not therefore be treated as coincidental that the Arab revolutions were fuelled by the workers (proletariats), and by the downtrodden, *al-Kādihīn*. In Tunisia, the initiator of the revolution, Mohamed Bouazizi (1984–2011), was a fruit seller whose life was strangulated by the undignified practices of the Tunisian authorities, an arm of the dictatorial regime. The seeds of the Egyptian revolution were planted by striking factory workers in al-Mahala al-Kubrā and other Egyptian cities such as Alexandria, who called for pay-rises and better working conditions. The aforementioned poetry, in addition to other forms of expression, has therefore constantly played the role of torch-bearer in heightening the consciousness of the people regarding the state of their country and its needs. The vocabularies of this poetry endowed slogans and public speeches with urgent meanings. One of the slogans of the revolution that echoes the spirit of the poem quoted so far in Egypt is 'Life, freedom and human dignity'. All these aspects are vital to the fulfilment that workers want to be central to their lives, and have constantly been at the heart of revolutionary poetry in the Arab world.

Islamism: change and return

Alongside the trends of socialism and secular nationalism that flourished in the Arab world particularly from the 1950s until the 1980s came a new philosophy and poetry, inspired by the relatively new phenomenon of Islamism, championed with considerable enthusiasm by the intellectual godfather of modern Islamism, Sayyid Qutb (1906–1966) of Egypt. Qutb is known for his Islamist treatises, such as *Milestones*, in which he doggedly advocates a return to the principles of the original *umma*, or Islamic nation. He denounces both the materialism of the West and those in the Arab world who subscribe to Western ideology. As he wrote in the introduction to this influential book, 'if Islam is again to play the role of the leader of man-kind, then it is necessary that the Muslim community be restored to its original formation'.[22] Qutb's poetry encompasses various themes and forms. It struck a chord with the Muslim Brotherhood supporters not only in Egypt where the Muslim Brotherhood was founded, but wherever the movement found cognates, such as in the Palestinian resistance movement Hamas. One poem used to mobilise Islamic sentiments, which gained attention and is widely memorised and recited by the Muslim Brotherhood, is called '*Akhī* (My brother). The poem is essentially a call to arms, *kifāh*, for the sake of the restoration of the Islamic *umma*. It calls for and also predicts a new order:

> My brother, you will annihilate the armies of darkness
> And in the universe a new dawn shall rise
> So let your soul release its first rays
> You will see dawn gazing at us from afar.[23]

Qutb, who was hastily executed by the President of Egypt Jamal 'Abd al-Nassir in 1966 for allegedly plotting to overthrow the government, had his eyes firmly on a new dawn; one in which his Islamist ideology would reign with God as the ultimate point of reference in all affairs of the Islamic *umma*. In the poem he advises his 'brother', through the evocative case he adopts, to keep his eyes straight on his objective of establishing *al-Haqq* (righteousness), a term that in Islamist parlance suggests a narrow determination to make Islam central to governance. In light of the electoral success of Islamists in various parts of the Arab world, some Islamists reread Sayyid Qutb's strident views and saw vindication in his assessment and prediction that Islam and a society guided by Islamic principles would eventually win the upper hand. His aforementioned poem is widely chanted and memorised, used to express a strong belief that Islam should and will have a say in the regulatory powers of the state; particularly after many Islamists were imprisoned by secular Arab regimes, they recite it with confidence, assurance and faith.

The anatomy of dictatorship

Besides the poets of ideology, those who implied or propagated a particular system of governance in their poetry, such as socialism or Islamism, there have also been independent poets who observed the corrosive signs and effects of dictatorships, and stood on the side of the people. They deployed a variety of literary methods in their poetry to portray the depth of their frustrations; one of the most common is sarcasm, sometimes vulgar and biting and at other times subtle and theatrical.

The Iraqi poet Ahmad Matar (b.1952) has been one of the main champions of poetry of protest against the rulers, and against the people for not rebelling under their terrible conditions and their dictators. Most of his poetry offers a damning verdict on the dictator and searing lamentations over the state of the Arab world in general. In 'A tear over the corpse of freedom', Matar writes:

> *I do not write poems, but poems write me,*
> *I want silence so that I can live, but what I face compels language out of me,*
> *All I encounter is sadness, sadness and sadness again,*
> *Can I write as if I am alive in my coffin?*
> *Can I write I am free when every letter ripples with enslavement?*
> *I have mourned a ravishing woman,*
> *She is called destruction and terror in the Arab land,*
> *And in violation of the divine laws,*
> *By God, I swear...*
> *Her real name is freedom.*[24]

The poet suggests that freedom has been trampled upon in the Arab world. It has been replaced by references to the divine and by misconceptions of a variety of fundamental human capacities and meanings. In short, the poet, staring into the deep abyss of the Arab world, sees nothing but sorrow and meaninglessness, which in turn forces poems of rebellion and protest out of him, crying out for the lost human ideal of freedom. The type of freedom that Matar evokes is one that has been voiced by many revolutionaries in the Arab world during the Arab Spring. Among them is the President of Tunisia,

Muncif al-Marzouqy, who replaced the dictator through a popular vote after a transitional period in the wake of the Tunisian revolution. In his writings, al-Marzouqy laments the years of despotism and calls for an ethos of freedom and humanity that does not cheapen others but respects human rights, moving on from the years of squandering, rhetorical vacuity, ideological abuse and reductionism that found fertile ground under Arab dictatorships.[25]

Another poet who has been a visionary thinker on dictatorship and despotism in the Arab world is the Palestinian poet Mahmoud Darwish (1941– 2008). Though renowned as the Palestinian national poet, using his poems to register the effects of the Israeli occupation on Palestine and the Palestinians with vividness and worldliness, Darwish also contributed to poetic engagement against authoritarianism and dictatorship. His 1987 poem, *khutab al-dictātūr al-mawzūnah*, 'The rhymed speeches of the dictator', ripples with prophecies as well as humorous snapshots as to how the dictator perceives himself and his realm.[26]

Ironically, Darwish was hesitant about incorporating the poem into his poetic oeuvre, whether for artistic or political reasons.[27] The poem is divided into the dictator's speeches, arranged chronologically. Thus it begins with the speech of taking power, when the dictator starts his reign:

From the speech of taking power

I will choose my people...
I will choose the intelligent people, the lovely and the successful,
I will choose you according to the constitution of my heart:
Whoever of you is without fault, he is the guardian of my dog,
Whoever of you is without a doctor, I will appoint him a politician to my new horse,
Whoever of you is a man of letters, I will appoint him a standard-bearer for the direction of the anthem,
Whoever of you is wise, I will appoint him a councillor for the coinage of money,
Whoever of you is handsome, I will appoint him a chamberlain for scandals
Whoever of you is strong, I will appoint him a deputy for eulogies...
And whoever of you is without gold, or talents, he should go away...

From the speech of annoyed boredom

Who amongst you could sit for thirty years on one chair,
without becoming a piece of wood himself...?
Which chest can afford as many badges of honour as mine...?...

From the speech of peace

> *...O people, it is time for us to correct our history*
> *So that we can compete with civilisations in word and deed...*
> *What do they want?*
> *All Palestine? Welcome,*
> *Do they want the edges of Sinai? Welcome*
> *Do they want the head of the Sphinx—this trickster of time?—welcome*
> *They want the heights for attack on Shām (Syria)? Welcome*
> *They want the rivers of Lebanon? Welcome*
> *They want to amend Uthmān's Qur'an? Welcome*
> *They want Babylon so that they can take the head of 'Nabū' as a spoil of war?*
> *Welcome...*

From the speech of 'The Prince'

> *And our oil is your blood*
> *And industry is the production of the orphans our war has generated...*

From the speech of the grave

> *I have reached eighty, but I will live for another eighty and another ninety...*

From the speech of the idea

> *I say to you what the party decides, and the party is our absolute authority...*
> *I will announce a revolution from our land,*
> *The revolution of the poor against the poor...*

From the speech of the women

> *How can I liberate the bodies of our wives from the fingers of (my) others...?*
> *And each woman has a Scheherazade in her*
> *And each tyrant has a tortured shahrayār in him...*

From the speech of the speech

> *It is in my language that the affairs of the country are run...*
> *My speech is the reality of this speech*
> *Because the speech of the system*
> *Is the system of speech...*

Darwish insightfully relays a variety of dictatorial patterns and scenarios picked up from observing the Arab political scene. But these scenes and scenarios are also universal to wherever there is absolute power, institutionalised

237

corruption and widespread practices of gross inhumanity. Dictatorships all share delusion, grandiosity, messy playfulness, recklessness and cruelty. Darwish touches on eight vital elements which can represent Arab dictators, ranging from economy to politics to religion.

In the first speech, we see the random choice of people the dictators put in place; the wrong person for the wrong job, creating a psychological displacement of human energies. Later we come across the image of Mubarak who, having been president for thirty years, reached the age of eighty but still insisted on continuing to rule. We see the defeatist position of Arab leaders, accepting unacceptable alleged peace deals for the sake of a facade of stability and patriarchal continuity. We see the unworthy rich propped up by oil revenues. We see the dictator clinging to the edge of life, ruling by iron fist even in his speech of the grave. Then we have an image of Qaddafi of Libya in the speech of the idea, flimsily claiming to be the father of revolutions and equality, while in reality creating hierarchies of submission to him and his rule. Then there are the rulers who exploit and cheapen their people's conceptions of women, investing their desires with grandiose masculinity cloaked in darkness and oppression. And finally, in the speech of the speech, language becomes an object of oppression, suppression and deception in itself, when reality is made not by what it is but by discourses of absolute power.

It goes without saying that all the aspects ridiculed in Darwish's poem have been exhibited by Arab dictatorships in one form or another. They represent the serious flaws that have been depicted by all the poets examined so far. They are another testament to the long tradition of protest against political elites and unjust rulers in the Arab world who have abused their power and downgraded their people's abilities. What Darwish playfully satirises above are the sorts of practices and realities that provoked the Arab Spring, which I turn to now.

The poetry of the Arab Spring

The Arab Spring is hardly a 'Spring'; it is more like an enormous pile of frustrations that could no longer be contained by the times in which we live. The initial phase of the revolution in Tunisia did not create a widespread eruption of unstoppable momentum in the Arab world until Ben Ali suddenly fled to Saudi Arabia with his family. Egypt then carried the flame; from then onwards, revolution became a part of the imagination as well as the actual lives of the people of the region. The Libyan revolution with its violent showdowns gave way to Syria with its ongoing blood-drenched conflict, too dark and tragic to have any affinity with the image of spring promised by the Tunisian revolution. Yet it is as an 'Arab Spring' that this outbreak of revolutions has come to be known. In this case, the Arab Spring is a category of convenience, holding hope and possibility after decades, if not centuries, of decadent misrule and oppression. Whichever bright or dark alleys it has entered at the time of this current writing, the Arab Spring is a historical moment of momentous transition which has to be treated with cautious hope, even though the human loss and destructive consequences of the revolutions in Syria and Libya in particular have been heart-wrenching to watch and live through. Dictatorships are by nature violent and stubbornly dark, as they negate the presence of other citizens and their capacity for governance. Dictators entrench themselves in positions of power that, as historical experience teaches us, should be diffused into many hands and legally and institutionally protected, rather than being paternalistically and selfishly seized. Considering that the revolutions started with the aim of replacing dictatorships with democracy and freedom, these original noble objectives should be borne in mind first and foremost regardless of whatever courses the revolutions then ran into. All the voices of free poets, as opposed to strictly ideological poets, assert the uncompromising necessity of freedom as a way of life that respects the roots of human essence and gives each individual the socio-political avenues and opportunities needed to realise themselves. In this sense, the scope of poetic politics is wider and more promising than that of formal politics with its entrenchment in the present moment and its lack of flexibility.

Against this background, poets rising to the occasion of the Arab Spring responded with compositions of varied quality, relevance and meaning. No one poet can be singled out for her or his uniqueness and overall qualities, however. The political scene in this sense corresponds to the literary one, as no single political leader of solid stature stepped up to seize attention in this revolution. With this in mind, the poetry that emerged in the course of these revolutions is worthwhile for its dynamism and interaction with the moment. And as always in Arab lives, poetry reflects a rich repository of expressive powers congruent with certain aspects of history, culture and political events and values. In addition, some of the poetry in question includes poetry written in local dialects, such as the Egyptian or Palestinian dialects. In particular, the Egyptian dialect has occupied pride of place among Arab dialects for its popularity and Arab-wide resonance perhaps because the poetry written in it tends to draw on common Arab imagery and classical sources. Noha Radwan refers to such poetry, called *Shi'r al-'Ammiyya*, as 'a modern movement that originated in the 1950s and in the poetry of Fu'ād Haddād (1927–85) and Salah Jāhīn (1930–86)...as a fusion of the new poetic sensibilities that had been developing among Arab poets and critics for a few years by then and some of the features and poetics of older, more traditional forms.[28]

Such poetry draws on and also heightens the immediacy of political events. It popularises them and stokes collective passion to innovate, interact and respond. In addition to Jāhīn and Haddād, some of the most important practitioners and popularisers of this poetry have been the late Ahmad Fuʾād Najm and Abdel Rahmān al-Abnūdī. In particular, the beginning of the Arab Spring constituted such a political moment with an immediate poetic output because of the emotional response it engendered. It provoked poets with a talent for immediate interaction and collective embodiment to recite and write poetry to accentuate everyone's consciousness and record what people were feeling at this authentic time, when people were seen as the holders and shapers of their own fate. To this end, in what follows, I highlight fragmentary samples from a few Arab poets who responded to the revolutions and made them central to the subject of their poetry, whether in classical or in colloquial Arabic.

At the height of the Egyptian revolution, the veteran Egyptian poet Abdel Rahmān al-Abnūdī wrote and recited the following poem on one of the Egyptian television stations while people were congregated in Liberation Square in Cairo and in other cities of Egypt. The poem is titled, *al-maydān*, 'The Square':

> Old men, tough, ravenous, they totally ate our country,
> All alike in greed, cheapness and form,
> But the brilliant young men emerged
> And turned their autumn into a spring
> And they achieved the miracle of waking up the murdered from his murder...
> It is impossible that lying can wear the mask of truth again.∴
> They have written the first lines on the page of the revolution.

This is an extract from the long poem that al-Abnūdī recited in Egyptian dialect. It conveys an intimate connection between the people and the poet as an intellectual with an educational message. Each line reflects an issue regarding dictatorship. The poet lambasts dictators, echoing similar sentiments to that of al-Shābbī, as mentioned at the beginning of the chapter. Al-Abnūdī also writes in a realistic, wise tone, steeped in the historical knowledge that revolutions often take time to ripen. The people who protested have just written the first line on the empty page of revolution, suggesting a long road ahead. It is only poetry that could say so much through so little.

Another significant popular Egyptian poet was Ahmad Fuʾād Najm.[29] His death in 2013 engendered an outpouring of affection and respect for a figure that had been since the 1950s, alongside his comrade Sheikh Imām, a champion of the poor and the downtrodden.[30] It seems appropriate to refer to him as a walking revolution. He had always called for change in an inclusive revolutionary tone that voiced people's grievances in a way that endeared him to the entire spectrum of Arab society, excepting the regimes that imprisoned him and subjected him to harsh treatments many times over. His poems interacted with major political events and issues along socialist, internationalist and pan-Arab lines, as was highlighted in previous chapters. His poetry constituted a part of the counter-literature and counter-culture that opposed the regimes in power and their desire for hegemony; and it derives its inspiration and lexicon from the political concerns of the Arab world.[31]

One of his moving poems evokes the death of the revolutionary Che 'Ernest' Guevara (1928–1967). It depicts him as a model human being who is uncompromising on what is right and just and is engaged in achieving justice on the battlefield and in the forests, rather than remaining removed from the people in palaces or private places, as Arab dictators have done. In addition, Najm is characterised as having an acerbic sense of humour. Referring to the raging conflict in Syria and the tension between the Sunni and Shī'a, he highlighted the subservient nature of Arab politics and its consuming absurdity: 'The Sunnis have America; the Shī'a have Russia and the atheists have God.'[32] Yet, he is also critical of exploitative political groups, an indication of his wisdom as to the political sensibilities in place at the time of the unfolding revolutions. He wrote one poem in the context of the evolving revolutions, entitled 'This is a poor people' (*Dah sha'b fa'ir*), in which he drew a picture of a people who are effectively ignorant, unable to organise the revolution productively in order to move forward towards freedom and responsibility, and addicted to subservience and humiliation. As he says:

These people most certainly do not understand
O the leader, evict them from the realm of your mercy
And if you are tempted by authority
Stay in your place
I will dive and go up and down
And come back with people obedient to you...
All that they can say is
'Long live the leader,'
'Long live the leader.'[33]

Najm celebrated Arab revolutions and championed them. In this poem, however, he highlights the entrenched difficulties of achieving emancipation when people are disunited and various groups are pursuing power through

241

exploitative means that perpetuate the old status where the leader is idolised by the people, rather than being subject to criticism and accountability. People are not acting as citizens with responsibility towards the collective welfare of their states, but as uncritical affiliates of their ideological groups. In a way, Najm puts into critical verse Lisa Wedeen's thesis about Syria, which is applicable to other dictatorial contexts where people seem to reproduce the regime's platitudes and unreservedly show reverence to its leader. Wedeen writes:

> The regime produces compliance through enforced participation in rituals of obeisance that are transparently phony to those who orchestrate them and to those who consume them.[34]

Yet, Najm does not excuse people for blind submission to corrupt rulers, suggesting oppression by habitual compliance. Najm is an advocate of institutional reforms and purposeful actions that yield collectively valued results that serve the people and elevate their place as agents. This sentiment was something the initial discourse of the Arab Spring capitalised on. The poetry of the Arab Spring therefore concerned itself with the power of the people, as well as the condemnation of dictatorship, waste and oppression. To this end, the Libyan poet Khaled Mattawa was active during his own revolution. The following poem of his was first published in English following the cruel death of the Libyan dictator Mu'ammar al-Qaddafi:

> *The dictator, a young man, a shy recluse assumed the helm, bent in piety,*
> *the dead sun of megalomania hidden in his eyes...*
> *the radio thundering hatred, retching blood-curdling song—*
> *Signs that went unread...*
> *Factories built and filched, houses stolen, newspapers shut down,*
> *decades of people killed, 42 years...*
> *Wait 42 years—five years old when my father was killed*
> *standing in front of a hotel.*

This poem, called 'After 42 years', is based on a poignant story. The poet narrates the emergence of the young leader of Libya, Mu'ammar al-Qaddafi, in 1968. Soon after assuming power, he began a series of practices that ensured ultimate and absolute loyalty to himself and his regime, constituted in what he called the revolutionary committees. Qaddafi was merciless in suppressing any sign or hint of dissent or opposition. He styled and modelled everything on his insubstantial personality, dragging a world of potential into one of waste and total brutality. It is the pain of forty-two years of chaos that the poet is exorcising, recounting the incident, one that must have derailed his life, when his father fell victim to al-Qaddafi's system.

Furthermore, it is evident that the poetry of the Arab Spring has generally focused on the leaders and their corruption, unlike pre-revolution poetry when protest was often directed against the rulers and the ruled, the latter for their silence, collusion, or submission to corrupt authorities. In the poetry of the Arab Spring, the people are often singled out and praised for collectively taking the initiative to improve their conditions. In this sense, the poetry of the Arab Spring is bound to the moment of protest, and is as focused as the revolutionaries themselves on ridding the people of oppressive authorities. The poetry often takes its inspiration from the language of the protesters themselves, as can be seen from the opening word of the Egyptian poet Farūq Shūshah's poem '*Irhal*': 'leave', a word that the protesters used to direct at the dictator, framing their simple demand for him to leave so that they could choose their leaders and representatives.

Finally, in the ongoing Syrian revolution, the birthplace of 'Abd al-Rahmān al-Kawākibī who once protested against despotism, the killing and mutilation of one singer, Ibrāhīm al-Qawūsh, has demonstrated beyond doubt the depth of human depravity that dictatorship breeds. The song that particularly angered the authorities, sung in colloquial Syrian Arabic like many other revolutionary poems, is the following:

> *O Bashār* [the dictatorial President of Syria], *you are not one of us,*
> *Take Māher* [his brother] *and go away from us,*
> *Your legitimacy had been stripped by us,*
> *O Bashār, the liar, you torment and give a speech;*
> *Freedom is at the doorstep,*
> *O Bashār, damn you and all those who salute you...*
> *O Bashār, the parasite, your speeches are incomprehensible,*
> *Your news is that of the owl...*[35]
>
> *We will remove him* [Bashār], *and with our strong determination,*
> *Syria needs Freedom...*
> *Without Māher and without Bashār, and this savage lot...*
> *Syria needs freedom...*

The colloquial leanings of the song, chanted around a crowd that repeated and confirmed his sentiments after him, rang out in the squares of Hama in an atmosphere as electric as it was good-natured. A few days later, Ibrāhīm al-Qawūsh was abducted and murdered. His vocal cords were cut out and his mutilated body was thrown into a river. His murder, along with thousands more, is the strongest statement on the savagery of dictatorship that al-Qawūsh sang against with youthful fervour, as did so many other Arab poets, singers and writers before him. He and other victims of the revolutions have been commemorated by poets from across the Arab world, such as the Omani poet 'A'isha al-Saifi, the Lebanese poet Shawqī Bazīqh and the Algerian poet 'Ayāsh Yahyāwī. They recited their poems in poetry festivals held in Arab capitals, such as Cairo, Muscat in Oman and Amman.

The Syrian revolution has taken a prolonged and bloody trajectory. Various forces, including extremist oppositional Islamist groups, have targeted the country and its citizens. As well as being a revolution, it is now also a complex and intractable tragedy. All the forces involved are accused of war crimes and inhumane conduct on a huge scale. Against this background, there emerged a poetry which depicts the suffering of the Syrians as a people engulfed by violence, displacement and degradations from multiple forces within the country, including the regime, the Lebanese Shi'ā movement Hizbullah, Sunni Islamist groups and other actors, with some acting as proxies for regional powers such as Saudi Arabia and Iran.

One story tells that the Syrian refugee poet, Nadir Shalīsh, from the town of Kafr Nbūdah near Hama, was in the middle of reciting the following poem when he was forced to stop midway as his town was being bombarded. He later had a chance to recite his poem in full in the refugee camp of Atmah on the borders between Syria and Turkey. The poem is written in the traditional Arabic style of Qaṣīdah, brimming with rhythmic cadence and studded with imagery that draws on classical Arabic poetry and its themes of lament over ruins:

> *I sent my soul to my home to circulate around it*
> *When our steps to reach it had become untenable*
> *I delegated my soul to ask if the house still remembers us*
> *Or if it has forgotten since its people left it*
> *To ask the ceiling if it was still proudly on top of the wall*
> *Despite what they* [the regime's forces] *have done*
> *Or it has crumbled to the ground and prostrated*
> *Lamenting to God in sorrow and supplication...*
> *My soul would still inhabit the house*
> *I have nothing in Atamah, neither herds nor livelihood...*
> *The night will be followed by a morning that dispels it*
> *And light will prevail and darkness will fade away...*
> *How trivial that they had thought of us as animals*
> *As if we were bereft of leaders.*[36]

The poem registers the gloominess of the moment, with painful nostalgia for the house left behind and the intimate ordinary scenes that once surrounded the poet who weeps as he recites his poem. Turning the soul into a migrating object or a caring bird, one that possesses the human ability to ask questions and declare loyalty to a place, is quite common in Arabic poetry. In addition to the poem's echoes of Imrū al-Qays' lament for a ruined place, which was referred to in the first chapter, links can also be made with Darwish's long poem, '*Lāʿib al-Nard*', 'The dice player'. The Syrians have been experiencing what the Palestinians once suffered as refugees in 1948, a shattering experience centred on the loss of the home that constitutes the primary sense of psychological security and stability. Darwish writes:

> *I could not have been a swallow*
> *Had the winds wished me to,*
> *And the wind is the luck of the traveller...*
> *I travelled north, east and west*
> *But the south was too hard and forbidden to me*
> *Because the south is my country*
> *I became a metaphor for a swallow...*
> *Flying over my ruins...*[37]

In fact one Palestinian poet, Nabīl al-Muʿajil, has written a letter tellingly entitled 'A letter from a Palestinian refugee to a Syrian refugee'. It registers the traumatic experience of dispossession and the lingering pain of losing the homeland and the nation-state. The Palestinian says to the Syrian refugee in a poetic narrative style:

> I was told by an unknown source that the tent will be disturbing in the first night. Thereafter, it will emit warmth and tenderness as if it is one of the family members. But be warned of falling in love with it, as we did...do not be happy if they find a health centre or an elementary school. This is not good news at all.[38]

Having experienced dispossession for so long, the Palestinian refugee advises the Syrian refugee to keep struggling to return to home, and not to resign her or himself to a tent elsewhere. The tent is a symbol of loss, not settlement or stability. The letter is acutely aware of the political dynamics of the various actors in play. It highlights a hegemonic international practice: the parties responsible for refugees' dispossession and suffering often treat them as victims of humanitarian rather than political crises. The refugees are therefore given handouts and treated with gestures, rather than being offered political rights that address the root causes of their predicament, or the opportunity of seeing those who caused their dispossession held responsible for their crimes.

The references and allusions in the Syrian poet's poem, shared among poets in a process known as intertextuality, are notably moving. Such intertextuality is further underlined by shared sensibilities shaped by similar experiences, as

Shalīsh is writing at a moment of acute crisis. Despite his humble peasant origins, he adopts the structure of classical Arabic poetry and fuses it with modern language and references to treat the tragedy at hand. Meanwhile, he resorts to stock images of hope, resurrection and return to recapture what has been lost, because there is an ongoing struggle to retrieve the loss. The poem is grounded in hopeful faith in divine justice and human will for the ultimate triumph of good over evil. This hope has been popularised by the Tunisian poet Abū al-Qāsim al-Shābbī, as seen above. The Syrian poet/refugee appears as an old man. He is made destitute by a ravaging war in which cruelty is a daily reality. His poem addresses his own tragedy of displacement and humiliation, and puts his grief into a metrically ordered language that mourns it and suggests the possibility of another future, an essential ingredient of therapeutic recovery.

Stefan Sperl has highlighted how poetry can serve as a healing force in the face of shattering traumas.[39] His illuminating study uses as examples the poetic texts that respond to the tragedies that afflicted cities from the Sumerian era in Mesopotamia in 1940 BC to the destruction of Jerusalem in 586 BC, as recorded in the Biblical book of Lamentations; and also to one poem of Ibn al-Rumī composed in AD 871, which invokes the destruction of the Iraqi city al-Basra. Such poetry reorders the lost old world through language that reconstitutes the trauma in mournful and transcendental ways. Al-Rumi makes from language houses of remembrance, comfort and possibility:

> We are here faced with the fundamental unity of the human psyche which resurfaces more clearly in the confrontation with extreme events and the reactions they cause. Much in contrast to this, the texts also show that this same psyche seeks meaning and coherence in the construction of identities whose hallmark is the exclusion of others and hence the very denial of that unity.[40]

Through poetry, a Syrian poet attempts to retrieve and reassert an identity, albeit a lost one, to affiliate her or himself with a familiar, ordered and secure world. Moreover, while the Syrian tragedy continues, its victims vary and their traumas deepen. In particular, Syrian children have borne the brunt of the devastation, with the United Nations estimating that as many as 1.1 million Syrian children are refugees in neighbouring countries; haunted, as their counterparts in Syria, by the war and its traumas.[41] The Syrian poet Hussein Habasch, in his collection *Malāk Tāʾir* (A Flying Angel), concentrates on their plight. In modernist sombre verse with a terse narrative style, Habasch depicts the painful targeting of innocence and the haunting scenes of violence with children as victims, a violence that shatters their world and introduces them to scenarios and places beset by utter abnormality, utterly lacking in peace and humanity:

> *The boy who ascended the ladder*
> *To tell the neighbours*
> *About the approaching aeroplane*
> *And the beginning of bombardment*
> *Carried on his ascendance to Heaven!*[42]

Another haunting piece records the predicament of another child:

> *From the awesome fear and the savagery of the massacre*
> *The tongue of the boy got tied*
> *With his trembling hands*
> *He narrated the complete story of his miraculous escape.*[43]

In another fatal incident, the child was not fortunate enough to survive to tell her story:

> *The killer forgot to stab the doll*
> *Alongside the little girl who owned it*
> *From the shock, the doll woke up*
> *Clung to the girl*
> *Refusing to be buried except with her.*[44]

The symbolism of a childhood brutally cut short rings out in these poems through poignant symbols, most notably the loyal grieving doll whose owner has been killed. The world depicted in these poems suggests that the Arab revolutions are far from being an easy story to narrate or celebrate. The poems show the many tragedies that have ravaged families, divided communities and wrecked countries where the idea of living as more than surviving has to many become a dream. Yet, this should not obscure the essential fact that the Arab uprisings represent a long journey towards freedom, justice and dignity, where human progress may have been achieved by surviving the tragic and hopeful struggles.[45] The poetry in this chapter should therefore be seen as seeds of hope sown from a constant vision of a better future and fairer conditions. In this respect, the English poet Percy Bysshe Shelley (1792–1822) is apt, with his enlightening ideal of a humanity free from oppression and with values of love, hope and forgiveness at its heart:

> *To suffer woes which Hope thinks infinite*
> *To forgive wrongs darker than death or night;*
> *To defy Power, which seems omnipotent;*
> *To love, and bear; to hope till Hope creates*
> *From its own wreck the thing it contemplates...*[46]

Conclusion

It is evident that there is a long-standing narrative of poetry of rebellion and revolution in the Arab world. Since the nineteenth century, when the Arab world lay in the shadow of colonialism, many Arab intellectuals and poets called for, discussed and prophesied revolution. The poets examined here have all been outraged by the corruption of authority and vocal in their desire to see it overthrown. Meanwhile, there have also been a number of poets, writers and intellectuals who went along with authority and offered legitimacy to the cruellest of dictators and authorities. What has been presented above shows one solid strand of the Arab poetic culture that was brought to the fore by the Arab Spring with vitality, passion and promise.

The poetry of the Arab Spring offers an insightful record of the engagement of poets and writers with the rich culture, history and politics of the Arab world. While the revolutionaries tapped into Arabic traditions and employed lines of inspiration from across the centuries, they also found poets in their midst who expressed their long-held frustrations and rendered them with vividness and passion through recitation or singing. The voice of the people took over, as they were hailed for their courage as vociferously as their leaders were condemned for their corruption. In speaking out, the poets of the revolution stepped up their criticism of their leaders, seeing in them the brutal human beings they are, and eviscerating the God-like facades they had unsuccessfully attempted to maintain. The poets have also been forthcoming in recording the traumas of the Arab Spring and its victims.

To this end, there is promise in the poetry of the Arab Spring, that it will open up to broader questions of social, political, existential and aesthetic considerations, rather than regurgitate existing forms of literary and by implication political authority.

One value of the poetry in question is perhaps best expressed in the words of the Egyptian poet Salah Jahīn (1930–1986), who also had great insights about the people's power and spirit:

> *O the spring has taken a long time to come,*
> *For the weather to warm up and the flowers to blossom*
> *The spring has returned rapturously, injected with youth's passion...*
> *What made me erupt?*
> *O my world...'agabī!*
> *Tomorrow, our struggle will be an ode*
> *That describes to us*
> *The days of a glorious revolution...*[47]

AFTERWORD

From the room where I am sitting, two scenes attract my attention in particular; one born of nature, and another of nurture through human labour, attesting to humankind's capacity for constructive creation. Firstly, I can see leaves on the trees bathed in sunshine. Secondly, I can see a golden-coloured Renaissance church with grand windows, communicating stable delight and hope. The comparison between these two scenes in turn relates to Arabic poetry in so far as it uses the building blocks of language to represent experiences derived from diverse human realities, both natural and man-made, amidst conditions in which humans are subjects as well as objects. The Arab poets, and indeed all poets, employ and explore the nature of language and subject it to their will and vision to produce an outcome concurrent with their understanding and wishes. To this end, the story of modern Arabic poetry is multi-layered and vast—it would take many books to do justice to its breadth and depth. Be that as it may, I hope that this book represents a modest contribution towards the task of highlighting the range of conceptual ground on which modern Arabic poetry has stood since it came to the fore in the nineteenth century, particularly as linked to the major political currents and events that have shaped the modern Arab world. The unique value of Arabic poetry is that it shows how the Arabic language is a force not only of expression but also of action. The sense of action within which the Arabic language can be understood entails an expressive variety of concerns, ranging from appeals to emotion to direct calls for mobilisation. In this sense, Arab nationalism as crystallised in literature is actively embedded in acts of expression that have accentuated the consciousness of the Arabs about their society and their needs. The Arab world represents a language community *par excellence*, in that its language has been a barometer of its past and present as well as its highs and lows.

The story of Arab nationalism with all its political implications and diversity would be incomplete and unrepresentative without an acknowledgement of the role that poetry has played in its inception and continuity. The aesthetic value of poetry is encompassed not only in its literary form, but also in its performative articulation. The artistic use of language has created and continues to create immense aesthetic and political effects. This is illustrated by the fact that, at the time of writing, one of the major global news items is about the young Palestinian singer from Gaza, Mohammad Assaf (b. 1989), who rose to fame on the grounds of his accomplished performance. His unique voice, with its confident depth, flexibility and fluidity, coupled with his lively and charming personality, have endeared him to the Arab world; he won a major singing competition in 2013 and brought memorable scenes of celebration to Palestine and the Arab world.[1] He follows a line of notable Arab singers immersed in the poetic traditions and concerns of their countries and the Arab world at large, such as the iconic Umm Kalthūm and 'Abd al-Ḥalīm Ḥāfiẓ of Egypt, Kādhim al-Sāhir of Iraq, Sabāḥ Fakhrī and Fayrūz of Lebanon and Mohammad 'Abdū of Saudi Arabia. It is nationalist songs, sung with evident vocal competence and spiritual power, invoking Palestine and Arab pride as well as love and human relations, that continue to show how alive and animated the Arabic language is, and how art is effective and potentially transformative, both socially and politically.

Anyone looking at the Arab world and its political and cultural landscape today would notice long-standing customs alongside modern characteristics, coexisting as well as vying with each other. The Arabic language is one such facet of Arab life, one that continues to exhibit its historical roots as well as its dynamism in today's cultural life, including the modern media. Within such a complex world that demonstrates its history through its own language, poetry has often showcased this vitality, giving birth to what the German philosopher Heidegger calls acts of 'founding':

> Poetry is a founding; a naming of being and the essence of all things—not just any saying, but that whereby everything first steps into the open, which we then discuss and talk about in everyday language. Hence poetry never takes language as a material at its disposal; rather poetry itself first makes language possible.[2]

The poet communicates to their audience the perceptual, musical and spiritual gifts of language, carving spaces for renewal through which existing and continuing human life is reborn with expressions and constructs that reveal the inner and outer shells of existence. Not all Arab poets can be considered founders in Heidegger's sense. Many poets choose to recycle existing reality in

archaic or ideological poetic discourses that amount to no more than reproducing the past, narrowing the present to the dimension of a past life that no
longer exists. Yet, several poets since the nineteenth century have been pioneers in reinvigorating Arab life and language, effecting changes in form,
content, image and tone. The Lebanese poet Gibran Khalil Gibran, the Iraqi
Badir Shākir al-Sayyāb, the Egyptian Salāh 'Abd al-Sabūr, the Syrian Adonis
and the Palestinian Mahmoud Darwish are amongst the brilliant poets who
have transformed the landscape of poetry in the Arab world with their visionary powers of articulation, synthesising time so that the past, the present and
the future are given living voices and universal resonance.

This could scarcely have happened without the turbulent political times
through which these poets lived and with which they were aesthetically and
personally engaged. The Arab national has been at the convergence of multiple
loyalties encompassed within political, social and religious affiliations, so that
the vital fruits of freedom appeared to elude many people and poets, who
restricted their poetry to narrower streams of expression and invocation. But
the poets who broke open the ceiling of external domination, internal despotism and patriarchal control have kept alive the flame of the Arabic language.
Through their commitment to human values and ideals of aesthetics and conceptual enrichment, their understanding of the Arab world and its dilemmas
and challenges, and most importantly their liberated vision, they have succeeded as free poets, unencumbered by the deadweight of ideologies and their
overblown slogans that have held back the Arab world developmentally and
politically for so long. Theirs is a world of engaged continuity and renewal.

Commenting on the abused concepts and discourse of modernity in the
Arab world, the great poet and visionary critic Adonis asks in kālām al-bidāyāt,
'The language of beginnings':

> Did not modernity within Arab cultural circles become a surplus of speech, like the
> surplus of revolution, unity, progress and socialism (addition: *Islamism*)...etc? Or
> a surplus of bullets, arms, parties, organisations, charities, groups, and gatherings...
> etc?
>
> Indeed, let us talk about modernity.
>
> Let us speak, if you wish, about poetry.
>
> The poet does not think of the rule when he writes. Language is inside him, before
> the rule.[3]

Against this background, Adonis concentrates on the individual and her or
his inner maturity as a source of poetry. Adonis believes that poetry, unlike

science, 'exists on a different level, nearer to man and more expressive of the inwardness of his being'.[4] In another instance, he refers to poetry as 'an innate quality. It is not a stage in the history of human consciousness but a constituent of this consciousness.'[5] Adonis sees the poet as a 'metaphysical being who penetrates to the depths', and in so doing 'keeps solidarity with others'.[6] It is the introspective individual as a creative force that animates Adonis' vision of poetry, rather than collective society on a manifest level. Other poets, however, have incorporated the collective in the individual in a way that lessens this separation and duality between the individual and society. Mahmoud Darwish reflects that poetry is a case of metaphorical human wandering and effectively existential expansion, moored in its historical and socio-political context, but not trapped inside it.

> Perhaps the source of poetry is one, it is our human identity, from the past of its alienation on this earth to its alienated present. Poetry was born from the first questions of the astonished wonder about our existence, in that past distance in which our human child wondered about the secrets of his primary existence. Therefore, and since the beginning, internationalism was but localism.[7]

At the present time, avant-garde Arabic poetry seems less visible on the performative cultural scene; the novel has been moving closer towards consumerist popularity. Yet as Darwish put it, 'the future is for poetry as much as it is for the novel'.[8] It is unlikely that poetry will ever be dethroned from Arab life: its brevity and the sense of historical connectivity and warmth it conveys; its intimate associations with music and protective spirituality; the sheer philosophical strength and wisdom that fine poetics can enshrine in people; its socio-political roles of mobilisation, imaginative cohesion and memorialisation; all these dimensions make Arabic poetry an enduring living testament to the Arab world's resonant desire for continuity as well as change.

NOTES

NOTES

1. For reference, see http://web.gc.cuny.edu/ijmes/docs/TransChart.pdf, accessed 3 June 2013.

INTRODUCTION

1. Vincent B. Leitch, *Deconstructive Criticism: An Advanced Introduction*, New York: Columbia University Press, 1983, p. 47.
2. For a nuanced perspective on naming in Arabic, see Yasir Suleiman, *Arabic, Self and Identity: A Study in Conflict and Displacement*, Oxford: Oxford University Press, 2011, pp. 142–236.
3. For a general introduction about early Arabic poetry, including pre-Islamic poetry and the issues (*aghrād*) it concerned itself with, see Stefan Sperl, Introduction, *Classical Traditions and Modern Meanings*, Leiden: Brill, 1996, mainly pp. 1–15.
4. See Michael Zwettler, *The Oral Tradition of Classical Arabic Poetry: Its Character and Implications*. Columbia: Ohio State University, 1978. See also James T. Monroe, Oral Composition in Pre-Islamic Poetry, pp. 1–55, in Suzanne Pinckney Stetkevych, *The Formation of the Classical Islamic World: Early Islamic Poetry and Poetics*, London: Ashgate Variorum, 2009.
5. See Atef Alshaer 'Towards a theory of culture of communication: the fixed and the dynamic in Hamas' discourse,' *Middle East Journal of Culture and Communication*, 1, 2 (2008), pp. 101–121.
6. Ibn Khaldun in James T. Monroe, Oral Composition in Pre-Islamic Poetry, in Suzanne Pinckney Stetkeych (ed.) *The Formation of the Classical Islamic World: Early Islamic Poetry and Poetics*. London: Ashgate Variorum, 2009, pp. 1–55, P.31.
7. Ibn Rashiq in Suzanne P. Stetkevych, *The Mute Immortals Speak: Pre-Islamic Poetry and the Poetics of Ritual*, Ithaca and London: Cornell University Press, 1993, p. 82.
8. I draw on the Italian philosopher Giambattista Vico's insight here: '...The first poets

were natural poets, for poetry laid the foundation of pagan civilization, which in turn was the sole source of all the arts.' Giambattista Vico, *New Science*, London: Penguin Classics, 2001 [1744], p. 94.

9. See Stefan Sperl, Islamic Kingship and Arabic Panegyric Poetry in the Early 9th Century, in Suzanne Pinckney Stetkeych (ed.) *The Formation of the Classical Islamic World: Early Islamic Poetry and Poetics*. London: Ashgate Variorum, 2009, pp. 79–95.

10. It is noteworthy to quote Saleh Said Agha here: "Setting poetics aside, Arabic versified speech and the history of the Arabs are, in the Arabic sources, almost inseparable; so much so that one may even conjure up an outline (*or a silhouette*) of at least the major contours of early Arab history by solely tapping Arabic verse." See Saleh Said Agha, *Of Verse, Poetry, Great Poetry and History*, in Ramzi Baalbaki, Saleh Said Agha and Tarif Khalidi (eds.), *Poetry and History: The Value of Poetry in Reconstructing Arab History*, Beirut: AUB Press, pp. 1–39, p. 7.

11. See Edward W. Said, *Beginings: Intention & Method*, London: Granta Publications, 1975, p. 379.

12. See Yasir Suleiman, *Arabic In the Fray: Language Ideology and Cultural Politics*, Edinburgh: Edinburgh University Press, 2013.

13. See Wen-chin Ouyang, *Politics of Nostalgia in the Arabic Novel: Nation State, Modernity and Tradition*, Edinburgh: Edinburgh University Press, 2013.

14. See http://www.aljazeera.net/news/pages/546a4ca2-a306–4632-abb6–2cda06 106860, accessed 18 June 2013.

15. Marlé Hammond, *Beyond Elegy: Classical Arabic Women's Poetry in Context* (British Academy Publication), Oxford University Press, 2010, p. 2.

16. Michel Foucault, *Power/Knowledge: Selected Interviews and Other Writings 1972–1977*, Colin Gordon (ed.), New York: Pantheon Books, 1980, p. 142.

17. See Charles Tripp, *The Power and the People: Paths of Resistance in the Middle East*, Cambridge: Cambridge University Press, 2013. Also, Arshin Adib-Moghaddam, *On the Arab Revolts and the Iranian Revolution: Power and Resistance Today*, London: Bloomsbury Academic, 2013.

18. Adonis, *Dīwān al-Shiʿir al-ʿArabī*, Damascus: Dār al-Madā, 1996, p. 12.

19. See Khaled Mattawa, *Mahmoud Darwish: The Poet's Art and His Nation*, Syracuse, NY: Syracuse University Press, 2014. See also, Atef Alshaer, 'Adonis'. *The Literary Encyclopaedia*. 13 January 2014 http://www.litencyc.com/php/speople. php?rec=true&UID= 13116, accessed 15 January 2014.

20. Yasir Suleiman, 'The Nation Speaks: On the Poetics of Nationalist Literature', in Suleiman and Muhawi (eds.), *Literature and Nation in the Middle East*, Edinburgh: Edinburgh University Press, 2006, p. 229.

21. See Yasir Suleiman, 2013, op.cit., p. 110.

22. Salma Khadra Jayyusi, *Modern Arabic Poetry*, New York: Columbia University Press, pp. 1–42.

23. See Ouyang, *Politics of Nostalgia in the Arabic Novel*, p. 145–146.

24. In Craig Raine, *T. S. Eliot*, Oxford: Oxford University Press, 2006, p. 74. See also Victor Shklovsky, 'Art as Technique', in *Russian Formalist Criticism: Four Essays*, trans. L. T. Lemon and M. J. Reis, Lincoln, NE: University of Nebraska Press, 1965, p. 155.

1. POETRY IN THE SHADOW OF THE OTTOMAN EMPIRE

1. In George Antonius, *The Arab Awakening: The Story of the Arab National Movement*, London: Hamish Hamilton, 1955, p. 152. The poem appears in the cited book in English.

2. See Albert Hourani, *A History of the Arab Peoples*, London: Faber and Faber, 1991, pp. 273–5.

3. Antonius, op. cit., pp. 54–5.

4. Yasir Suleiman, 'The Nation Speaks: On the Poetics of Nationalist Literature', in Suleiman and Muhawi (eds.), *Literature and Nation in the Middle East*, Edinburgh: Edinburgh University Press, 2006, p. 208.

5. Abū-Hāqqa-Ahmad, *al-iltizām fī al-shi'r al-'Arabī*, Beirut: Dar al-'ilm lil-malayyīn, 1979, p. 138.

6. This attitude of pan-Arabism was particularly associated with the Syrian educationalist Sāti' al-Hursī, who advocated pan-Arabism on the basis of the Arabic language and shared history; and in this respect he was influenced by the new areas of independence and nation-state, advocated in Europe and elsewhere.

7. It is noteworthy that the Islamism that emerged in the latter part of the twentieth century in particular differs from that of the preceding century, as it is officially constituted within Islamist political parties rather than being an intellectual force and ideological current, as represented in the Wahhabi movement in Saudi Arabia. In particular, the Islamism of the twentieth century begins with the establishment of the Muslim Brotherhood in Egypt at the hands of Hassan al-Banna (1906–1949) in 1928. Yet he was influenced by earlier thinkers such as Mohammad 'Abduh and Mohammad Rashid Rida, who advocated Islamic governance in various ways.

8. The title of the poem serves as the title of the famous book by George Antonius, *The Arab Awakening*, first published in 1939.

9. See Arthur J. Arberry, *Modern Arabic Poetry: An Anthology with English Verse Translations*, Cambridge: Cambridge University Press, 1967, pp. 15–16.

10. See Suzanne Pinckney Stetkevych, *The Poetics of Islamic Legitimacy: Myth, Gender and Ceremony in the Classical Arab Ode*, Indiana: Indiana University Press, 2000.

11. The Qur'an, 35:28–29.

12. There are numerous interpretations of this verse. Orthodox interpretations tend to emphasise that 'authentic scholars' are not those who only know and under-

stand, but those who fear God as well (see http://islamqa.info/ar/ref/52817, accessed 3 December 2012). But others, such as the former President of Egypt Mohamed Morsi, offered what amounts to a neutral/non-controversial reading of it (even though it sparked a number of criticisms), suggesting that God does not fear scholars, but he reveres them; His fear emanates from reverence, not fear as such (see the video where Morsi's remarks appear: http://www.youtube.com/watch?v=xLnAZO5peTw, accessed 3 December 2012).

13. Yāsir al-Za'ātreh (18 June 2012), *mādha ba'du tarāja'i al-'ulāmā'i 'an nazriyyati al-tā'ati*, 'What after the scholars gave up on the theory of obedience?'; see http://www.aljazeera.net/pointofview/pages/d2705673–919d-4352-a247–9b46ddb2fb7f?GoogleStatID=1, accessed 18 June 2012.

14. See Albert Hourani, *A History of the Arab Peoples*, London: Faber and Faber, 1991, pp. 207–48.

15. A culture of communication is defined as 'the process of enactment that stems from the historical-anthropological rootedness of action in language and culture… a culture of communication is a communicated compendium of religious, historical, literary and mythological references used by a community as valid tropes for all times and, as such, are acted upon and treated as having authenticity. Authenticity in a culture of communication serves to manipulate language as a residue of resonant power embodied in culture as an anthropological-historical space in which the powerful, the spiritual and the pertinent (to the moment) are drawn on, selectively, produced, idolised, talked of and visualised.' Atef Alshaer, 'Towards a Theory of Culture of Communication: The Fixed and the Dynamic in Hamas', Communicated Discourse, in *Middle East Journal of Culture and Communication*, 2008, vol. 1(2), pp. 101–21, p. 104.

16. See Yasir Suleiman, *The Arabic Language and National Identity: A Study in Ideology*, Edinburgh University Press and Georgetown University Press, 2003.

17. See Jonathan Lyons, *The House of Wisdom: How the Arabs Translated Western Civilization*, New York, Berlin, London: Bloomsbury Press, 2009.

18. *Shawqiyyāt li-amīr al-Shu'arā Ahmad Shawqī*, Cairo: Dār kunūz al-ma'rifah, 2002, pp. 969–71.

19. Hourani, op.cit., 1991, pp. 404–5.

20. Hourani, op.cit., 1991, pp. 257–8.

21. Mohammad Ali led campaigns to Sudan, Syria and Arabia, but as Hourani writes, 'Egyptian rule in Syria and Arabia did not last long; he was forced to withdraw by a combined effort of the European powers, which did not wish to see a virtually independent Egyptian state weakening that of the Ottomans. In return for withdrawal, he obtained in 1841 recognition of his family's right to rule Egypt under Ottoman suzerainty (the special title his successors took was that of Khedive). Egyptian rule continued, however, in the Sudan, which for the first time constituted a single political unit' (Ibid., p. 273).

22. Albert Hourani, *Arab Thought in the Liberal Age: 1798–1939*, Cambridge: Cambridge University Press, 1963, p. 120.

23. *Ijitihād* can be understood as a process of reasoning on matters relating to the well-being of the Muslim community and their adaptability to change. For further reference, see: http://www.britannica.com/EBchecked/topic/282550/ijtihad, accessed 29 November 2013.

24. Ibid., p. 144.

25. Al-Kawākibī, A-*Istibdād wa-mas-Istiʿbād*, Bayrūt: Dār al-Nafāʾis, 1902, 2006, p. 186. For further delineations and understanding of al-Kawākibī's ideas, see Ryuichi Funatsu, 2006, pp. 1–40.

26. See http://www.omandaily.om/node/124188, accessed 2 June 2013.

27. See http://www.muslm.org/vb/showthread.php?266806, accessed 2 June 2013.

28. See http://www.adab.com/modules.php?name=Sh3er&doWhat=shqas&qid=66861&r=&rc=14, accessed 2 June 2013.

29. See http://www.adab.com/modules.php?name=Sh3er&doWhat=shqas&qid=66728, accessed 2 June 2013.

30. For the poem in question, see http://www.odabasham.net/show.php?sid=48255, accessed 6 December 2013.

31. Ibid.

32. M. M. Badawi, *A Critical Introduction to Modern Arabic Poetry*, Cambridge: Cambridge University Press, 1975, p. 15.

33. See Kadhim Hussein, *The Poetics of Anti-Colonialism in the Arabic Qasidāh*, Brill, London, Boston: Leiden, 2004, pp. 36–7.

34. See Asef Bayat, *Life as Politics: How Ordinary People Change the Middle East*, Stanford: Stanford University Press, 2010.

35. Badawi, A *Critical Introduction to Modern Arabic Poetry*, p. x.

36. Ibid., pp. 15–16.

37. See A. Nicholson, *Literary History of the Arabs*, London: Adelphi Terrace, 1907, pp. 109–13.

38. http://www.adab.com/modules.php?name=Sh3er&doWhat=lsq&shid=297, accessed 2 June 2013.

39. Ibid.

40. Badawi, *A Critical Introduction to Modern Arabic Poetry*, p. 29.

41. Ibid., p. 33.

42. The Ottoman Constitution (1876), which was abetted by the highest vizier in the Ottoman Empire under Sultan Abdelhamid, namely Midhat Pasha, represented the first constitution of the Ottoman Empire. The constitution aimed to reform the empire and provide checks on the powers of the Sultan; and it followed from the Tanzimat era (1839).

43. See http://www.adab.com/modules.php?name=Sh3er&doWhat=shqas&qid=9515, accessed 2 June 2013.

44. Sultan Abdulhamid paid closer attention to the Arabs to ensure their ultimate loyalty to him, and as such 'more than a quarter of the approximately 280 deputies in the 1908 parliament were Arabs'. Interestingly, Abdulhamid was advised by his grand vizier Ahmad Cevdet Pasha to respect the Arabs more, as their loyalty was essential to the survival and durability of the Ottoman Empire, warning him 'of the importance of respecting the Arabs, since their language was the language of Islam, and had pointed out the damage wrought by the state officials who insulted Arabs by referring to them as *fellahin*, peasants.' See Caroline Finkel, *Osman's Dream: The Story of the Ottoman Empire 1300–1923*, London: John Murray, 2005, p. 522.

45. See Arshin Adib-Moghaddam, *A Meta-History of Clash of Civilisations: Us and Them Beyond Orientalism*, London and New York: Hurst & Co. and Columbia University Press, 2012.

46. Caroline Finkel, op. cit., 2005, p. 495.

47. See http://www.adab.com/modules.php?name=Sh3er&doWhat=shqas&qid=19509, accessed 2 June 2013.

48. The political significance of Saudi Arabia is evident in the annual Muslim pilgrimage ceremonies that the country hosts. The Ottoman authority in Istanbul recognised the political potency of the pilgrimage in giving legitimacy to its rule; and to this end, it oversaw the pilgrimage routes through Syria and other places under its control in the Arab world. With the advent of Arab nationalism, the Arab-Islamic values as manifest in Saudi Arabia and elsewhere increased at the level of discourse as well as poetry. See Hourani, op. cit., 1991.

49. Jabra I. Jabra, 'Modern Arabic Literature and the West', *Journal of Arabic Literature*, Leiden: Brill, 1971, v.2 (pp. 76–91), pp. 78–9.

50. See Diwān Jamīl Sidqī al-Zahāwī, Dār al-'Awdah, Bayrūt, 1972, p. 178–179.

51. Abū-Hāqqah, op. cit., pp. 139–40.

52. See A. J. Arberry, *The Seven Odes: The First Chapter in Arabic Literature*, London: George Allen & Unwin, New York: The Macmillan Company, 1957, p. 61.

53. See Suleiman, *The Arabic Language and National Identity*.

54. See Adonis, *An Introduction to Arabic Poetics*, London: Saqi Books, 1990, p. 76.

2. POETRY IN THE SHADOW OF COLONIALISM

1. Edward Said, *Orientalism*, London: Penguin Classics, 1978, p. 82.

2. Juan Cole, *Napoleon's Egypt: Invading the Middle East*, London: Routledge, 2007, p. 11.

3. Hourani, op. cit., 1991, p. 283.

4. Said, op. cit., 1987.

5. In this context, Cole wrote, 'Bonaparte was playing the role of a Muslim sultan, honouring the progeny of the Prophet, and they (some Muslim scholars) in turn pledged to support the status quo and employ their religious aura to mediate dis-

putes between ruler and ruled...Bonaparte appears to have believed that even a public debate about whether the French might become Muslims benefited his cause.' Cole, op. cit., 2007, pp. 135, 128.

6. Michel Foucault, *The Archaeology of Knowledge*, London: Routledge, 2006 [1969].

7. Stefan Sperl and Christopher Schackle, *Classical Traditions and Modern Meanings*, Leiden, New York and Köln: Brill, 1996, pp. 1–15.

8. Barbara Harlow, *Resistance Literature*, New York and London: Methuen, p. 33.

9. Frantz Fanon, *The Wretched of the Earth*, London: Penguin, 1963.

10. See Yasir Suleiman, *The Arabic Language and National Identity*, Edinburgh: Edinburgh University Press, 2003, pp. 69–158.

11. Ibid.

12. Salma K. Jayyusi, *Trends and Movements in Modern Arabic Poetry*, vol. 1, Leiden: Brill, 1977, p. 193.

13. Salma K. Jayyusi, *An Anthology of Modern Arabic Poetry*, New York: Columbia University Press, 1987, p. 95.

14. Hussein N. Kadhim, *The Poetics of Anti-Colonialism in the Arabic Qaṣīdah*, Leiden: Brill, 2004, pp. 85–130.

15. Maʿruf al-Rasāfī, *al-Diwaan*, Beirut: Daar al-ʿAwdah, 1972, p. 416.

16. The Qur'an: Al-Baqara, 2/205.

17. Al-Rasāfī, op. cit., p. 235.

18. Ibid., p. 301.

19. Karl Marx, *The German Ideology*: http://www.marxists.org/archive/marx/works/1845/german-ideology/ch01a.htm, 1845, accessed 25 March 2013.

20. Kadhim, op. cit., 2004, pp. 91–129.

21. Frantz Fanon, op. cit., 1963, p. 183.

22. Albert Hourani, *Arab Thought in the Liberal Age*, Cambridge: Cambridge University Press, 1991, p. 174.

23. In Ahmad Abu Haqqa, *al-iltizām fi al-shiʿr al-ʿArabī*, Beirut: Dar al-ʿilm lil-malayyīn, 1979, p. 215.

24. Said, *Orientalism*.

25. Ahmad Abu Haqqa, op.cit., p. 211.

26. Hourani, op. cit., p. 186.

27. In Ahmad Abu-Haqqa, op. cit., pp. 211–12.

28. Ibid., p. 208.

29. Taha Hussain was castigated by al-Azhar and other religious and populist authorities and forums in Egypt for casting doubt on pre-Islamic poetry, suggesting that it was written after Islam. 'This', according to Hourani, 'aroused opposition both because it suggested a critical method which, if applied to the texts of religion, might cast doubt on the authenticity, and because it struck at the roots of the traditional structure of Arabic learning by which the faith was buttressed.' Hourani, op. cit., 1991, p. 327.

30. See Muncif al-Marzouqy, *al-Huriyyah*: http://moncef-marzouki.net/spip. php?article536, accessed 18 June 2012.

31. In Ahmad Abu-Haqqa, op. cit., p. 118.

32. Fanon, op. cit., p. 181.

33. In Ahmad Abu-Haqqa, op. cit., p. 180.

34. See Hourani, op. cit., p. 404–7.

35. For the poem, see: http://www.adab.com/folk/modules.php?name=Sh3er&do What=shqas&qid=83251&r=&rc=1, accessed 10 December 2013.

36. Ibid., p. 201.

37. M. M. Badawi, *Anthology of Modern Arabic Verse*, Oxford: Oxford University Press, 1970, p. 20–21.

38. Bernard Shaw, *John Bull's Other Island*, London: Constable, 1931, p. 60–61.

39. Hourani, op. cit., p. 164.

40. In Ahmad Abu-Haqqa, op. cit., p. 158.

41. On the educative elements in Ibrāhīm's poetry particularly regarding the Arabic language, see Yasir Suleiman, *Arabic in the Fray: Language Ideology and Cultural Politics*, Edinburgh: Edinburgh University Press, 2013, pp. 112–119.

42. See Hussein Kadhim's interpretation of the poem, op. cit., 2004, pp. 2–19.

43. Hussein Kadhim translates this line as 'when you departed, the country said the Shahādah [praise to God], as if you were an incurable disease from which it had recovered'. Kadhim, op. cit., 2004, p. 10.

44. Badawi, op. cit., pp. 17–19.

45. See Khadim, op. cit., 2004, p. 17.

46. Edward Said, op. cit., 1978, p. 40.

47. Hourani, op. cit., p. 199.

48. Ibid., p. 201.

49. *Nakbat Bayrūt* is another poem authored by Shawqī to condemn the Italian attack against Beirut in 1912.

50. Kadhim, op. cit., pp. 37–8.

51. Khoury in Kadhim, ibid., p. 42.

52. In Kadhim, pp. 44–6.

53. Stefan Sperl, 'O City Set Up Thy Lament': Poetic Responses to the Trauma of War', 2013, pp. 1–39, in Hugh Kennedy (ed.), *Warfare and Poetry in the Middle East*, London, I.B. Tauris, p. 28.

54. In Kadhim, op.cit., p. 49.

55. Ibid., p. 80–81.

56. Ibid., p. 82.

57. See Stefan Sperl and Christopher Shackle, Introduction to *Classical Traditions and Modern Meanings*, Leiden, New York, Köln: Brill, pp. 1–34.

58. Ahmad Abu-Haqqa, op. cit., pp. 664–87.

59. Ahmad Abu-Haqqa, op. cit., pp. 432–42 and 617–37. See also Mustafa Bitām,

al-thawra al-Jazāiriyyah fī shi'ir al-Maghreb al-'Arabī: 1954–1962, al-Jazāir: Diwān al-matbū'āt al-markaziyyah, pp. 122–3.

60. See Nazik al-Mala'ika's poem, 'Jamilah and Us', in Reza Aslan (ed.), *Tablet and Pen: Literary Landscapes from the Modern Middle East*, London and New York: Norton & Co., 2011, pp. 584–5.

61. Tunisia's most notable poet is Abū al-Qāsim al-Shabbī. I discuss his significance in the following chapter. I perceive his sensibility to be modernist, even though he still followed the metrical norms of the classical Arabic Qaṣīdah.

62. See also Mustafa Bitām, *al-thawra al-Jazāiriyyah fī shi'ir al-Maghreb al-'Arabī: 1954–1962*, al-Jazāir: Diwān al-matbū'āt al-markaziyyah, p. 19.

63. Jabra I. Jabra, 'The Rebels, the Committed and the Others—Transitions in Arabic Poetry Today, 1980', pp. 191–206 in Issa J. Boullata, *Critical Perspectives on Modern Arabic Literature: 1945–1980*, Washington: Three Continents Press, p. 193.

64. http://ejabat.google.com/ejabat/thread?tid=27720bae920c1ae5, accessed 13 January 2014.

65. Edward Said, *The Question of Palestine*, London: Verso, 1979.

66. See Muhammad Y. Muslih, *The Origins of Palestinian Nationalism*, New York: Columbia University Press, 1988.

67. See Victor Kattan, *From Coexistence to Conquest: International Law and the Origins of the Israeli–Arab Conflict, 1891–1949*, London: Pluto, 2009.

68. Said, op. cit., pp. 3–55.

69. Barbara Harlow, *Resistance Literature*, New York and London: Methuen, p. 68.

70. Khalid A. Sulaiman, *Palestine and Modern Arab Poetry*, London: Zed Books, 1948, p. 18.

71. See ibid., pp. 18–20.

72. In Ilan Pappé, *The Rise and Fall of a Palestinian Dynasty: The Husaynis 1700–1948*, London: Saqi Books, 2010, p. 165.

73. See Amin Maalouf, *The Crusaders Through Arab Eyes*, London: Saqi Books, 1984.

74. Sulaiman, op. cit., p. 20.

75. Ibid., pp. 17–18.

76. Ibid., p. 22.

77. In Sulaiman, op. cit., p. 52.

78. Pappé, op. cit., p. 239.

79. Ibrahīm Diwān Touqān, *Ibrahīm: a'māl shā'ir falastīn Ibrahīm Tauqān*, Beirut: Dār al-Quds, 1975, pp. 82–3.

80. In Sulaiman, op. cit., p. 32.

81. See Laleh Khalili, *Heroes and Martyrs of Palestine: The Politics of National Commemoration*, Cambridge: Cambridge University Press, 2007.

82. In Sulaiman, op. cit., pp. 28–30.

83. See Nels Johnson, *Islam and the Politics of Meaning in Palestinian Nationalism*, London: Kegan Paul International, 1982.

84. In Touqān, op. cit., p. 75.
85. See Pappé, op. cit.
86. In Roger Allen, *The Arabic Literary Heritage: The Development of its Genres and Criticism*, Cambridge: Cambridge University Press, 1998, p. 209.
87. In Sulaiman, op. cit., p. 30.
88. Jabra I. Jabra, op. cit., p. 193.

3. POLITICS IN THE AESTHETICS OF MODERN ARABIC POETRY

1. Adonis, *Fātiḥa li-nihaiyāt al-qarn: bayanāt min ajil thaqāfah ʿArabiyyah jadidah*, Beirut: dār al-ʿawdah, 1980, p. 14.
2. Edward Said, *Culture and Imperialism*, London: Vintage Books, 1993, p. 379.
3. Adonis, *An Introduction to Arab Poetics*, London: Saqi Books, 1990, p. 76.
4. Ibid., p. 79.
5. These last two paragraphs appear in an encyclopedia entry I wrote. For the reference, see Atef Alshaer, 'Adonis (b.1930)', *The Literary Encyclopedia: Exploring Literature, History and Culture*, The Literary Dictionary Ltd, 2014.
6. Adonis, *Aghānī Mihyār al-Dimashqī wa qaṣāʾid aukhrā*, Beirut: al-Mada, 1996, p. 502.
7. Marshal Berman, *All that Is Solid Melts into Thin Air: The Experience of Modernity*, London: Verso, 1983.
8. Edward Said, *Beginnings: Intention and Method*, London: Granta Publications, 1997 [1975].
9. Muhsin J. al-Muswai, *Arabic Poetry, Trajectories of Modernity and Tradition*, London: Routledge, 2006, p. 85.
10. Adonis, op. cit., p. 199.
11. See Adonis, *Kalām al-bidayyāt*, Beirut: dār al-Adāb, 1989, pp. 41–51.
12. The correspondence between Adonis' poetics and Spinoza's philosophy deserves a separate study, which will be undertaken by this author in the future.
13. See Younkins, 'Edwards, Spinoza on Freedom, Ethics and Politics', http://www.quebecoislibre.org/06/060507-2.htm, accessed 19 April 2013.
14. Salma Khadra Jayyusi, *Modern Arabic Poetry: An Anthology*, New York: Columbia University Press, 1987, p. 72.
15. I am mindful of Carl Joung's embrace of individuation, as opposed to individualism, which marks an earlier stage in life. Joung refers to individuation as 'a spiritual journey' explaining that 'only the man who can consciously assent to the power of the inner voice becomes a personality.' In *The Essential Jung, Selected Writings* Introduced by Anthony Storr, Princeton: Princeton University Press, 1983, p. 19.
16. Adonis in Atif Y. Faddul, *The Poetics of T. S. Eliot and Adonis: A Comparative Study*, Beirut: Alhambra Publishers, 1992, p. 147.
17. Salma Khadra Jayyusi, *Trends and Movements in Modern Arabic Poetry*, vol. 2, Leiden: Brill, 1977, p. 364.

18. See M. M. Badawi, *An Anthology of Modern Arabic Verse*, Oxford: Oxford University Press, 1970.

19. See M. M. Badawi, *A Critical Introduction to Modern Arabic Poetry*, Cambridge: Cambridge University Press, 1975.

20. It is worth quoting Jayyusi here: 'Thanks to its influence the Romantic trend in modern poetry in the Arab East established itself, a trend which helped poets to arrive at a relative individuality and originality by which they were able to fight, in their limited ways, the more formal and repetitive elements of traditional poetry. Poetry became an aesthetic adventure sought for itself.' Jayyusi, op. cit., 1977, p. 387.

21. Khalil Gibran, 'The Future of the Arabic Language', in Reza Aslan, *Tablet and Pen: Literary Landscapes from the Modern Middle East*, New York, London: Norton & Co., 2011, pp. 5–11, p. 11. See also Yasir Suleiman's reference to Gibran's view of the Arabic language as understood and practiced by traditionalists in forms that deplete the language of dynamism, manifesting a cultural trope which Suleiman calls, 'the fossilisation trope'. Referring to Gibran's piece, 'You have your language. And I have mine', Suleiman comments that 'it is a scathing attack on the traditionalists, who would rather have a pure form of Arabic, even though it is a corpse, than evolving form of the language, which can keep pace with modern life.' Yasir Suleiman, *Arabic in The Fray: Language Ideology and Cultural Politics*, Edinburgh: Edinburgh University Press, 2013, p. 129.

22. Khalil Gibran, 'From a Speech by Khalil the Heretic', in Suheil Bushrui and James M. Malarkey, *The Literary Heritage of the Arabs: An Anthology*, London: Saqi Books, pp. 299–302.

23. Faddul, op. cit., 1992, p. 244. With the émigré poets in perspective, it is instructive to quote Moreh on this: 'romanticism took hold of the *Mahjari* poets as the result of their education but also through various movements that flourished at the time in the United States, such as Freemasonry and theosophy. These romantic poets furthered the development of Arabic poetry in that they succeeded in diverting it from concern with the outer world to the expression of the inner world of the poet's soul; they transformed it from a tool in the hands of ruler and an ornament at their festivities into a vehicle suited to the exposition of the "philosophical ideas".' S. Moreh, *Modern Arabic Poetry, 1800–1970: The Development of its Forms and Themes under the Influence of Western Literature*, Leiden: Brill, 1979, p. 121.

24. The Apollo group was initially headed by the neo-classist poet Ahmad Shawqī, and included poets such as Khalīl Mutrān and the prolific and important Egyptian poet Ahmad Zakī Abū Shādī. After Shawqī's passing, the Apollo poets took to expressing subjective, symbolist and meditative themes, and al-Shābbī emerged as one of the prominent talents among them.

25. Abū al-Qāsim al-Shābbi, *al-khayyāl al-shiʻri*, in Mohammad Qaubaʻa, *al-shiʻir fī*

kitabāt al-Shābbi al-nathriyyah, dirasāt fī al-shi'riyyah, al-Shābbi namūdhajan, Qartāj bayt al-hikmah, 1988, p. 193.

26. *Diwān Abū al-Qāsim al-Shabbi,* Beirut: Dār sādir, 1996, pp. 149–52.

27. See the last chapter in this book for further analysis of excerpts from al-Shābbī's poetry.

28. Ibid., pp. 42–3.

29. Hourani, *The History of the Arab Peoples,* London: Faber & Faber,1992, p. 396.

30. Nazik al-Malāika, *shazāyā wa ramād,* Beirut: Dār al-'awdah, 1971, p. 19.

31. Hourani, op. cit., p. 396.

32. Yasir Suleiman, 'The nation speaks: on the poetics of nationalist literature', in Y. Suleiman and M. Ibrahim (eds.), *Literature and Nation in the Middle East,* Edinburgh: Edinburgh University Press, 2006, pp. 208–31, p. 12.

33. Terri Deyoung,'New Reading of Badr Shākir al-Sayyāb's "Hymn of the rain"', in *Journal of Arabic Literature,* Leiden: Brill, vol. 24, no. 1 (March 1993), pp. 36–61, 59–61.

34. Wen-chin Ouyang, *Poetics of Love in the Arabic Novel: Nation-state, Modernity and Tradition,* Edinburgh: Edinburgh University Press, 2012, p. 40.

35. Deyoung, op. cit., p.xxiv.

36. Faddul, op. cit., 1992, p. 244.

37. Ouyang, op. cit., p. 40.

38. In Abu-Haqqah, op. cit, p. 413.

39. Medusa is a mythical Greek character with eyes which, whatever falls on them, turn into stones.

40. In Abu-Hāqqah, op. cit., pp. 413–24.

41. T. S. Eliot, *Selected Poems,* London: Faber & Faber, 2009 [1954], p. 41.

42. Hisham Sharabi, *Neopatriarchy: A Theory of Distorted Change in Arab Society,* Oxford: Oxford University Press, p. 7.

43. See Halim Barakat, 'The Community of Old Cleavages: Tribe, Village, City', *The Arab World,* California: University of California Press, 1993, pp. 48–70.

44. This theme involving village and city dynamics is also treated in the poetry of the prominent Egyptian poet Salah 'Abd al-Sabūr (1931–1981); see Paul Starkey, *Modern Arabic Literature,* Edinburgh: Edinburgh University Press, 2006, p. 84.

45. Quoted in Jayyusi, op. cit., p. 581.

46. Initially, the debate about the notion of commitment in literature took place between the Lebanese thinker Ra'īf Khoury and Taha Hussein and was published in the journal *al-Adāb* in 1955. The former emphasised the importance of commitment on the part of writers towards their society.

47. In Abu-Hāqqah, op. cit, p. 361.

48. Ibid., op. cit., p. 361.

49. Ibid., op. cit., pp. 443–80, see the last chapter in the book for this.

50. See the poet Hijāzī reciting his poem on https://www.youtube.com/watch?v= TKZcroVEY34, accessed 10 May 2013.

51. 'Abd al-Wahhāb al-Bayyātī, *Diwān*, Bayrūt: Dār al-'awdah, 1971, p. 6.
52. Hijāzī, op. cit.
53. See Suzanne Pinckney Stetkevych, *The Poetics of Islamic Legitimacy: Myth, Gender and Ceremony in the Classical Arabic Ode*, Bloomington, IN: Indiana University Press, 2002.
54. Salma Jayyusi, 1987, p. 277.
55. See Salma Khadra Jayyusi, 'Modernist Poetry in Arabic', in M. M. Badawi (ed.), *Modern Arabic Literature*, Cambridge: Cambridge University Press, 1992, pp. 132–80.
56. Ibid.
57. For more on Qabbānī and his love poetry, see Stefan Wild, 'Nizār Qabbānī's Autobiography: Images of Sexuality, Death and Poetry', in R. Allen, H. Kilpatrick and E. de Moor (eds.), *Love and Sexuality in Modern Arabic Literature*, London: Saqi Books, 1995, pp. 200–219.
58. In Habiba Muhamadi, *al-Qasīdah al-Siyāsiyyah fī shi'ir Nizār Qabānī*, mufim lil-nashir, 2001, p. 62.
59. Ibid., p. 72.
60. Ibid., p. 74.
61. Fouad Ajami, *The Arab Predicament: Arab Political Thought and Practice since 1967*, Cambridge: Cambridge University Press, p. 31.
62. In Sulaiman, op. cit., 1984, pp. 137–8, trans. by Sulaiman.
63. I thank Mr Mohammad Said who drew my attention to this poem; see: http://dvd4arab.maktoob.com/f785/3214338.html, accessed 15 June 2013.
64. See Jayyusi, op. cit., 1977, pp. 583–95.
65. Mozaffar al-Nawwab, 'Bridge of old wonders', in Reza Aslan (ed.), *Tablet and Pen: Literary Landscapes from the Modern Middle East*, New York: Norton & Co. 2011, pp. 196–213, trans. by Carol Bordenstein and Saadi A. Simawe.
66. See the poem of Qabbānī, 'Love and petroleum', pp. 58–60, in Issa Boullata, *Modern Arab Poets: 1950–1975*, Washington: Three Continents Press. It is noteworthy that the attacks of some poets on the Gulf countries and their politics of oil do not all merely seem to be borne of objective inclinations. These countries have long been seen by people of the Levant as constituted of unsophisticated Bedouins; and therefore it is possible to imagine that their sudden oil-induced wealth provoked unconscious jealousy, which others built into claims of cultural and moral superiority. Qabbānī's poem abounds with references to certain habits of the Gulf countries, such as polygamy, references which harbour prejudices and reduce the complexity of these societies to a set of traditional stereotypes. See Jeff L. Patty and Samia T. Reading (ed.), *An Anthology of Contemporary Arabian Gulf Poetry: Gathering the Tide*, Ithaca Press, 2011.
67. See http://www.adab.com/modules.php?name=Sh3er&doWhat=shqas&qid=65804, accessed 15 March 2013.

68. See Edward Said, *The End of the Peace Process*, London: Granta, 2000.
69. See http://www.adab.com/modules.php?name=Sh3er&doWhat=shqas&qid= 469, accessed 15 March 2013.
70. For a sung version of the poem, see the following link: http://www.youtube.com/ watch?v=8-royNKOOGY, accessed 14 April 2013.
71. On the contrary, there are poets in the Arab world who belong to minority groups which do not fit the state's definition of the national; they tend to develop their own cultural and political facets subversively. They have not been recognised within the state system, as is the case of those who are known as the Bedūn poets in Kuwait. In this sense, the centralised nationalism of the state tallies with several national-istic examples which operate according to the paradigm of exclusion and inclu-sion. Gifted poets such as Sa'diyyah Mufarrih, Dkheil Khalifah and other Bedūn poets in Kuwait are excluded from the official routes to belonging. Likewise in Algeria, the state has been more inclined to celebrate Algerian poets of Arab rather than Berber descent, to the point that a professor of poetry was banned in 1980 from teaching a lecture on Berber poetry, sparking what is called the Berber Spring against the residing government of the first Algerian President Ahmad Ben Bella with its exclusivist practices in favour of Arabic culture (for more on the latter case, see http://www.aljazeera.com/indepth/opinion/2013/02/201321913479 263624.html). I register my gratitude to Tareq Alrabei for information on the Bedūn.
72. Jayyusi, op. cit., 1992, p. 169.
73. Adonis, *An Introduction to Arab Poetics*, London: Saqi Books, 1990, p. 69.
74. See the review by Atef Alshaer of *Embers and Ashes* by Hisham Sharabi: http:// electronicintifada.net/content/embers-and-ashes-intellectuals-exile-struggle-and-success/8319, accessed 15 June 2013.
75. Atif Y. Faddul, *The Poetics of T. S. Eliot and Adonis: A Comparative Study*, Islamabad: Alhambra Publishing, 1988, p. 160.
76. Adonis, *Aghānī Mihyār al-Dimashqī wa qasā'id aukhrā*, Beirut: Dār al-Madā, 1996, pp. 177–8.
77. Albert Camus, *The Rebel*, London: Penguin Classics, 1951, pp. 30–31.
78. Roger Scruton, *A Short History of Modern Philosophy*, London: Routledge, 2001, p. 41.
79. Edward Said, *Culture and Imperialism*, London: Vintage, 1994, p.xiii.
80. In Nabīl Munasar, *al-Khitāb al-muwāzī: al-Qasīdah al-'Arabiyyah al-Mu'āsirah*, Casablanca: Dār Tubqāl lil-nashir, 2007, p. 168.
81. See Unsī al-Hāj, *Lan*, Beirut: Dār al-Jadīd, 1994, p. 18.
82. See Atef Alshaer, 'Ahmad 'Ali Said, Adonis (b.1935)', in *The Literary Encyclopedia*: http://www.litencyc.com/index.php, accessed 15 June 2013.
83. Adonis, 'Grave for New York' (excerpt), in Reza Aslan, op. cit., 2011, pp. 189–90.
84. Adonis, op. cit., 1989, p. 137.

85. Noam Chomsky, *The Fateful Triangle: The United States, Israel and the Palestinians*, Cambridge, MA: South End Press, 1999.

86. Translated by Sinan Antoon, cited in Laleh Khalili, *Time in the Shadows: Confinement in Counterinsurgencies*, Stanford: Stanford University Press, 2013, pp. 248–9. For an alternative translation, see http://behindthelinespoetry. blogspot.co.uk/2009/09/saadi-yousefs-tormented-of-heavenan.html, accessed 20 April 2013.

87. Ibid., pp. 136–7.

88. Ibid.

89. Mohammad Benis, in Salma Khadra Jayyusi, op. cit., 1987, pp. 181–2.

90. In Issa J. Boullata, op. cit., 1976, p. 83, translated by Boullata.

91. For another sample of his poems and writings, see Saadi Yousif's website: http:// www.saadiyousif.com/home/, last accessed 20 April 2013. He has poems which exhibit the severity of depravity to which his native country, Iraq, has been made to sink as a result of the American atrocities, particularly after the 2003 invasion.

92. Jayyusi, op. cit., 1992, p. 174.

4. THE POETRY OF MAHMOUD DARWISH: HUMANISM, NATIONALISM AND VIOLENCE

1. Oscar Wilde, *The Complete Short Stories of Oscar Wilde*, New York: Dover Publications, 2006, p. 11.

2. For discussion regarding modernity and tradition in modern Arabic literature, see Wen-chin Ouyang, *Poetics of Love in the Arabic Novel: Nation-state, Modernity and Tradition*, Edinburgh: Edinburgh University Press, 2012, pp. 1–34.

3. Ibid.

4. On modernity, see Stuart Hall, 'The Question of Cultural Identity', *The Polity Reader in Cultural Theory*, London: Polity, pp. 119–25.

5. For example, see Atif Y. Faddul, *The Poetics of T. S. Eliot and Adonis: A Comparative Study*, Beirut: Alhambra Publishers, 1992, and also Nabīl Munasar, *al-Khitāb al-muwāzī lil-qasīda al-'Arabiyyah al-mu'āsirah*, Casablanca: dār tūbiqāl lil-nashir, 1997.

6. Modernity and postmodernity is underpinned by the de-centring and fluidity of the human subject rather than its fixed core and nature, as emphasized in the Enlightenment. The de-centring is situated within Marx's thought on economic production and its consequences, the saliency of the unconscious for Freud, the social rather than individual nature of language according to Saussure, the effect of disciplinary power on the human subject for Foucault, and the revolutionary impact of feminism. See Stuart Hall, et al., *The Question of Cultural Identity*, in *Modernity: An Introduction to Modern Societies*, Oxford: Blackwell Publishers, 1996.

7. Darwish, *al-bayt wa-tarīq* (The house and the road) in *Hīrat al-ʿaʾid*, selected articles, Beirut: Riad El-Rayyes Books, 2007, p. 150.

8. See Salma Khadra Jayyusi, 'Mahmoud Darwish's Mission and Place in Arab Literary History', in H. Nassar and N. Rahman (eds.), *Mahmoud Darwish: Exile's Poet*, Northmpton, MA: Interlink Publishing, 2008, pp. iv–1.

9. Rajāʾ Naqqāsh, *Mahmoud Darwish: Shāʿir al-ard al-muhtalla* (Poet of the Occupied Territories), Beirut: al-Muaʾsassah al-ʿArabiyya lilddrasāt wa-nashr, 1972, p. 100.

10. Dina Matar, *What It Means to be Palestinian: Stories of Palestinian Peoplehood*, London: I. B. Tauris, 2011.

11. Naqqāsh, op. cit., p. 113.

12. See Bassam K. Frangieh, in H. Nassar and N. Rahman (eds.), *Mahmoud Darwish: Exile's Poet*, 2008, pp. 11–40.

13. Naqqāsh, op. cit., p. 107.

14. See Sigmund Freud, *Civilisation and its Discontents*, London: Penguin Books, 2004 [1930].

15. Jacqueline Rose, *The Last Resistance*, London: Verso, 2007, p. 6.

16. Rose, op. cit., p. 48.

17. Rose, op. cit., p. 85.

18. Freud, op. cit., p. 18.

19. Frantz Fanon, *The Wretched of the Earth*, London: Penguin Books, 1963, p. 70.

20. Frantz Fanon, *Black Skin, White Masks*, Paris: Gallimard, 1952, p. 224.

21. Fanon, op. cit., 1952, p. 156.

22. Edward Said, *Freud and the Non-European*, London: Verso, 2003, p. 25.

23. Said, 'On Mahmoud Darwish', *Grand Street*, 12/4, 1994, p. 113.

24. Mahmoud Darwish, *Diwān Mahmoud Darwish*, Beirut: Dār al-ʿawdah, 1964, p. 135.

25. Fanon, op.cit., 1963, p. 73.

26. Darwish, *Yawmiyyāt juruh falastīni*, (Diaries of a Palestinian Wound), Beirut: Dār al-ʿawdah, 1964, pp. 383–97.

27. Fanon, op. cit., 1963, p. 74.

28. Perhaps Darwish's most notable poem which dramatises this theme of nature and its ultimate knowledge by those who live for and amongst it is 'The Speech of the Native Indian', where he gives voice to the Native Indians against the white settlers: Darwish, *Eleven Planets*, Syracuse, NY: Syracuse University Press, 1992, pp. 129–45.

29. See Angelika Neuwirth on Darwish's incorporation of historic and mythic figures and themes in his poetry: *Hebrew Bible and Arabic Poetry: Mahmoud Darwish's Palestine—From Paradise Lost to a Homeland Made of Words*, Northampton, MA: Olive Branch Press, 2008, pp. 167–90.

30. Darwish, *rad alfiʿil*, A reaction, p. 112.

31. Darwish, *jawāz safar*, Passport, p. 40.

32. Darwish, *jawāz safar*, p. 41.

33. Darwish, *Unfortunately, It Was Paradise*, trans. by Munir Akash and Carolyn Forché, Berkeley, CA: University of California Press, 2003, pp. 165–8.

34. Naqqāsh, op. cit., p. 233.

35. Frantz Fanon, op. cit., 1963, p. 74.

36. Darwish, 1972, p. 68; for the entire poem, see pp. 63–9.

37. Laleh Khalili, *Heroes and Martyrs of Palestine: the Politics of National Commemoration*, Cambridge: Cambridge University Press, 2007.

38. See Rose, op. cit., pp. 62–92 for a discussion of Freud's view of nationalism, resistance, individual and social identities. See also Atef Alshaer's review and critique of the book in *Studies in Ethnicity and Nationalism*, 8/2, London, 2008, pp. 376–8.

39. Fanon, op. cit., 1963, p. 74.

40. Darwish, op. cit., 2007, pp. 32–3.

41. Rose, op. cit., p. 42.

42. Robert Fisk, *Pity the Nation: Lebanon at War*, Oxford: Oxford University Press, 2001.

43. Fanon, op. cit., p. 29.

44. Darwish, *madih az-zill al-ʿāly* (In Praise of the High Shadow), Beirut: Dār al-ʿawdah, 1984, pp. 35–7.

45. Roman Jakobson, *Selected Writings: Poetry of Grammar and Grammar of Poetry*, edited with a preface by Stephan Rudy, New York, London: Duke University Press, 1981, pp. 86–97.

46. Fanon, op. cit., 1936, p. 73.

47. Jean-Paul Sartre, Preface to Frantz Fanon, *The Wretched of the Earth*, London: Penguin Books, 1961, p. 25.

48. See Wen-Chen Ouyang's chapter in her book for an interesting discussion on the theme of madness in the work of Darwish and other Arab authors, namely *Madness: In the Ruins of Dream and Memory*, Edinburgh: Edinburgh University Press, pp. 39–49.

49. Fanon, op. cit., 1963, p. 73.

50. Darwish, *madih az-zill al-ʿāly* (In Praise of the High Shadow), p. 124.

51. See Patrick Sylvain's article where he attributes to Darwish this appellation: philosopher–poet or poet–philosopher. He also engages theoretically with his poetic creations, identifying several stages to Darwish and his poetry, namely the formative, the sublime and the global. Sylvain, 'Darwish's Essentialist Poetics in a State of Siege', in *Human Architecture: Journal of the Sociology of Self-Knowledge*, VII, Special Issue, 2009, pp. 137–50.

52. See Rose, op. cit., p. 89.

53. Darwish, *Hālat hisār* (A State of Siege), Beirut: Riad El-Rayyes Books, 2002, p. 64.

54. Darwish, *t'axxara huzni ʿalihi* (My sadness over him has been delayed), op. cit., 2007, p. 92.

55. Darwish, *al-bahith 'an at-tabī'ī fi al-lā tabī'i*, op. cit., 2007, p. 22.

56. Rose, op. cit., p. 80.

57. Darwish, *Hālat Hisār*, p. 50.

58. Neuwirth, op. cit., p. 189.

59. Darwish, *Hālat Hisār*, op. cit., 2002, p. 79.

60. Fanon, op.cit., p. 165.

61. Max Weber, *Politics as a Vocation*, Munich: Duncker und Humblot, 1921, pp. 396–450.

62. Rose, op. cit., p. 76.

63. Darwish, July 2007, online: http://www.bintjbeil.com/A/literature/darwish_gaza.html

64. Darwish, 2008, online: http://www.darwish.ps/dpoem-127.html, accessed 27 June 2013.

65. Mohammad Abed al-Jābry, *Fikr Ibn Khaldūn al-'asabiyya wa-dawla*, Beirut: Dār al-'awdah, 1992, p. 168.

66. Darwish, *lā uridu li-hadhi al-Qasīda an tantahi*, op. cit. 2009, pp. 74–5.

67. Edward Said, *Culture and Resistance: Conversations with Edward Said*, Interviews by David Barsamian, Cambridge, MA: South End Press, 2003, pp. 163–4.

68. Josh Cohen, *How to Read Freud*, London: Granta Books, 2005, pp. 104–5.

69. Darwish, *madīh az-zill al-'āly*, (In Praise of the High Shadow), p. 79.

70. In Taha Hussein, *Hadīth al-arabu'ā*, Cairo: Dār il-Ma'ārif, 1935, p. 69.

71. Darwish, *Hīrat al-'ā'id*, op. cit., p. 149.

72. Darwish, *Hālat Hisār*, op. cit., p. 14.

5. THE POETRY OF HAMAS

1. For one example of Hasan al-Banna's writing, see 'Toward the Light', in Roxanne L. Euben and Muhammad Qasim Zaman (eds.), *Princeton Readings in Islamist Thought: Texts and Contexts from al-Banna to Bin Laden*, Princeton: Princeton University Press, pp. 49–79.

2. See in ibid., Roxanne L. Euben & Muhammad Qasim Zaman, Introduction, pp. 1–49.

3. See in ibid., Sayyid Qutb, 'Signposts along the Road', pp. 129–45.

4. See http://www.adab.com/modules.php?name=Sh3er&doWhat=shqas&qid=79 178&r=&rc=52, accessed 15 April 2013.

5. The quoted poetry is taken from collections published on the internet, where pages are unnumbered. For the original sources, see the following website for the poetry of 'Abd al-azīz al-Rantīsī; http://ikhwanwiki.com/index.php?title=; for the poetry of Ibrāhīm al-Maqādmah, see the following website: http://www.ikhwan.net/forum/showthread.php?4952-; and for the extract quoted from al-Masrī's poem, see https://www.paldf.net/forum/showthread.php?t=207053; all accessed 2 June 2013.

6. All Palestinian Islamic parties have prominent figures in them who have written poetry concerned with Palestine. This includes the other active Islamist Palestinian party, namely Islamic Jihad. Fathī al-Shiqāqī, the founder leader of Islamic Jihad who was assassinated by an Israeli intelligence unit in Malta in 1995, wrote poetry, sometimes incorporating it in his letters to other prominent Palestinian leaders, such as the Palestinian President Yasir Arafat, to convey the intensity of his concern and emotions over Palestine and Palestinian affairs. See Fathī Shiqāqī (1995), *rihlat ad-dam al-dhī hazama as-sayif*, Markaz Jafa li d-dirāsāt wa al-abhāth, edited by Rif'at sayyed Tawfīq, 1997:31, pp. 615–17.

7. Atef Alshaer, 'Towards a Theory of Culture of Communication: The Fixed and the Dynamic in Hamas Discourse', *Middle East Journal of Culture and Communication*, October 2008, vol. 2, pp. 101–21.

8. Taha Hussein, *Hadīth al-arbu'ā'*, Cairo: Dār al-ma'ārif, 1998.

9. Jeroen Gunning, *Hamas in Politics: Democracy, Religion, Violence*, New York: Columbia University Press, 2008, p. 125.

10. Hamas as a movement is heavily engaged in producing and promoting literature. Another prominent Hamas leader who has written literature is Mahmoud al-Zahar, who published seven novels. There are also many paintings produced by Hamas members. These aspects are yet to be studied.

11. Loren L. Lybarger, *Identity and Religion in Palestine: The Struggle between Islamism and Secularism in the Occupied Territories*, Princeton: Princeton University Press, 2007, p. 3.

12. In this context, it is noteworthy to highlight Jayyusi's point with regard to modern Arabic secular poetry: 'by the end of the forties, Arabic poetry had gained great flexibility. Its imagery and language had undergone major transformations, its diction gained a new capacity for obliquity and mystery, its rhythms attained greater lyricism, its tone a wider expressive range. It was rich, full of nuance, pulsating with spirit of adventure, open to everything.' Jayyusi, op. cit., 1987, p. 8.

13. See http://woman.islammessage.com/article.aspx?id=6321, accessed 15 April 2013.

14. In her book, Lila Abu-Lughod highlights Bedouin poetry and songs amongst some Bedouin communities in Egypt (Awlad Ali), where poetry and songs serve as mediums of coded expression with regard to areas for which there is social disapproval, such as honour, betrayal and lack of love and so forth. Thus, what could not be expressed in normal, unblemished language could be said in poetry or songs, hence the title of her book, *Veiled Sentiments*. Some of Hamas leaders' poetry mentioned in this article can be correlated with this concept of 'veiled sentiments', where poetry says what the poet could not say in plain language for ideological or pragmatic reasons, be they social or political. Lila Abu-Lughod, *Veiled Sentiments: Honour and Poetry in a Bedouin Society*, California: University of California Press, 2000.

15. Al-Banna, op. cit.
16. Qur'an, Fatir/28.
17. Gunning, op. cit., 2008, p. 129.
18. Jayyusi, op. cit., 1987, p. 36.
19. Jayyusi, op. cit., 1987, p. 31.
20. Khalid Hroub, *Hamas: Political Thought and Practice*, Washington, DC: Institute for Palestine Studies, 2000, p. 241.
21. During this incident in Hebron, 29 Palestinians were gunned down by Goldstein and 125 were wounded, causing much Palestinian distress, turbulence and reaction through suicide bombings.
22. Jayyusi, op. cit., 1987, p. 21.
23. In Stefan Sperl, 'Crossing Enemy Boundaries: Al-Buhturi's Ode on the Ruins of Ctesiphon Re-Read in the Light of Virgil and Wilfred Owen', *Bulletin of the School of Oriental and African Studies*, 2006, 69 (3), pp. 365–79, p. 30.
24. Alshaer, op. cit., 2008.

6. THE POETRY OF HIZBULLAH

1. Yasir Suleiman, 'Introduction: Literature and Nation in the Middle East: An Overview', in Yasir Suleiman and Ibrahim Muhawi (eds.), *Literature and Nation in the Middle East*, Edinburgh: Edinburgh University Press, 2006, pp. 1–16.
2. I have argued in an earlier paper that authenticity is paramount in any culture of communication rooted in past convictions; see Atef Alshaer, 'The Poetry of Hamas', *Middle East Journal of Culture and Communication* 2, 4 (2009), pp. 214–30. Similarly, Arshin Adib-Moghaddam writes, 'I have argued that Islamisms advocate authenticity; they define autonomy as a virtue'; see *A Metahistory of the Clash of Civilisations: Us and Them Beyond Orientalism*, London: Hurst & Co., 2011, p. 248.
3. See Mohammad Mahdi Shams ad-Din, '*Khitāb al-Imām al-Sadr al-thaqāfī* (The cultural discourse of Imam Musa al-Sadr), in *al-Hawiyya al-thaqāfiyya: Qir'āt fi al-bu'ud ath-qāfi limasirat al-Imām as-Sayed Musa al-Sadr*, Beirut: Markaz al-Imām al-Sadr lil-abhāth wa-dirāsāt, 2000, p. 43.
4. See Joseph Alagha, *Hizbullah's Identity Construction*, Amsterdam: Amsterdam University Press, 2011, pp. 178–81.
5. See Ahmad Abu-Hāqqa, *Al-iltizām fi al-shi'r al-'Arabī*, Beirut: Dar al-'ilm lil-malayyīn, 1979.
6. As mentioned in the text, the dictatorial Iraqi leader Saddam Hussein was such an example who found many poets to praise and adulate him. In return, he lavished on them gifts and honours. One such a poet was 'Abd al-Razzāq 'Abd al-Wāhid, who wrote several poems in praise of Saddam Hussein; see Stephan Milich, 'The positioning of Ba'athist intellectuals and writers before and after 2003: the case of the Iraqi poet Abd al-Razzaq Abd al-Wahid', *Middle East Journal of Culture and Communication*, 4, 3 (2001), pp. 298–338.

7. See Laurence Louër, *Transnational Shia Politics: Religious and Political Networks in the Gulf*, London: Hurst & Co., 2011, pp. 211–19.
8. Clifford Geertz, *The Interpretation of Cultures*, New York: Basic Books, 1983, p. 24.
9. See Michel Foucault, *The Archaeology of Knowledge*, London and New York: Routledge, 1972, pp. 24–33.
10. There are other oaths to Hizbullah; but the ones mentioned here are the most widespread. One noteworthy oath to highlight, which evokes several past and present Shi'ite figures and ends with Hizbullah, is the following: 'We have pledged our allegiance, O Khomeini...in the name of al-Mahdi... the soul of God...of Sayyed Abbas...the martyr of God...and Khamenai...the shadow of God...we will continue to honour the pledge, O Nasrallah...'
11. See Louër, op. cit., pp. 204–5.
12. See ibid., p. 9.
13. See Naim Qassem, *Mujtama' al-muqāwwamah: irādat al-shahādah wa-sinā'at al-intisār*, Beirut: Dār al-ma'ārif al-hakmiyya, 2008.
14. See *al-'Ahd*, 3 September 1993 supplement, issue 482, pp. 17–24, where there is a discussion of the Prophet Mohammad's life and meaning to Muslims from cultural, spiritual and political perspectives. See also the 26 March 1999 issue 790, pp. 12,14,16, with references on the life of Hassan and Hussein and other model roles of the Shi'ites.
15. The poetry of this era represents a break from the past of the Shi'ites of Lebanon, who did not link themselves so organically (through Hizbullah in particular) in their culture in general (poetry included) to the Iranian system before the Iranian revolution of 1979. Instead, the poetry that emerges from south Lebanon includes themes such as the beauty of nature, particularly that of the Levant (Syria, Lebanon and Palestine), the Arab heritage, valour, nobility, loyalty and generosity. The latter are aspects which are generally associated with the classical period in Arabic literature. If there are references to Shi'ite figures or places, it was often to Iraq, where there are seminal Shi'ite places and historical memories, such as Najaf and Karbala respectively (see Hassan al-Amin, *'asir Hamad al-Mahmūd wa al-haiyaah al-shi'riyyah fii jabal 'Amil*, Beirut: dār al-Turāth al-Islāmī, 1974).
16. See *al-'Ahd*, 15 February 1985, issue 34, p. 1.
17. See ibid., p. 7.
18. See the undated *al-'Ahd* newspaper special edition from June 1989, entitled 'Farewell the Imam of the umma,' p. 4.
19. See Kamran Scot Aghaie, *The Martyrs of Karbala: Shi'i Symbols and Rituals in Modern Iran*, Seattle: University of Washington Press, 2004.
20. The quoted poems above of Mohammad al-Qabisi were recited to me by a Lebanese citizen who agreed for his name to be mentioned, namely Khalil Ahmad Issa from the village of Ramiyyah in south Lebanon. Khalil Issa confirmed that the poems

in question were widespread in south Lebanon. Though he did not know the poet in question very well, he referred to his poetry as an important part of what he called 'the poetry of resistance'.

21. There are a number of choral singers and singing teams affiliated with Hizbullah. They have become particularly important since 2006 as they perform several functions, such as at social occasions like weddings or political rallies. These include *Firqat al-Fajr, Firqat al-Isrā', al-Mahdi*, etc.

22. See Augustus Richard Norton, *Hizbullah: A Short History*, Princeton and Oxford: Princeton University Press, 2007, p. 80.

23. *Al-'Ahd*, 2 June 2000, issue 852, p. 8.

24. Ibid.

25. Ibid., p. 19.

26. Ibid.

27. Ibid., p. 31.

28. The poem '*Rijāl Allah*' was one of the poems that al-Farra recited to a packed audience of Hizbullah supporters during his poetry reading evening at the International Arab Book Fair in Beirut on 10 May 2007.

29. Omar Al-Farra, *Umsiyya* (DVD), Dar al-Manar lil-intaaj al-fani wa-tawzii', 2007.

30. Barbara Harlow, *Resistance Literature*, New York, London: Methuen, 1987.

31. Geertz, op. cit., p. 220.

32. Rida Shu'ayb, the choral group al-Fajr; the poem was adapted by Tarik Sharifa and produced by Hizbullah's Dar al-Manar, 2006.

33. Norton, *Hizbullah*, op. cit., p. 285.

34. Atef Alshaer, 'Towards a Theory of Culture of Communication: the Fixed and the Dynamic in Hamas's Communicated Discourse', *Middle East Journal of Culture and Communication*, 1, 2 (2008), pp. 101–21.

35. Hamid Mavani, 'Ayatullah Khomeni's concept of governance (*wilayat al-faqih*) and the classical Shi'i doctrine of Imamate', *Middle Eastern Studies*, 47, 5 (2001), pp. 807–24.

36. Ibid.

37. It merits attention to quote Amal Saad-Ghorayeb on the concept and institution of the *wilayat al-faqih* and Hizbullah's relationship to it, in the sense that the *faqih* (the one on whom religious authority is invested, in this case, Khomeini) recognises 'the national boundaries dividing the umma and the consequent limits of his *wilayat*. Hizbullah's claim that it is "enlightened enough to decide for itself" on other political issues which are not religiously problematic, such as its vote of confidence in the government or its promulgation of laws, further limits the scope of the *faqih*'s political authority. Thus, the party is able to balance its intellectual commitment to the concept of the *wilayat* with its allegiance to the Lebanese state.' See Amal Saad-Ghorayeb, *Hizbullah: Politics and Religion*, London: Pluto Press, 2002, p. 68.

38. Dawisha, Adeed, *Rise and Fall of Arab Nationalism*, Princeton: Princeton University Press, 2003, pp. 24–41.

39. Ibid.

40. Ibid.

41. Phillip Hitti, *History of the Arabs: From the Earliest Times to the Present*, London, New York: Palgrave Macmillan, 1937 [2002].

42. Salma Khadra Jayyusi, *Anthology of Modern Arabic Poetry*, New Nork: Columbia University Press, 1987.

43. See Dina Matar, 'The Power of Conviction: Nassrallah's Rhetoric and Mediated Charisma in the Context of 2006 July War', *Middle East Journal of Culture and Communication*, 1, 2 (2008), pp. 122–37.

44. Atef Alshaer, 'The poetry of Hamas', *Middle East Journal of Culture and Communication*, 2, 4 (2009), pp. 214–30.

45. Haidar (lion in classical Arabic) is one of the titles of Imam Ali to evoke his courage and powerful leadership.

46. An example of this is to be found in an interview with the Palestinian poet Mahmoud Darwish, where he refers to the tenth-century Arab poet Al-Mutanabbi as 'my grandfather of poetry', *jaddi al-shi'ri*. See Wazan Abdu, *Al-gharib yaqa'u 'ala nafsihi*, Beirut: Riad El-Rayyes Books, 2006, p. 93.

47. For the poem in question, see http://alorobanews.com/vb/showthread.php?t=503, accessed 3 March 2013.

48. See http://www.jebchit.com/article.php?arid=18, accessed 25 September 2012.

49. The German philosopher Heidegger quotes the German poet Hölderlin who wrote, 'that is why language, the most dangerous of goods, has been given to man... so that he may bear witness to what he is...' (IV, 246). On poetry as the essence of language and humanity, see the beautiful essay by Heidegger, *Hölderlin and the Essence of Poetry*, New York: Prometheus Books, 1981, pp. 5–65; see also Adonis, *An Introduction to Arab Poetics*, Beirut: Dār al-Sāqī, 2003, pp. 55–75.

50. For the entire words of the letter and the song itself, see: http://lachyab.jeeran.com/archive/2006/10/106267.html, accessed 13 September 2012.

51. Al-Farra, *Umsiyya* in Beirut, 13 June 2007.

52. See the following video, where the remarks of Najm appeared: http://www.youtube.com/watch?v=jhUVXG12j1c, accessed 12 January 2013.

53. Lila Abu-Lughod, *Veiled Sentiments: Honour and Poetry in a Bedouin Society*, Berkeley, CA: University of California Press, 1989 [2000].

7. POETRY AND THE ARAB SPRING: A HISTORICAL PERSPECTIVE

1. In M. M. Badawi, *A Critical Introduction to Modern Arabic Poetry*, Oxford: Oxford University Press, 1975, p. 23.

2. *Egypt Independent*, 16 June 2012.

3. Albert Camus, *The Rebel*, London: Penguin Books, 1951 [2000], p. 76.

4. In Adonis, *An Introduction to Arab Poetics*, London: Saqi Books, 1990, p. 56.

5. Ibid.

6. R. A. Judy, 'Introduction: Tunisia and the Poetry of Emergent Democratic Criticism', *Boundary* 2 (2), 2012, p. 15. I heartily thank Professor Gilbert Achcar for sending this article to me.

7. See Salām al-Kawākibī, Abdel Rahmān Al-Kawākibī fikr lam yafqid hadāthatuhu wa-ahmiyatuhu fī 'srinā al-halī al-muthlim, Majallat Ibn Rushd; for reference, see: http://www.ibn-rushd.org/typo3/cms/ar/magazine/14th-issue-summer-2013/salam-kawakibi/, accessed 13 January 2013.

8. Abdel Rahmān al-Kawākibī, *Tabai' al-Istibdād wa-masāri' al-Isti'bād*, Bayrūt: Dār al-Nafā'is, 1902 [2006], p. 183.

9. Ibid., p. 180.

10. For further delineations and understanding of al-Kawākibī's ideas, see Ryuichi Funatsu, 2006, pp. 1–40.

11. As Funatsu (2006, p. 11) writes of al-Kawākibī's thought, 'without the ability to act on free will, progress is impossible and decline is inevitable'.

12. See a translation of a section of the poem by Elliott Colla: http://arablit.wordpress.com/2011/01/16/two-translations-of-abu-al-qasim-al-shabis-if-the-people-wanted-life-one-day/, accessed 5 June 2012.

13. Ibid. On the evocation of dignity in the poem and its humanist associations in the poem, see R. A. Judy, 'Introduction: Tunisia and the Poetry of Emergent Democratic Criticism', *Boundary* 2 (2), 2012.

14. Translated by Adel Iskandar. For reference, see: http://aasilahmad.net/abu-al-qasim-al-shabi-the-poet-of-the-tunisia-and-egyptian-revolution/, accessed 5 June 2012.

15. The French philosopher Derrida advances this idea of malleability of language and makes it a centrepiece in his philosophy with regard to literary text. See Edward Said's discussion of Derrida and other philosophers on this in *The World, the Text and the Critic*, Cambridge, MA: Harvard University Press, 1983, pp. 178–225.

16. See Jayyusi (1977, pp. 410–24) and Ronak Husni (1995, pp. 81–92) for further treatment of al-Shābbī's poetry.

17. Jayussi, *Modern Arabic Poetry*, 1987, pp. 1–40.

18. In Abū Hāqqah, 1979, pp. 443–4.

19. See Frangieh, op. cit., 2008, pp. 11–40.

20. Abū Hāqqa, op. cit., p. 445.

21. In Hutash, 1987, p. 354.

22. Sayyid Qutb, *Milestones*, Chicago, IL: Kazi Publications, 1964, p. 6.

23. See http://www.adab.com/modules.php?name=Sh3er&doWhat=shqas&qid=79125&r=&rc=11 for a sample of Sayyid Qutb's poetry, accessed 2 July 2012.

24. See a sample of Ahmad Matar's poetry: http://www.adab.com/modules.php?name=Sh3er&doWhat=shqas&qid=1641&r=&rc=6, accessed 2 June 2012.

25. See al-Marzouqy's articles in Aljazeera on 30 December 2009, *lā hal fī al-Islām huwa al-Hal:* http://www.aljazeera.net/pointofview/pages/2d28640e-5988–443e-9ca8–94fcf4a5da1e, accessed 5 June 2012; and also his article 10 April 2012: http://www.aljazeera.net/pointofview/pages/4f355c57–2d8a-434a-a56f-556158cca3cc.

26. Nonetheless, in November 2007 Darwish accepted a prize from the former Tunisian President Zine El-Abidine Ben Ali, who was the first to be deposed in the Arab Spring.

27. See http://alkarmelj.org/userfiles/pdfs/4.pdf, republished in 2011 by Khadar Hassan in *al-Karmel*, no. 1, accessed 2 June 2012.

28. Noha Radwan, 'The Land Speaks Arabic: Shi'r al-Ammiyya and Arab Nationalism', in R. Baalbaki, S. S. Agha and T. Khalidi (eds.), *Poetry and History: The Value of Poetry in Reconstructing Arab History*, Beirut: American University of Beirut Express, 2011, p. 413.

29. Haddad, Najm and other colloquial poets can be seen as being influenced by the important Tunisian–Egyptian poet Bayram al-Tūnisī (1893–1961), whose popular poems are known as *zajal*. These were concerned with political and social issues in the Arab world and were written in a vernacular tone; see Radwan, op. cit., p. 434.

30. See Chris Stone and Elliot Colla's article: http://www.jadaliyya.com/pages/index/15670/negm-mat, accessed 13 January 2014.

31. Noha Radwan, op. cit., p. 429.

32. See http://arabic.cnn.com/2013/middle_east/12/3/najm.passed-away/, accessed 13 January 2014.

33. See http://www.nmisr.com/vb/showthread.php?t=250809, accessed 13 January 2014.

34. Lisa Wedeen, *Ambiguities of Domination: Politics, Rhetoric, and Symbols in Contemporary Syria*, Chicago, IL: Chicago University Press, 1999, p. 6.

35. The owl is a bird that embodies and carries bad omens in Arab culture.

36. See the poem in Arabic: http://syrianchange.wordpress.com/2013/07/28/, accessed 13 January 2014.

37. See Atef Alshaer, 'Identity in Mahmoud Darwish's poem, "The Dice Player"', in *Middle East Journal of Culture and Communication*, 4 (4), Leiden: Brill, pp. 90–110.

38. See http://mojil.net/site/?p=24650, accessed 13 December 2014.

39. Stefan Sperl, '"O City, Set Up Thy Lament": Poetic Responses to the Trauma of War', in H. Kennedy, *Warfare and Poetry in the Middle East*, London: I. B. Tauris, 2011, pp. 1–39.

40. Ibid., p. 28.

41. For this statistic, see https://www.un.org/apps/news//story.asp?NewsID=46615&Cr=Syria&Cr1, accessed 13 January 2014.

42. The fragments taken from the collection appeared on Aljazeera: http://www. aljazeera.net/news/pages/4269cec2–14f0–4439-aef6-d8fd3a74bef9, accessed 13 January 2014.

43. Ibid.

44. Ibid.

45. See Gilbert Achcar's book, which views the revolution as a long protracted process towards a genuine transformative change: *The People Want: A Radical Exploration of the Arab Uprising*, London: Saqi Books, 2013.

46. http://andromeda.rutgers.edu/~jlynch/Texts/prometheus.html,   accessed 13 January 2014.

47. In Zyād Shalyūt's article, '*Nubūā't al-thawrah fī ash-shi'r al-masrī*' (The prophecies of the revolution in Egyptian poetry), http://www.diwanalarab.com/spip. php?article27246, accessed 6 June 2012.

AFTERWORD

1. The annual competition on MBC television is called 'Arab Idol': http://www.mbc. net/ar/programs/arab-idol-s2.html, accessed 27 June 2013.

2. Martin Heidegger, 'Hölderlin and the Essence of Poetry', in *Elucidations in Hölderlin's Poetry*, New York: Prometheus Books, 1981, pp. 5–65, p. 60.

3. Adonis, *Kalām al-Bidayāt*, 1989, p. 178.

4. Adonis, *An Introduction to Arab Poetics*, London: Saqi Books, 1990, p. 94.

5. Ibid., p. 97.

6. Adonis in Khalid Mattawa's introduction, *Adonis: Selected Poems*, New Haven & London: Yale University Press, pp.x-xxii.

7. Darwish, '*al-bayt wa-tarīq*' (The house and the road), in *Hīrat al-'a'id*, The Perplexity of the Returnee, selected articles, Beirut: Riad El-Rayyes Books, 2007, p. 158.

8. Ibid., p. 91.